CONCORDIA

H. Armin Moellering

Victor A. Bartling

CONCORDIA PUBLISHING HOUSE

COMMENTARY

1 Timothy
2 Timothy
Titus

Philemon

SAINT LOUIS   LONDON

The Bible text in this publication is from
the Revised Standard Version of the Bible,
copyright 1946 and 1952 by the Division
of Christian Education, National Council
of Churches, and used by permission.

Concordia Publishing House, St. Louis, Missouri
Concordia Publishing House Ltd., London, E. C. 1
© 1970 Concordia Publishing House
Library of Congress Catalog Card No. 71-121107
MANUFACTURED IN THE UNITED STATES OF AMERICA

CONTENTS

PREFACE

The preparation of commentaries on the Bible is a continuing task of scholarship and faith, for the unchanging Word of God must speak to the varying needs of each age. Furthermore, new knowledge of ancient cultures and languages adds to the insight into the world and meaning of the Bible. A commentary is thus a means of listening to the text.

The Concordia Commentary offers its readers a running narrative interpretation of the Revised Standard Version of the Bible. Writers are free to criticize the translation since their work is based on the Hebrew, Aramaic, and Greek texts of the original Bible. Footnotes and foreign language expressions are generally omitted. Brief bibliographies provide direction for further study.

The writers of this series accept the Bible as the source of faith and the directive for life. They pursue their task in confessional commitment to Biblical revelation. Yet in their role as Biblical scholars it is their function to subordinate personal reflection and private or sectarian views to the unique and original direction of the text.

This commentary, therefore, is addressed to the devout who may often be mystified or frightened by the Bible's vastness and depth. The commentary attempts to provide a contemporary understanding of the ancient text rather than to develop practical implications for modern life. Theological, historical, and literary interests are uppermost. However, the writers are aware not only of the difference between the past and the present but also how little basic human problems have changed and how directly helpful the Biblical perspective and commitment remain.

The contributors to this series hope that their words may bear worthy witness to that Word which alone abides.

WALTER J. BARTLING AND ALBERT E. GLOCK

Editors

INTRODUCTION

(Pastoral Epistles)

Although the designation of the two letters to Timothy and the one to Titus as the "Pastoral Epistles" has become standard only since the 18th century, the pastoral character (*pastor*=Latin for "shepherd") was recognized also by writers of the ancient church. Differing from the letters of Paul to entire congregations, the Pastoral Epistles are still not strictly private messages as, for instance, the note to Philemon. Timothy and Titus are addressed as co-laborers in the service of specific congregations, and the members are not lost from sight when the apostle formulates his message. (Note the plural "you" at the close of each letter.)

The Persons Addressed

Both Timothy, who was in Ephesus, and Titus, who was in Crete, were veteran co-workers of Paul. Timothy, the son of a heathen father and a Jewish-Christian mother (Acts 16:1; 2 Tim. 1:5), was perhaps converted on Paul's first missionary journey (Acts 14:6 ff.) and then taken along as a helper on the second missionary journey after he had been circumcised (Acts 16:3). Thereafter Timothy frequently accompanied Paul (Acts 16:1 ff.; 1 Thess. 1:1; 2 Thess. 1:1; Phil. 1:1; 2 Cor. 1:1, 19) and was also sent on special missions. (1 Thess. 3:1 ff.; 1 Cor. 4:17; 16:10; Phil. 2:19, 23; Acts 19:22; see also Acts 20:4; Col. 1:1; Philemon 1; 1 Cor. 16:10; Heb. 13:23)

Titus, a convert from heathenism, is not mentioned in Acts. His name first occurs in Gal. 2:1, 3 as a companion of Paul who accompanied him to Jerusalem where Paul stoutly resisted the demands of the Judaizers that he be circumcised. In the difficulties Paul experienced with the Corinthian congregation, Titus was of special service, delivering the first letter and skillfully representing the apostle's interests. (See 2 Cor. 2:13; 7:6 ff., 13 ff.; 8:6, 16 ff.; 12:18. 2 Tim. 4:10 mentions a journey from Rome, where he had been with Paul, to Dalmatia.)

The Question of Authorship

Since the publication of Friedrich Schleiermacher's essay disputing the Pauline authorship, *The So-Called First Letter of Paul to Timothy* (1807), the great and vexing problem of the Pastoral Epistles has been: Did Paul really write them? Respected scholars are arrayed on both sides of the question, though the preponderant opinion still seems to be that Paul is not the direct author. (The general reader will find helpful orientation in reading the introductions of C. K. Barrett, disputing Pauline authorship, and J. N. D. Kelly, defending Pauline authorship. See "For Further Reading" at the close of this commentary on the Pastoral Epistles.)

The question of Pauline authorship revolves in the main around the following problems:

1. Chronological Setting
2. Religious and Theological Concepts
3. Congregational Organization
4. The Heresies Combated
5. Peculiarities of Language and Style
6. The Problem of Pseudonymity and the Pastorals

Before considering these difficulties in order, one should note that the witness of the ancient church to authenticity, though not without its puzzles, is favorable. Because of their obviously related and similar character and peculiarities the Pastorals may be rightly considered as a unit. There are apparent allusions and echoes in 1 Clement (about A. D. 95) and Ignatius (about 110). The plainer and more frequent references in Polycarp (no later than 135) have led so noted a scholar as Hans von Campenhausen to advance the amazing theory that Polycarp wrote the Pastoral Epistles ("Polykarp von Smyrna und die Pastoralbriefe," *Sitzungsberichte der Heidelberger Akademie der Wissenschaften,* Phil. – his. Klasse, 1951). This theory is rendered incredible by the fact that differences between the letter of Polycarp and the Pastorals are greater than those between the Pastorals and the admittedly Pauline epistles. The insistent and unanswered question is: Why should Polycarp be capable of such great changes and transformations in style and Paul be incapable of lesser ones? One is reminded of the caustic observation of George Bernard Shaw: "The chaos of mere facts . . . in which Paul is only the man who could not possibly have written the epistles attributed to him . . ." (*Androcles and the Lion,* Preface, Baltimore: Penguin, 1951, p. 98). After the middle of the second century the Pastorals are frequently cited (Irenaeus, Tertullian, Clement of

11

Alexandria). The omission of the Pastorals from the canon of Marcion can be explained as deliberate rejection because they were hostile to his theological ideas. A more serious problem is posed by the fact that the Pastorals are not in the Chester Beatty Papyrus (P 46), the oldest codex of the Pauline letters. But even here the difficulties are not insuperable. Since several pages are missing from the codex, it is possible that the Pastorals may originally have been included. Thus the total witness of the early second century is favorable to authenticity.

However, the Pauline authorship cannot be blandly assumed. The practice of publishing one's own writings under assumed names taken from the Biblical past is said to have been common, so that it is necessary to give some attention to the specific points of objection if one is to entertain a reasonable conviction as to authorship.

Chronological Setting

The attempt to fit the data of the Pastorals into the historical framework of Acts is futile. If the Pastorals are to be accepted as historical, they must relate to situations and events that occurred after the Roman imprisonment described in Acts 28. This is not at all impossible, for there is no intimation in Acts that at the conclusion of the two-year imprisonment Paul was executed. The early and strong tradition that Paul was released after his first imprisonment (Acts 28) and then carried out his plan to visit Spain (cf. Rom. 15:24) may well be true. It is likewise entirely natural that Paul would use this freedom to visit his old mission territories and also take full advantage of an opportunity to begin mission work on the island of Crete. After this brief interlude Paul may have been arrested a second time, condemned, and executed.

The presence in the Pastorals of data that are difficult to fit into the known framework of Paul's career, rather than arguing against authenticity, favors it. Why would a forger write what could not be incorporated into the chronology and events of Acts and thus risk exposure?

Religious and Theological Concepts

In the Pastorals there are unmistakable shifts in the meaning of some terms and the usage of certain words not found in the undisputed Pauline letters. The question is whether these changes and novelties are irreconcilable with Pauline authorship. Some examples will illustrate the nature of the problem.

The *Law* now becomes a disciplinary institution for the godless (1 Tim. 1:8 ff.). However, this emphasis, occasioned by the teachings of the errorists (1 Tim. 1:7), is not without its parallel in another Pauline letter (Gal. 5:18 ff.). *Faith* has been modified to an objective signification meaning the faith of the church, that is, Christian doctrine (1 Tim. 4:1; 6:21; Titus 1:4), or has come to mean only another in the series of Christian virtues (1 Tim. 2:15; 4:12; 6:11; 2 Tim. 2:22; 3:10; Titus 2:2). And yet the meaning of faith as trust in and committal to Jesus is not lacking in the Pastorals (2 Tim. 3:15; cf. 1 Tim. 1:16). God is frequently called *Savior*, a term reminiscent of Hellenistic emperor worship (1 Tim. 1:1; 2:3; 4:10; Titus 1:3; 2:10; 3:4). Also the designation of the Lord's Second Coming as the *appearing* of the Lord is frequent (1 Tim. 6:14; 2 Tim. 4:1, 8; Titus 2:13), but not without precedent (2 Thess. 2:8). But why should Paul not use, and being in Rome, use with greater frequency, expressions from the Hellenistic environment, which he could invest with new and Christian meaning? (Perhaps in Phil. 3:20 usage of the term *Savior* is meant to establish a contrast to emperor worship.)

The general emphasis on orthodoxy, so suspicious to some, is natural and to be expected when one keeps in mind that the general purpose of the Pastorals was to steady and strengthen the Christian community against the intrusion of error. It is therefore reasonable to argue on the grounds of the basic Pauline structure of the Pastorals and the understandable novelties that these are the writings of the apostle himself.

Congregational Organization

The evolution of congregational organization is believed to have followed a general line from the beginnings, when the Spirit ruled, to a later period of definite hierarchical positions, when the office was all-important. At first the congregations were served by traveling, Spirit-endowed preachers who were later supplanted by local officials with a bishop at their head. Those who deny the Pauline authorship maintain that the congregational organization reflected in the Pastorals is so late that Paul could not have been the author.

In general it is to be noted that there apparently always were officials of some kind in the churches Paul established. (See, for instance, 1 Thess. 5:12; 1 Cor. 12:28.) Phil. 1:1 even speaks of *bishops* and *deacons*, terms occurring also in the Pastorals. And even the designation *elder*, not found in the acknowledged Pauline writings, is employed by Luke in Acts 20:17, where it may well reflect Pauline usage. Moreover, the vagueness about the specific functions of the various offices indicates an early or intermediate state of development, quite different from that even of Ignatius' description of the so-called "monarchical" episcopate as it obtained in Asia Minor about 110. Timothy and Titus are not monarchical bishops but assistants of the apostle on a special mission with limited powers. Though the significance of the office is increasing in the situation presupposed by the Pastorals, the functioning of the Spirit is by no means minimized (see, for instance, 1 Tim. 1:18; 4:14). Thus the further development of offices discernible in the Pastorals is no compelling argument against authenticity.

The Heresies Combated

Are the heresies denounced in the Pastorals too late to fall within the life span of Paul? To answer this question it is necessary to determine, from the descriptions given in the Pastorals, the nature of the heresies combated. It is also to be noted that the problem of authenticity does not hinge on whether the heresies were distinct assaults on the faith or an amalgam. In fact, the situation on Crete (Titus) and in Ephesus (Timothy), though sharing certain similarities, would naturally tend to differ in some details.

In the broadest terms the heresy that agitates the mind of the author of the Pastorals is Jewish-Christian Gnosticism. This clumsy designation calls for definition. Gnosticism (*gnosis*, Greek for knowledge) is a comprehensive term embracing a baffling swirl of doctrines and systems that developed in the interactions of the Greco-Roman and Oriental civilizations. As the name itself indicates, a common feature was the promise of esoteric knowledge necessary for salvation (cf. 1 Tim. 6:20). The content of this knowledge varied considerably with time

15

and system. The Jewish ingredient in the heterodoxy denounced in the Pastorals is not identical with the legalism scored in Galatians. In the Pastorals the errorists presume to teach the Law but are really ignorant of it (1 Tim. 1:7). They do not seem to insist on the necessity of observing the Law as a way of winning heaven. Rather, they are bungling theologians because they spin out fantastic speculations on the basis of Old Testament genealogies (Titus 3:9; cf. 1:14 and 1 Tim. 1:4; 4:7.) The false distinction between clean and unclean (Titus 1:15; 1 Tim. 4:3) also derives from Judaism.

If then, the grand heresy of the Pastorals is Jewish-tinged Gnosticism, there is no necessity for identifying this aberration with the fully developed Gnostic systems of the middle of the second century, associated with such names as Valentinus and Marcion. On the contrary, the relationships appear to be much closer to the syncretistic Jewish-Christian Gnosticism of Colossians with its ascetic rules and regulations.

Peculiarities of Language and Style

The problems of language and style are slippery and elusive. The critic must be careful to make due allowance for variations within the language and style of a single author as occasioned by differences of time, circumstance, and topic. One must also consider that all the undisputed letters of Paul do not yield the complete picture of his vocabulary. Even the use of the same words with different meanings does not unambiguously indicate variant authorship, for who is to say that a single author cannot use one term in a variety of significations? Since the Pastorals constitute a special group of letters both in content and time of composition, some peculiarities are to be expected. Are the variations so many

16

and striking as to render Pauline authorship of the Pastorals uncertain or even untenable?

There are, be it noted first of all, undisputed similarities to the acknowledged writings of Paul. Sections like 1 Tim. 1:12 ff.; 2:7; 4:11 ff.; 2 Tim. 1:3 ff., 15 ff.; 2:8 ff.; 3:10 ff.; 4:6 ff.; Titus 3:3 ff. are generally conceded to have an unmistakably Pauline flavor. The layout and characteristic formulas are those of the admittedly Pauline letters.

However, in style and vocabulary there are differences. Painstaking labor has been lavishly expended in examining grammar and word usage and in making comparisons with church fathers, noting and analyzing the minutest variations, such as comparison of the average number of letters in a word. The great name in this area of investigation has been P. N. Harrison. (*The Problem of the Pastoral Epistles*, London: Oxford, 1921. A readily accessible, conservative critique of Harrison's work is given in the appendix to Donald Guthrie's commentary. See the suggestions under "For Further Reading.") Most recently computers have been used in analyzing the linguistic data of Paul's epistles. The conclusion of A. F. Morton that six authors wrote the New Testament letters commonly attributed to Paul has been rejected by another scholar, John W. Ellison, who charges that the method of Morton is "an abuse of both computers and scholarship."

It has been correctly pointed out that characteristic Pauline terms are lacking (for instance, "the righteousness of God," "works of the Law," "flesh"). The usual particles and prepositions are wanting. New terms occur ("sound doctrine," "good conscience," etc.). Expressions and terms are more freely borrowed from the philosophic and cultic environment ("goodness and loving-kindness of God," "godliness," "appearing," etc.). The style is smoother and more prosaic.

How are such departures from the admittedly authentic letters to be explained? There are two possibilities: (1) They are written by different authors; (2) They are written by the same author at different times and under different circumstances.

The presence of undeniably Pauline elements is evidenced by two theories which agree that such elements are in the letters but endeavor to account for them without accepting the apostolic authorship of the epistles as such. There is first the "Fragments Theory." According to this hypothesis some unknown Paulinist wrote the Pastorals and, in order to lend an air of apostolic authority to his composition, inserted portions of genuine Pauline material he had in his possession. However, there are weighty objections to this theory. On the face of it there seems little likelihood that any writer should have had in his possession letters of Paul that he might dissect and then insert at various points in the material he was forging. Why can the supposed fragments not be reassembled into a coherent whole? If they are only parts and do not add up to the whole, what happened to the complete letters? And if the fragments came into the hands of the author simply as fragments, how can this strange occurrence be explained?

The second hypothesis is the "Secretary Theory," which seeks to account for the Pauline and non-Pauline elements by ascribing the composition to a secretary working with considerable freedom, albeit under Paul's supervision. It is argued that since writing was so difficult because of the materials used (2 Timothy even coming from a prison), correspondence was regularly committed to an amanuensis who was given certain directions and was supervised in carrying out the actual composition. Paul's letters too, it is urged, should be understood as having been written in this fashion.

Such a theory seems to account adequately for the perplexing combination of Pauline and non-Pauline features. It is rather an attractive hypothesis, even for the conservative Bible student, particularly if, as has been proposed by some, Luke was the amanuensis. However, the whole theory is subject to attack, and a secretarial role for Luke is also questionable. The possibility that Luke may have been the secretary seems to be ruled out by the fact that the style is more Pauline than Lucan, whereas the reverse should be true if Luke were writing as an amanuensis with considerable freedom. Further, no other likely candidate for the role presents himself, this difficulty indicating a weakness in the whole theory. It also seems that the sweeping contention that Paul did not dictate his letters may be an overstatement. (Cf. Rom. 16:22. Tertius likely took dictation and did not have a hand in the formulation of the letter.) Although the imprisonment of 2 Timothy is more severe (cf. 2 Tim. 1:16; 2:9) than that of Acts 28, the possibility of dictation is not utterly and automatically precluded. According to 2 Tim. 4:10 Paul seems to have been in free contact with his co-workers, and 4:21 indicates communications with individual Christians and through them with the entire Christian community in Rome. An inescapable implication of the "Secretary Theory" should also be noted. If the possibility of word-for-word dictation is rejected, then minute stylistic comparisons are complicated to the point of futility. Changes in freewheeling secretaries will bring changes in style and vocabulary that will make analysis baffling and conclusions unconvincing.

At the time of the Pastorals Paul was older, and we would expect his vocabulary to be expanded and modified by his experiences. He had been living in the West, where Latin would tend to influence his style. Arguments that Paul was so "dominated by language" that his style was fixed rather than flexible seem incompatible with the blithe assumption of secretarial cooperation. Such factors combined with other serious difficulties inherent in alternate theories still leave it a reasonable belief that Paul is the author of the Pastorals and that the deviations in style and vocabulary are adequately accounted for by changes in time and circumstance.

The Problem of Pseudonymity and the Pastorals

The difficulty suggested by this title can be simply stated: Is it conceivable that an author with the ability and moral sensitivity evident in the Pastorals could perpetrate the "pious fraud" of issuing these letters as the work of Paul?

The answers are sharply divided. Some scholars warn against the use of terms such as "forgery" to describe this kind of literary production. They contend that the attempt to gain acceptance for one's own composition by publishing it under the name of an apostle was in keeping with a standard literary convention and did not involve the stigma of forgery in the minds of the ancients as it does for us.

Others affirm the opposite point of view, arguing that pseudonymous publication was an anomaly always demanding an adequate explanation wherever it is assumed to have occurred. Moreover, in the specific case of the Pastorals the psychological prerequisites for a pseudonymous composition are wanting. Would the church countenance the publication of works under an apostolic name in order to recall a later generation to apostolic teaching when this dubious method was being used by Gnostic heretics? (See Donald Guthrie, "The Development of the Idea of Canonical Pseudepigrapha in New Testament Criticism," *Vox Evangelica*, London: Epworth Press, 1962, p. 57.) Another New Testament scholar came to the emphatic conclusion: "It seems to me that this conception of the letters, namely, that they are a drama in three acts composed both with ethical purposes and cunning calculation, confronts us with an author-personality which is psychologically inconceivable. Such a bizarre individual has never lived." (Frederik Torm, *Die Psychologie der Pseudonymität*, Gütersloh: Bertelsmann, 1932, p. 52)

More recently a scholar, rejecting the ethico-psychological approach as inadequate, has advanced the thesis that in early Christianity the modern understanding of authorship was unknown. According to this theory, those who composed sacred writing were believed to be "but the pen moved by the Spirit." Hence the identity of the human instrument remains unimportant. This hypothesis leads to a startling conclusion: "In my opinion we do not have to explain the phenomena of anonymity or pseudonymity in early Christian literature. It is the other way round: We need an explanation when the real author gives his name." (Kurt Aland, "The Problem of Anonymity and Pseudonymity in Christian Literature of the First Two Centuries," *The Journal of Theological Studies*, New Series, Vol. 12, 1961, p. 45)

Misgivings immediately suggest themselves. Aland can reach this conclusion only by lumping together patristic writers (church fathers of the second century)

21

and New Testament authors. This is an audacious procedure since it scarcely seems warranted to mingle the self-understanding of New Testament authors with that of church writers in the second century. Quite evidently apostolic authorship was held in high esteem from the earliest times and distinguished from that of other Christians. (See, for instance, 2 Thess. 2:2; 2 Peter 3:15, 16.) Aland's hypothesis thus appears to be self-contradictory. The identity of the human writer who is nothing but an instrument of the Holy Spirit is unimportant (anonymity is the ideal), and yet the human writer takes great pains to make his production look like and pass for the work of an apostle (pseudonymity). Indeed, if anonymity is the ideal, pseudonymity demands explanation. All the while pseudonymity is virtually impossible of explanation.

Although Aland believes that he can take care of the problem of 2 Peter and 1 Timothy with relative ease, 2 Timothy confronts him with such difficulties that he must concede: "But the information about the sojourn of the various co-workers in the fourth chapter of 2 Timothy, the first trial of Paul, the instructions for the addressees, as well as the end of the epistle to Titus evince such a thorough knowledge, such a simulated perspective, and such a reconstruction of Paul's personal affairs, that we can hardly avoid assuming an intended forgery" (p. 46). But if we are confronted by a forgery, the psychological objections of Torm are pertinent. He protests (p. 8) against the euphemism "pious fraud" (*fraus pia*) and contends that in many instances a question mark must be placed behind the term "fraud" and most especially behind the word "pious" unless this latter designation is to be utterly devoid of all meaning.

An important New Testament reference bearing on the problem of pseudonymity seems not to have received the attention it deserves. In his second letter to the Thessalonians Paul exhorts the brethren "not to be quickly shaken in mind or excited, either by spirit or by word, or by letter purporting to be from us" (2 Thess. 2:2). The somewhat ambiguous expression "purporting to be from us" (literally, "as from us") may very well refer to a forged letter. But even if it be conceded that the meaning is rather a wrong interpretation of a letter Paul had actually written, it still remains true that apostolic authorship and inspiration are sharply distinguished from nonapostolic authorship and the ecstatic utterances of some other member of the Christian community. Candlish links this reference from 2 Thessalonians with 1 Tim. 4:1 ff. and comments: "That Paul anticipated that such practices (forgery) would increase among those who departed from pure Christianity appears from 1 Tim. 4:1, where he characterizes the seducers of the last days as 'speaking falsely in hypocrisy' (Authorized Version), that is, acting a part, a phrase which in its proper meaning exactly describes the literary forgeries that were so largely associated with Gnostic, Manichaean, and ascetic errors, such as he describes in the following verses" (J. S. Candlish, "On the Moral Character of Pseudonymous Books," *The Expositor*, 4, 4 [1891], p. 105). If these observations are at all correct, the sweeping assertion that "at the time when the New Testament was written, pseudonymity was an accepted literary form" (J. C. Fenton, "Pseudonymity in the New Testament," *Theology*, 58 [1955], 55) becomes an impossibility.

At least one other serious objection to the theory of pseudonymity in the case of the Pastorals must be mentioned. Psychological grounds for most spurious works are readily forthcoming. The Infancy Gospels attempt to fill the gap left by the canonical gospels. Gnostic writings seek to clothe their heretical novelties with venerable, apostolic authority. But in the case of the Pastorals there is no such gap to be filled, no point of contact beckoning. There is no ancient tradition putting Timothy in Ephesus and Titus on Crete. Why fabricate letters adapted to situations that are difficult to fit into the tradition? An invented story should have seized on something like the reference to Spain (Rom. 15:24) or the remark of Paul in Philemon 22 asking that a guest room be prepared for him. Also it would have been easier for a forger to have Paul writing more generally to a congregation rather than to specific individuals in very concrete historical situations.

Thus the swarm of difficulties besetting the whole problem of New Testament pseudonymity and the Pastorals in particular adds credibility to Pauline authorship.

The Time of Writing

According to the interpretation accepted here, 1 Timothy and Titus were written after the first Roman imprisonment in conjunction with a final journey of the apostle through the mission territory of Asia Minor. 1 Timothy was likely sent from Macedonia (see 1 Tim. 1:3). It is not possible to determine whether Titus came before or after 1 Timothy, nor can the place of composition be fixed. 2 Timothy was written from Rome, where Paul was in prison awaiting execution. The similarity of the letters link them closely together in time. However, the scarcity of data makes it impossible to speak with finality concerning chronology.

Possible dates are:

59 – 61 Paul's First Roman Imprisonment
62 – 63 First Timothy and Titus
63 (fall) Second Timothy
64 Neronian Persecution Begins
64 or 67 Execution of Paul

The Pastorals introduce the reader to a theological climate different from that of the other Pauline epistles for the obvious reason that they derive from a later and more settled situation. This is no reason for depreciating their importance and relevance as some have tended to do. The current ecclesiastical situation is perhaps more accurately reflected in the Pastorals than in the earlier epistles. The problems besetting contemporary church life are in closer correspondence to those of the Pastorals than to those seen in the ferment and first enthusiasm of young churches addressed in Thessalonians, Galatians, Romans, or Corinthians. The present age is a time of buffeting and trial as the faithful seek to maintain the Gospel tradition in its purity. It may be more romantic and more exciting to plant the truth in new areas than to maintain it intact in the old. But who is to say that the former task is more important? Or more difficult? Because the latter assignment is different, it is not necessarily less important than the former. Indeed, for honest seekers the Pastorals continue to yield refreshment for their aridity, guidance for their perplexity, and encouragement for their despair.

1 Timothy

OUTLINE

Commentary on First Timothy

EXHORTATION TO COMBAT HERESY   1:1-20

Greeting   *1:1-2*

¹ **Paul, an apostle of Christ Jesus by command of God our Savior and of Christ Jesus our hope,**
² **To Timothy, my true child in the faith:**
Grace, mercy, and peace from God the Father and Christ Jesus our Lord.

1 Paul begins this letter with a special adaptation of the customary ancient formula of greeting. Among the unusual features is the emphasis on his apostleship. Although Timothy does not dispute Paul's authority, it is to be clear from the outset that Paul issues directives relative to church affairs on the basis of his apostolic office, not on the basis of a mere personal relationship between the two men. It will also be salutary for the congregation to be aware that Paul's directives are not unwarranted instrusions but that they are legitimated by his apostolic office. As an *apostle*, that is, one sent by Jesus, he functions as a representative of Jesus.

31

The obligation which has been placed upon him is intensified by the word "command," used here as well as Titus 1:3 and Rom. 16:26 instead of the milder and more customary term "by the will of God." (Cf. 1 Cor. 1:1; 2 Cor. 1:1; Eph. 1:1; Col. 1:1; 2 Tim. 1:1)

It seems unusual to find God called "Savior" since we more regularly refer to Jesus as Savior. However, the Septuagint (ancient Greek translation of the Old Testament) uses the term broadly, applying it not only to God but even to men. Despite this precedent, there may be a subtle hint (note *our* Savior") that whereas the heathen had used the title for their gods (for instance, Zeus, Apollo, and Aesculapius) and were now hailing the emperors, even Nero, as Savior, the Christian had Another for whom he reserved this title. Compare Titus 2:11 ff. and the comment there. The Christian appropriation of this term for Jesus and God would then mean setting up a rival claim. What the benighted pagan vainly sought or foolishly believed he had found in his rulers or his gods was more than fulfilled in God, who saved through His Son Jesus, the Savior. Jesus is called "our hope," emphasizing the fact that though our salvation has been fully won, we on earth still live in a state of expectancy, awaiting the full possession and realization of what we now enjoy by faith. This hope differs from irrepressible optimism by reason of the fact that it builds on the promise of God. And since the Lord in whom the believer hopes will return to demand an accounting, this hope does not tranquilize but rather galvanizes the congregation of believers.

2 Paul expresses the close relationship between himself and Timothy by calling him his "true child." Paul had brought Timothy to faith in Christ, and this Paul considers a spiritual fatherhood (cf. 1 Cor. 4:15 to

17). Perhaps Paul also means to hint that there is a father-son similarity of spiritual virtues between him and Timothy.

Whereas the apostle more frequently uses a doublet (grace and peace), he here employs a triplet ("grace, mercy, and peace") as the form of his benediction. The insertion of "mercy" into the formula serves to freshen and clarify the meaning of grace. In amazing condescension God has drawn near to us and on our level helped us by ending the hostilities between us and Himself through the declaration of peace in Christ. Regardless of how long or how strikingly one has enjoyed the grace, mercy, and peace of God, the prayer for their continuance is necessary. They do not need to be accomplished—God has done that—but they do need to be made effective in the lives of individuals and congregations. This happens through the power of God. Thus Paul acknowledges the power of God in this benediction, for he is beseeching the Almighty, the Source of all blessing, to grant of His sovereign goodness, grace, mercy, and peace through the one Mediator, Christ Jesus.

The Fight Against the Heretics   *1:3-11*

3 As I urged you when I was going to Macedo'nia, remain at Ephesus that you may charge certain persons not to teach any different doctrine, 4 nor to occupy themselves with myths and endless genealogies which promote speculations rather than the divine training*a* that is in faith; 5 whereas the aim of our charge is love that issues from a pure heart and a good conscience and sincere faith. 6 Certain persons by swerving from these have wandered away

a Or *stewardship*, or *order*

into vain discussion, [7] desiring to be teachers of the law, without understanding either what they are saying or the things about which they make assertions.

[8] Now we know that the law is good, if any one uses it lawfully, [9] understanding this, that the law is not laid down for the just but for the lawless and disobedient, for the ungodly and sinners, for the unholy and profane, for murderers of fathers and murderers of mothers, for manslayers, [10] immoral persons, sodomites, kidnapers, liars, perjurers, and whatever else is contrary to sound doctrine, [11] in accordance with the glorious gospel of the blessed God with which I have been entrusted.

When Paul was leaving Ephesus for Macedonia, Timothy was apparently eager to accompany him. However, Paul ordered him to stay behind to fight against errorists. This commission, once given orally, is so important that it is now repeated in writing. Since Timothy is to order the errorists to be silent, it is evident that they were still in the congregation or else Timothy would have had no authority over them. (This indicates an early date for the letter.) Before excommunication there is to be instruction. Dismissal from the congregation will finally be necessary, for continued toleration would mean hardening of errorists in their heresy and danger to the congregation. The prohibition is general, for neither are the errorists named nor is the error defined. Timothy is to "charge certain persons not to teach any different doctrine." Different from what? This is not immediately specified but becomes clearer in the context. For converts from Judaism and paganism there was always the tendency to drag along into their newly-found faith in Jesus elements of the old system or of their former way of life. Such Judaizing or paganizing elements had to be removed. A first symptom and a continuing source of the infection of heresy is the itch to go beyond the Scriptures. Compare 1 Cor. 4:6.

4 The child of God must be forearmed with the knowledge that error can be interesting. However, the worthlessness of heresy should be clear when contrasted with the Gospel. Whereas the errorists might be intriguing and captivating with their fanciful speculations, the Gospel makes a sober appeal that changes and reshapes lives once distorted by sin.

There is some obscurity about the precise nature of the myths and genealogies. They have been regarded as Gnostic fancies. Common to the various Gnostic (see the Introduction) systems was the belief in an Ultimate Being from whom there issued in a kind of overflow or radiation a series of emanations progressively farther withdrawn from the divine source. Some would link the genealogies with these emanation theories.

However, in view of the label "Jewish" applied to the myths in Titus 1:14, it may be better to regard the heresies more as Judaic in background. Substantiation for this view is also found in Titus 3:9, where genealogies are set into the context of wranglings about the Law, a very Jewish preoccupation (cf. 1 Tim. 1:7). Therefore, what may be meant is the allegorical and mythical trimming added to the Old Testament narratives and the mania for elaborate genealogies as seen, for instance, in the *Book of Jubilees* and the Pseudo-Philo *Book Concerning Biblical Antiquities*. All such legends and myths are worlds apart from the sober, factual history of Jesus Christ as narrated in the Gospel tradition. (Cf. 2 Peter 1:16)

Perhaps motivating the concern with genealogies was the desire of the errorists to make their fantastic doctrines more credible by exalting their own persons. This might be done by proving the purity and nobility of their own family tree. At all events, pride entered in, if not pride of ancestry then pride of ingenuity in expounding the supposed deeper mysteries and hidden meanings of the Scriptures. Luther once said: "Were pride to cease to exist, there would be no sin at all." If this is true, then the cessation of pride would also mean the end of heresy.

The craze for genealogies inevitably spawned a type of Bible interpretation that lost itself in trifles and fables to the neglect of what is important: "the divine training that is in faith." Such growth in faith occurs only through the exercise of faith, and it is not faith but idle fantasy that is exercised if energy is expended on myths and speculations.

5 In the clashes that are inevitable when Timothy opposes heresy, he is to remember the primacy of "love" (cf. Mark 12:30-31; Rom. 13:10; 1 Cor. 13). If the goal of instruction is love, this means something about motives and about manner of presentation. Love, however, never holds back from but rather impels to confrontation of error with the truth. Where love prevails, there is a corrective both for him who admonishes and for him who is admonished. The former is warned against the exaltation of his own person and private opinion; the latter is preserved from obstinacy and rebelliousness. That the goal of love is not reached by sentimental misinterpretations of love is emphasized by the word "charge" (several times: vv. 3, 5, 18), which in the original is a word of considerable force and energy, meaning not only to proclaim but also to com-

mand. However, whatever negative aspects the term may suggest (thrusting aside of heresy), all the force and energy are finally to serve the one positive purpose: teaching and inculcating love. But love cannot exist in a vacuum. It must derive "from a pure heart and a good conscience and sincere faith." This means that sinfulness has been renounced in the depths of one's being, that conscience can testify to the purity of motivation, that dependence on God's grace is a living reality. Loveless self-exaltation is humbled by penitent self-abasement. And yet, the humiliation of admitted sin does not paralyze the penitent in impotent self-recrimination, because God's forgiving grace releases him for a life of love.

6-7 Where these pure motives and the goal of love have been lost from sight, men slip into pompous pretensions. Because the errorist does not enjoy the satisfactions of faith, he restlessly casts about for a substitute and ends up with the miserable imitation of legalistic piety. Whatever form this legalistic tendency may take, be it subtleties in expounding the Old Testament law or rigorous, ascetic demands (cf. 1 Tim. 4:3 and Titus 1:14), all is rejected as missing the goal of the Gospel and wandering off into the wastelands of idle chatter. The upstarts are not only unable to distinguish accurately between Ceremonial Law (temporary) and Moral Law (permanent), but even in their application of the Moral Law, as summarized in the Ten Commandments, they are confused. Apparently they make the observance of moral laws a way of salvation. They add restrictions of their own to the prohibitions laid down in the Old Testament. Such multiplication of ascetic regulations usually betrays a basic conception of salvation as if it were by deeds. These would-be professors of the Old Testament deceive no one more than themselves, for their pretentious, inflated language is not understood even by themselves.

8-10 Law in v. 7 may be taken more narrowly as referring to the Mosaic Law. But the implications of Paul's observations make it legitimate to weigh his remarks in the context of the entire Old Testament. Here again in v. 8 the basic meaning of law may be the Mosaic Law. However, the digression on the law which follows makes it clear that the term must also be understood as specifying what is characteristic of law generally and is also of God's law. Mosaic Law, Law as opposed to Gospel, natural law, law as a principle in the government of society — none of these significations of the term is to be excluded in probing the import of Paul's observations on the function of law. However, even law given by God to Moses on Sinai is still Law and not Gospel. Therefore, this adamant stand against the would-be interpreters of the Law must not be misconstrued as repudiation of the Law as such. Only the error is decried. The Law is good, but the usage of the Law may be perverse (cf. Rom. 7:12). Basic to a proper understanding of the role of the Law is to see clearly that the Law was necessary in the first place only because of sin. Were it not for sin, there would be no antagonism between God and man, no need for the Law, which is necessary only if there is this conflict between the will of God and the will of man. But for the believer this discord has been overcome by Jesus Christ, in whom he believes, so that he has been elevated above the need for the Law. The Law as a means for attaining righteousness is superfluous for one who is just; just, that is, not because he himself has met the requirements of the Law, but because he has been declared righteous

38

through faith. For such the Law cannot be the way of salvation. Neither can the Law condemn them to separation from God because of their sin, for they are forgiven, and being forgiven, they are also renewed so as to be no longer under the dominion of sin.

However, the fact that salvation is not a prize for keeping the commandments but the unearned gift through faith in Jesus Christ does not mean that the Law no longer has any functions to perform for the believer. Total immunity from the Law is true for the Christian insofar as he is just. But even at their best, believers fall short of perfection. St. John's First Epistle (1:6 ff.) does not hesitate to combine as compatible the two emphases: (1) Believers are free from sin; (2) Believers must confess their sin. Believers are totally justified but not yet totally just. Therefore they need the Law, not indeed as a code book for meriting heaven but for the condemnation and direction the Law gives. According to Paul, all the vicious sins for which the Law is properly designed are simply various eruptions of the Old Adam, the rebellious nature of sinful man. And though subdued in the Christian, the Old Adam is still at work as the second "I" (cf. Rom. 7). The Christian's Old Adam is everything that is mentioned in vv. 9 and 10. Hence the Law must help to cage the beast, must reveal sin and the need for a Savior from sin, must mark out the forbidden way and illuminate the narrow way.

Moreover, there is rampaging lawlessness loose in the world, so that the reaffirmation of the Law is a standing need. As long as there are those who kill their fathers and mothers and who perpetrate the rest of the crimes listed in the catalog of vice, the Law cannot be expendable. The enumeration first of six general categories of sinners and then of sins against specific commandments is followed by the comprehensive denunciation of anything at all that is harmful to sound doctrine, so that no one escapes the need to consult his conscience and penitently to see himself as a sinner, righteous only by virtue of the gracious verdict of a forgiving God. The attitude of these verses toward the Law, sometimes regarded as un-Pauline, is not dissimilar to the emphases of Rom. 7:12 ff. and Gal. 5:13 ff.

The term "sound" literally means "healthy." This figurative sense is confined to the occurrences in the Pastorals. (See also 2 Tim. 4:3; Titus 1:9; 2:1; 1 Tim. 6:3; 2 Tim. 1:13; Titus 1:13; 2:2.) And yet, this epithet is not an invention of the apostle, for it has ancient antecedents and contemporary parallels. Though this may be a borrowing from the vocabulary of the Stoics, there is a shift in the precise meaning. Whereas for the Stoics "sound" meant, "in conformity with reason," for Paul the meaning is "in conformity with the Gospel of Christ" (cf. 1 Tim. 6:3 ff.). The contrast, then, is not between reason and unreason but between orthodoxy and heresy. In 1 Tim. 6:4 ("he has a morbid craving for controversy and for disputes about words") the original means literally "to be sick," indicating not only loss of vigor but also deterioration in function. Thus orthodoxy is spiritual health, heresy spiritual sickness. Such insistence on sound teaching presented in a vocabulary not found elsewhere in the apostle's writings hardly seems to betray the hand of a clever imitator of Pauline style, but rather is the kind of rigid emphasis one should expect at this late point in the apostle's career when the Gospel was in jeopardy.

11 In concluding the thoughts of this paragraph,

Paul relates what he has just said to the Gospel with which he has been entrusted. This provides Timothy with a weapon against those who would disparage Paul, for the Gospel of freedom from the Law which Paul proclaims is not his own invention but the Gospel, which reveals the glory of God. The Old Testament time of the Law is past; any hope of becoming righteous through the Law is illusory; to God alone be the glory! The Gospel is dedicated to revealing God's glory, which consists not only in His power and wisdom but also and especially in His forgiving love.

The designation of God as "blessed" (cf. 6:15) is unusual and interesting. The ancient Greek usage of this term for the gods was meant to describe them as happy because they are elevated above and beyond the cares and concerns of earthly existence. The Christian Gospel of the blessed God knows Him as the One who, though needing nothing, yet took pity on sinful man; who, though elevated above human woe, yet shared and conquered our misery.

The Power of the Pure Gospel
Illustrated in Paul   *1:12-17*

12 I thank him who has given me strength for this, Christ Jesus our Lord, because he judged me faithful by appointing me to his service, 13 though I formerly blasphemed and persecuted and insulted him; but I received mercy because I had acted ignorantly in unbelief, 14 and the grace of our Lord overflowed for me with the faith and love that are in Christ Jesus. 15 The saying is sure and worthy of full acceptance, that Christ Jesus came into the world to save sinners. And I am the foremost of sinners; 16 but I received

41

mercy for this reason, that in me, as the foremost, Jesus Christ might display his perfect patience for an example to those who were to believe in him for eternal life. ¹⁷ To the King of ages, immortal, invisible, the only God, be honor and glory for ever and ever.*ᵇ* Amen.

ᵇ Greek to the ages of ages

Having identified himself with the Gospel, Paul is so carried away that he must praise the grace of God in his own life as an impressive and instructive illustration of the meaning of the Gospel. He is a living example of the truth that Christians exist by reason of grace and not by virtue of the Law. And so Paul does not discuss and haggle; he demonstrates, and though he demonstrates by reference to himself, what he says is not egotistical, for it climaxes in the praise of God.

12 Paul's call to the apostolic office is marked with the impress of undeserved grace. Jesus Christ did not find the qualifications present in Paul and therefore select him as His ambassador, but rather in calling him Jesus empowers Paul with the strength and fidelity requisite for the task assigned to him. The potential is not really in man but in the forgiving, transforming grace of God. Therefore the motive force in Paul's work is not a grimly determined sense of duty in carrying out a disagreeable task, but throbbing, exultant joy in a forgiving Lord, so that even a difficult assignment is a privilege.

13 That his call was truly the result of grace is further emphasized when Paul describes his preconversion status with three terms designed to express all the virulence and violence of opposition to Jesus Christ. He "blasphemed" by denying that Jesus was the Messiah;

he "persecuted," and that fiercely; he "insulted" the Almighty by the insolence of his conduct (cf. Acts 9:1 ff.). In words and deeds Paul had rebelled against God, for in fighting against Christ's people, he fought against God. (If a later forger wrote the Pastorals, it is difficult to see how he would have had the audacity to apply these scurrilous designations to Paul.) Paul, here playing down his own achievements in true humility, sets his humble self in marked contrast to the grandiose and impressive teachers of the Law.

Paul's plea of ignorance is not meant to excuse and absolve himself. In v. 15 he confesses his guilt unreservedly. All that he is saying is that he was not frustrating the grace of God by deliberate sin in his preconverted state. Ignorance may reduce guilt; it does not eliminate guilt. There was much Paul could have urged in his behalf had he followed the typical pattern of self-justification. He knew the Law, was scrupulous and zealous in its observance, and where he erred, it was purely in ignorance and with the best of intentions. That sin committed in ignorance is really sin is evident also from Eph. 4:18. However, that there is a glimmer of hope where sins result from ignorance is also indicated in the New Testament (cf. Acts 3:17; 17:30; 1 Peter 1:14; Rom. 10:3; Heb. 5:2). God in His grace can and does overcome and forgive all kinds of sin. But perhaps nowhere does sin show its dread power more terrifyingly than when deliberate disobedience seeks to frustrate even the purpose of God to forgive and save.

14 Paul had no claim on God's mercy. It was only the superabundance (the original has a compound word to express the thought) of divine grace that could overwhelm the enormity of Paul's sin. And where grace has entered in, it does not come alone but is accompanied by faith and love, which find their sustenance in Christ Jesus. It is in the exercise of faith and love that the apostle does his apostolic work.

15 And so Paul has experienced in his own soul and life the truth that Jesus came into the world to save sinners (cf. Luke 19:10). Paul does not justify himself by making excuses but accepts God's justification by making confession.

The introductory formula, "the saying is sure" (limited in the New Testament to the other Pastoral occurrences: 1 Tim. 3:1; 4:9; 2 Tim. 2:11; Titus 3:8), evidently means more than merely to announce a familiar theme or just to affirm the reliability of the Gospel as such. Undeniably the author's main concern is to signalize the importance and reliability of what he is saying. (Compare 2 Cor. 1:18; Rev. 21:5; 22:6. For the content of the saying compare Mark 2:17; Luke 5:32; 19:10; John 12:47.) However, it may well be that the formula also implies the existence of sayings of Jesus in circulation in one form or another prior to and alongside our canonical Gospels. Such detached words of the Lord not found in the Gospels are recorded in Acts 20:35: "It is more blessed to give than to receive." The interesting question then arises whether such maxims of Jesus may have survived outside of the New Testament, so that "unknown words of Jesus" found in non-canonical sources may record authentic utterances of the Lord. Thus Paul may be quoting a saying of Jesus embodied in a baptismal hymn or some other liturgical formula, or taken from a collection of sayings of Jesus. At all events, there is no question that the apostle's main purpose is to underscore as absolutely certain that Jesus Christ is the Savior of sinners.

Overwhelmed by his own guilt, Paul immediately

adds that of sinners he is the foremost. The present tense is significant. The past rescue from sin is a vivid reminder that even now Paul can exist before God as one saved only by the mercy and forgiveness of God. Even in the present, the greatest sinner one can know is himself.

16 As Paul once again depicts his conversion, he describes it as an act of divine grace with a double emphasis: (1) "I received mercy"; (2) "His perfect patience." So great is the mercy and so longsuffering is the patience of Christ that the "foremost" sinner becomes the "foremost" example of God's forgiveness. Paul regards his own experience as an illustration and demonstration of what God wills for others.

17 Thinking of his own conversion and the salvation of many others to come, the apostle expresses his touched emotions in a doxology that likely came from the pre-Christian liturgy of the Hellenistic synagogs and was appropriated as part of the Christian worship. Being "of the ages," the eternal God is the One who is supreme ruler now over time and the events of history and who will both manifest and exercise His rule in the ages (also the eternal age) to come; being "immortal," He is the giver of all life; being "invisible," He is the God who dwells in the light no man can approach. He is, to put it in a word, "the only God." Therefore to Him belong the worship and praises of His people forever. The "Amen" is an invitation to all to believe and appropriate this doxology as their own.

This hymn of praise expresses the marvel of Christian worship, which is to recognize the exalted position of God and the humble status of sinful man, and yet to believe that the holy, sublime God is reached and touched by the praise of sinful but forgiven man.

Wage the Good Warfare!   *1:18-20*

¹⁸ This charge I commit to you, Timothy, my son, in accordance with the prophetic utterances which pointed to you, that inspired by them you may wage the good warfare, ¹⁹ holding faith and a good conscience. By rejecting conscience, certain persons have made shipwreck of their faith, ²⁰ among them Hymenae'us and Alexander, whom I have delivered to Satan that they may learn not to blaspheme.

18 The "charge" Paul commits to Timothy includes not only the order to remain in Ephesus but also the assignment of combating the errorists and defending the truth. The tender, affectionate form of address, "Timothy, my son," underscores the earnestness of Paul's exhortation to fight the good fight. In order further to fortify his fighting spirit, Paul reminds Timothy of an event that is not described for us in any detail. The plural, "prophetic utterances," may indicate a number of different occasions or may mean nothing more than that several prophets testified at one and the same time. These men, endowed with charismatic gifts of God's Holy Spirit (cf. 1 Cor. 12 and 14), testified to the fitness of Timothy for special service in the church. Whether the occasion referred to was the selection of Timothy as co-worker with Paul (Acts 16:1-3) or the assignment to a specific area (Ephesus), or both, is not clear. Possibly the situation was parallel to that of Acts 13:1 ff. Or perhaps the meaning here is that Paul's resolve to commit the important assignment in Ephesus to Timothy was confirmed by the pronouncements of men specially gifted with the Spirit. At all events, in times of stress and strain Timothy is to be reassured by

remembering that he has not brazenly intruded himself into the pastoral office but that he has been called by God.

Paul's fondness for the metaphor of warfare (cf. 2 Tim. 2:3-4; 1 Cor. 9:7) shows his virile understanding of the pastoral office, which involves both fighting and suffering. Peace and the reign of love cannot prevail until opposition has been hammered down. This is not to say that all fighting in the church has God's blessing. Haggling is not good warfare. The fighting spirit will best serve God's purposes if it is remembered that the warfare is waged not only against sin in others but also against sin in the self. (Gal. 5:17)

19 The vigorous expenditure of energy required for carrying out his ministerial functions means that Timothy will need the resources of "faith and a good conscience" (cf. v. 5). He cannot most effectively rouse faith in others unless he himself has faith, and he cannot fight nimbly if he is crippled by a bad conscience. A nautical metaphor serves to illustrate this. Faith and a good conscience are like an anchor. If the anchor is cut loose and thrown overboard, the vessel eventually shatters in shipwreck. And yet, though this accurately pictures the folly of the errorist, this is not to say that he deliberately chooses to be shipwrecked. Rather, shipwreck is an unforeseen disaster. Even so, alienation from God is the dread result of a hidden breakaway from God in the deep recesses of the soul.

20 This sad development is confirmed by two examples, "Hymenaeus and Alexander." In 2 Tim. 2:17-18 we read of a Hymenaeus who said the resurrection had already taken place, and in 2 Tim. 4:14 an Alexander called "the coppersmith" is mentioned as a personal opponent of Paul. Although one cannot press for the identification, there is no compelling reason for not assuming that those men are the same as those mentioned here.

The terminology describing excommunication from the congregation is identical with that employed in 1 Cor. 5:5, namely, "delivered to Satan." Though the details of the procedure are not known to us, the essentials are no mystery. Whenever crassly and stubbornly erring members were barred from the congregation, Satan gained easier access to them and might utilize his advantage to inflict physical harm. It is to be noted that man is never without a master. Either he is brought through faith under the lordship of Jesus Christ, or he is helplessly exposed to Satan's tyranny. The purpose of the whole procedure was pedagogical, that the persons excommunicated might learn not to blaspheme. Hence the motive was not the desire to satisfy personal vindictiveness but rather to save the congregation from corrupting contamination and to rouse the erring individual to an awareness of his sin, thus leading him to repent.

LIFE IN THE CONGREGATION   2:1 — 3:16

Chapters 2 and 3 prescribe forms necessary to bring order into the congregation lest exuberance get out of hand, a condition that threatened the Corinthian congregation (1 Cor. 14). Chapter 2 is concerned with the conduct of public worship, whereas chapter 3 concentrates on the officers of the congregation and their responsibilities.

Directive for Public Prayer   *2:1-7*

[1] **First of all, then, I urge that supplications, prayers, intercessions, and thanksgivings be made**

for all men, [2] for kings and all who are in high positions, that we may lead a quiet and peaceable life, godly and respectful in every way. [3] This is good, and it is acceptable in the sight of God our Savior, [4] who desires all men to be saved and to come to the knowledge of the truth. [5] For there is one God, and there is one mediator between God and men, the man Christ Jesus, [6] who gave himself as a ransom for all, the testimony to which was borne at the proper time. [7] For this I was appointed a preacher and apostle (I am telling the truth, I am not lying), a teacher of the Gentiles in faith and truth.

1 Most important of all the directives for worship is that which has to do with prayer. The congregation properly concerned with maintaining pure doctrine must also be concerned with prayer. The four different terms for prayer have differing connotations. "Supplications" derive from such an intense awareness of need that one does not hesitate to beg. "Prayers" include also the praise of God. "Intercessions" show that the believer's concern is not selfish, and "thanksgivings" result from an awareness that God's answers come of His goodness and are not elicited by man's merit. These varying emphases also are important in their cumulative stress that prayer is vital and that prayers are adaptable to the differing situations and requirements of life. None of the multiform types of prayer should be missing.

Immediately the universalism of the Christian faith is apparent. Prayer is to be made for all men, even the unbelieving pagan whom Judaism tended to despise. Dedication to the exclusive truth of the Gospel does not mean the exclusion of any from the congregation's intercession. On the contrary, if the Gospel is to be maintained in its purity, as chapter 1 requires, supplications must be made for all. The church is separated from the world and yet prays for the world. This is a unique kind of isolation.

2 Even when Paul gets specific and mentions kings as the concern of public prayer, his universalism is indicated by the plural. The absence of the definite article before "kings" makes it evident that universalism is intended and that there is no reference to a time, too late for Paul, when there were emperors in both East and West. Not only the present emperor, and not only the Roman emperor, but all rulers are to be remembered in congregational prayer. Even minor officials are not to be omitted. This attitude toward government is entirely in the spirit of Jesus (cf. John 19:11; Matt. 22:21). The exhortation does not intimate that Christians were inclined to be revolutionary and had to be restrained. Rather, the antagonisms on the part of the state might become so irritating that the proper attitude of obedience and concern could be poisoned with bitterness. To turn the other cheek requires strength from above. Also it may well be, as has been suggested, that prayer for those in supreme positions of power implies opposition to emperor worship, since the need for divine grace is a reminder that even the most exalted ruler is still under God.

It is an amazing audacity on the part of Christians to believe that their prayer for civil rulers moves God to control political events in a way that will be advantageous to the church. Only those who have stood at the foot of the cross can believe God cares that much. Neither is such prayer selfish. It is simply the awareness that what is good for the rulers is good for the church. The petition is not primarily concerned with escape from persecution but rather for that external quiet in which godliness best thrives. If a corrupt government tolerates disruptive explosions in society, the shock waves will rock the church. If there is a general decay of morals among the people unchecked by the rulers, the rot threatens also the health of the church.

Paul does not believe that the church must be magnificently imposing to be effective. Instead of noisily intruding itself on the public, the church quietly leads its godly life. However, if God so orders, the church is ready, in humble obedience to God, to take its stand before the public. And even if taking its stand for God in a hostile environment involves the church more tumultuously in the "good warfare" (1:18), the Christian life is still quiet and peaceable, since there is no hatred nor bitterness but rather intercession for all.

3 Such universal prayer pleases God, whose loving concern is universal. It is not always easy to pray for all, especially not those who place obstacles in the path of the church's progress. But God's love for all rules out selective, restricted prayer on the part of His people.

4 In order for all men to be saved, it is requisite that they come to the knowledge of the truth. The darkening of human understanding caused by sin and evidenced by pagan idolatry is enlightened and dispelled by the light of the truth in Christ. "The knowledge of the truth" comes from accepting the powerful and transforming proposition that in Jesus Christ God is good and forgiving. The depths of such knowledge cannot be intellectually probed, for in this knowledge there is also the awareness of sin and God's judgment upon sin. And yet God loves and forgives. It is too much for the mind.

51

Since God's loving will for "all men" is that they all should be saved, it cannot be that God has harshly decreed damnation for a certain irrevocably fixed number of people. (The Lutheran doctrine of predestination is treated extensively in the Formula of Concord, Article 11. John Calvin's doctrine of a double election [since some are predestined to be saved, it necessarily follows that others are predestined to be damned] is developed in the third book of his *Institutes*. In his comment on this verse Calvin can do no better than argue that "all men" really means all classes of men and does not refer to God's attitude toward specific individuals. This escapist interpretation is not new with Calvin.) The mysterious dread might of sin is that puny man, who cannot resist the absolute, imperative will of God, can, however, frustrate the will of God to save him. But then it is man, not God, who is at fault. God's will is that men should "*come* to the knowledge of the truth"; they are not forced. Man's power to reject does not necessarily imply the ability to accept the saving will of God. The saving response, the willingness to accept, is a gift of grace. (Cf. 1 Cor. 12:3; Eph. 2:1, 5; John 6:29)

5 "One God, one mediator," one humanity — this is a brief but full statement of the divine universalism (cf. Rom. 3:29-30). Because man is God's creation, God lovingly followed after erring man to recall him in the person of Jesus Christ.

The emphasis on the humanity of Jesus does not rule out His deity (cf. Titus 2:13) but simply shows that the divine-human Jesus is a qualified Mediator: by reason of His human nature adequate to represent man; by reason of His divine nature competent to deal with God. Also the stress on "one," marking out Jesus as unique in being the one and only Mediator, harmonizes with the belief in His deity. The Gnostic heretics taught that there were various mediators of an intermediate nature, neither totally divine nor completely human. Paul's stress here on the humanity of Jesus may then be designed to show a contrast between truth and error on this point.

6 The meaning of Christ's mediation is now explained. By giving Himself into death, Jesus has paid the "ransom" that releases man from enslavement to sin, death, and devil. The "many" of Matt. 20:28 is now emphatically revealed to be "all." Any limitation on the number finally saved, any exclusion from the ranks of the redeemed, is due to the perverse folly of unbelieving man, who shuts himself out. Again there is the theme of universalism. Even as Christ gave Himself to be the ransom for all, so His followers must pray for all.

"At the proper time," God's time (Gal. 4:4), the witness of Jesus Christ came with its clarity. And now the witness comes as a word of reconciliation. Only when the message of the cross is transmitted to us, do we know what has occurred for our benefit (cf. 2 Cor. 5:19). Christ accomplished His work of redemption, chose and commissioned His witnesses, and then gave them the Word they were to proclaim. The progress of the Gospel proclamation continues with its successes and reversals under the sovereign sway of God, who still determines the proper time.

7 Because of the attacks and insinuations of the errorists, Paul points to his special office with humble pride. Three terms describe his function: preacher, apostle, teacher. As a "preacher" he has a message from God to proclaim to man; as an "apostle" he is on a mission that God has assigned him; as a "teacher" he imparts instruction in the knowledge of God. As preacher, apostle, and teacher, Paul proposes to win the Gentiles for the faith that is the truth. He himself is so firmly persuaded of the truth of the Gospel that in God's hands he can be an effective messenger in communicating the same persuasion to others. Such confidence and zeal need the truth as their basis.

Conduct of Men and Especially Women at Worship　　　　　　　　　　　　　　　*2:8-15*

⁸ **I desire then that in every place the men should pray, lifting holy hands without anger or quarreling; ⁹ also that women should adorn themselves modestly and sensibly in seemly apparel, not with braided hair or gold or pearls or costly attire ¹⁰ but by good deeds, as befits women who profess religion. ¹¹ Let a woman learn in silence with all submissiveness. ¹² I permit no woman to teach or to have authority over men; she is to keep silent. ¹³ For Adam was formed first, then Eve; ¹⁴ and Adam was not deceived, but the woman was deceived and became a transgressor. ¹⁵ Yet woman will be saved through bearing children,ᶜ if she continues ᵈ in faith and love and holiness, with modesty.**

> ᶜ Or *by the birth of the child*　　ᵈ Greek *they continue*

8 The gesture alluded to here, customary for Jews, Christians, and pagans alike, is that of extending the hands, palms upward, a posture with rich symbolical meaning. The hands which are held out to receive the divine blessing, being also the symbols of human activity, must be pure if they are to grasp the pure gifts God bestows. The empty hands display human need and point to the divine source from which those needs must be supplied. It is the clean heart that means clean

hands. Therefore anger and quarreling are excluded, for those who would live by mercy must practice mercy.

9 The women are to be careful not to inflame the desires of the men by daring, unseemly dress. This is not to suppress but to sanctify the natural urge of the woman to adorn herself. It is not required that women be "defigured" any more than that they be disfigured. However, there is a propriety in dress that cannot be comprehended in any specific formula of length or thickness or looseness but must be controlled by an inward spirituality.

10 The proper santification of the desire to adorn herself will be effected if the woman keeps in mind that the true jewels of the professing Christian women are Christian deeds. (cf. 1 Peter 3:3-5)

11-12 In the background is the ferment in marital relationships. Misleading teachers with their doctrinal fantasies were inflaming the minds of women by their false asceticism (degrading marriage—1 Tim. 4:3; intoxicating the unstable with pretentious talk—2 Tim. 3:6-7) so that the home was being threatened with disturbance and disruption. Paul's directives are meant to halt this corrosion.

The directive to women now becomes more specific as Paul bars them from the teaching office in the public worship assemblies. In 1 Cor. 14:34 ff. his prohibition is more general since it is *speaking* that is forbidden, whereas here he more distinctly refers to *teaching.* Although the prohibition addressed to the Corinthians did not prevent the woman endowed with the special gift (charisma) of prophecy (1 Cor. 11:5) from speaking, the exercise of the public ministry was not open to her. This limitation does not degrade nor reject women; it assigns them to those roles for which they are best qualified, including even some forms of teaching (cf. Titus 2:3 ff.). Paradoxically, the way of humility is not impoverishment but enrichment, not weakness but power, not disgrace but honor.

13 The directive is now based on a twofold Old Testament foundation. First, the sequence of creation was man, then woman. The dignity of woman is assured by the fact of her creation by God. But the order was man first, then woman.

14 Secondly, Eve was deceived, and though Adam followed his wife into guilt so that in Romans 5 Paul can speak of Adam as the source from which original sin derives, yet Eve's susceptibility to the serpent's temptation is indicative of a weakness that justifies the role here assigned to women.

15 The differing role of the woman does not impede nor jeopardize her salvation. Various interpretations have been suggested for this difficult verse such as:

1. "She will be saved through the birth of the Child, that is, Jesus Christ." All women, as well as men, will be saved through the Son of Mary.

2. "She will be saved from the perils of childbirth."

3. "She will be saved by the religious upbringing of her children." (The original text has the plural verb: "if they continue." However, since "woman" is used collectively, the translation "if she continues" is correct.)

4. "She shall be saved even though she must bear children," as if bearing children were the continuing curse of Eve's sin.

5. Allegorical interpretations, for example, that bearing children is symbolical of producing good works.

All these fanciful dodges involve labored interpretations and are difficult to extract from the text. One thought must, because of the Pauline stress on salvation by grace alone, be immediately ruled out: Paul cannot mean that bearing children in any way atones for sin. He knows of only one atonement for sin: the sacrifice of Jesus Christ on the cross (cf. Titus 3:5). Therefore the substance of what Paul is saying must be that the sanctified life of the believing woman is demonstrated in the home, where she faithfully and lovingly performs her humble but important duties. God does not save women by making them men.

Extended Note: 1 Timothy 2:11-14 and the Position of Women in the Church

This section has caused considerable embarrassment because it seems to be in such strident contradiction to the voices of feminine emancipation heard in modern times. The pressure to adapt congregational arrangements to allow the participation of women in functions from which they have been traditionally barred is intense. The precise meaning of this section is therefore of great importance.

The possibility of a rigid stand and explicit pronouncements on specific questions (for instance, women in the ministry, feminine participation in the governing body of the congregation) seems to be complicated by a certain tension in the pertinent references. Gal. 3:28 ("There is neither male nor female; for you are all one in Christ Jesus") has been interpreted as meaning that Paul is pronouncing sexual differentiation quite without import for church offices and functions. 1 Cor. 14:34 ff. ("The women should keep silence in the churches") is apparently clear and explicit but must somehow be harmonized with 1 Cor. 11:5 ("Any woman who prays or prophesies with her head unveiled dishonors her head"), which concedes women the right to "prophesy" in the worship service. Then the ironclad restriction of 1 Tim. 2:11-14 seems by contrast to come with inflexible rigidity. But further to complicate the problem, certain historical features apparently indicate a free and unrestricted participation of women in the work of the church. The first converts, women as well as men, were mentioned in connection with services in their houses (cf. Rom. 16:5; 1 Cor. 16:19; Col. 4:15; Philemon 2). Phoebe was a "deaconess" (Rom. 16:1-2). Prisca (Priscilla) is a "fellow worker" as is also Aquila, her husband. (Rom. 16:3)

Varied solutions to these difficulties have been proposed. Among them are the following:

1. Enthralled by the traditional Judaic and by the contemporary Hellenistic attitude toward women, Paul regarded the female sex as inferior and relegated her to a second-rate, subordinate position. Though there may be glimmerings of greater respect and higher regard for women here and there (Eph. 5:25; cf. 1 Peter 3:7), these are soon extinguished. It is claimed: The traditional doctrine of feminine inferiority triumphs in the New Testament generally and in Paul specifically. It is then suggested that the contemporary church should disavow these obsolete ideas.

However, this antifeminist depiction of Paul will have difficulty with, among other things, his positive emphasis on matrimony, for though he recognizes that family obligations can engross attention and monopolize time (1 Cor. 7), he yet inculcates these very duties (Col. 3:19; Eph. 5:25). Marriage is not to be absolutely renounced because of the impending Parousia, since even when the Day of Judgment is imminent, matrimony is an estate in which the believer can be pleasing to God

(1 Thess. 4:1 ff.). Neither is there any peevish misogyny in 1 Tim. 5:5 ff., seeing that in 2 Thess. 3:6 a similar admonition is addressed to men.

2. The restrictions Paul imposed on the ecclesiastical activities of women were conditioned by the times and are therefore limited to a specific period. He did not mean them to be permanently binding. Perhaps the struggle against a particular heresy made the prohibition of 1 Tim. 2:12 a temporary necessity. Or, conceivably, the concession of 1 Cor. 11:5 had gotten out of hand, so that women were clamoring for unconditional permission for all to speak. (Are there implications concerning feminine loquacity in 1 Peter 3:1? "Likewise you wives, be submissive to your husbands, so that some, though they do not obey the Word, may be won *without a word* by the behavior of their wives.")

Against this interpretation it has been urged that the witness of later church history is to the permanency of the limitations imposed on women. However, can one argue back from the later period of certain church fathers to the earlier period of Paul? It is possible that the antifeminist position of the fathers was provoked by new emancipation movements. To suppress these, the enthusiastic-charismatic situation of 1 Cor. 11:5 may have been reinterpreted into something substantially different from what it originally was. Other difficulties in this position will be considered below in solution No. 4.

3. It is conceded that 1 Tim. 2:11-14 does restrict the churchly functions of women and bars them from the ministry. However, the force of this intractable passage is then evaded by accepting that the Pastorals are not directly from Paul but are the work of an admirer or disciple and therefore do not accurately reflect the apostle's convictions at this point.

In the interpretation of 1 Tim. 2:11-14 it will be important to keep in mind this concession as to the evident meaning of the words, for it is made by those who decline to accept this evident meaning. They will concede that these verses are plain and definite but will then immediately undercut this concession by accepting the opinion that the Pastorals are not strictly Pauline. The seemingly antifeminist viewpoint is allegedly an intrusion of the scribe's thought rather than a genuine sentiment of Paul.

4. It is Paul who here enunciates what he regards to be a permanent principle, but that principle cannot be mechanically applied. There are several indications in the texts suggesting that the apostle is laying down an abiding rule. When the forthright prohibition of 1 Cor. 14:34 ff. is modified in 1 Cor. 11:5, where the woman is described as prophesying, this concession is prefaced by the reminder: "The head of a woman is her husband" (v. 3). Therefore, whatever the nature of the exception, the different and permanent role of man must be respected. It thus appears that not the limitation but rather the exception is temporary and conditioned by peculiar circumstances prevailing at the time.

It is not exactly clear what functions Paul was willing to grant women in Corinth and what he was denying them. But it seems clear to many commentators that Paul tolerated no proclamation of the Word and surely no administration of the sacraments on the part of women in the congregations. Paul could the more readily permit the women to prophesy since this activity did not stem from their own initiative but rather was undertaken in obedience to the higher power of the Holy Spirit.

It would therefore appear that Paul's basic concern is to define the role of the sexes, securing the headship of man. The point is not to be belabored, but it does need the emphasis of repetition that even in 1 Cor. 14:3 ff., where the apostle grants the prophetically gifted woman the right to speak and pray, the permission is prefaced with the explicit reminder: "The head of the woman is her husband." The tension with 1 Cor. 14:34 thus avoids contradiction if it be understood that the general rule is for the women to keep silent in the assemblies and that the only exception to this rule is in the case of women prophetically gifted with the Holy Spirit.

Another indication that in 1 Tim. 2:12 Paul lays down what he regards as a permanent rule is to be found in the environmental context. Viewed in its historical setting, the limitation imposed on women is both a relaxing of the rigidities of Judaism and a stiffening of the current Gentile flexibilities. The religious position of women in Judaism tended to be harshly subordinate. In the pagan world, however, priestesses had long been common. Besides this, in more recent times women had come to enjoy new and more extensive privileges, including higher education and positions as magistrates. The fact that Paul departs from both areas of his environment indicates not the compromise of middle ground but the independence that asserts an abiding principle.

When viewing Paul in his environment, it is also instructive to note that antifeminist harshness is lacking in the apostle. Earlier the Greek dramatist Sophocles had made the sweeping assertion, quoted with approval by Aristotle, "Silence is a woman's glory." It remained for later church fathers to jibe that woman had once tried her hand at teaching (in the Garden of Eden) with disastrous consequences. (For instance, John Chrysostom, A. D. 347–407, Hom. 9)

Some exegetical niceties also suggest the permanency of Paul's regulation. The "became a transgressor"

61

in v. 14 has the perfect tense in the original and may, according to the usage of Greek tenses, suggest that the consequences of the initial act remain. Also, since Adam and Eve are archetypes having an enduring descriptive significance for their posterity, male and female, it becomes even clearer that Paul is not speaking merely to a passing situation.

However, even if the permanency of the principle is accepted, there still remains the complex problem of current application. Precisely what was Paul forbidding women to do and how are these prohibitions to be applied to the different, concrete circumstances of today's congregational life? If the apostolic restrictions are understood as barring women from public teaching, one is confronted by the exception that women did "prophesy" (1 Cor. 11:5) and that some women were among Paul's co-laborers (Rom. 16:3-5; Phil. 4:2-3). If the subordination of women is extended into the home, there are the complicating facts that Timothy was taught by his mother and grandmother (2 Tim. 1:5), that the older women "are to teach what is good" (Titus 2:3), that Priscilla and her husband Aquila impart instruction to Apollos (Acts 18:26). Do not these exceptions, it may be argued, so breach the principle that it is no longer possible to lay down restrictive rules?

It must be emphasized that though there were doubtless local developments that evoked the prohibitions of 1 Cor. 14:34 and 1 Tim. 2:12, one cannot know specifically what they were. However, the mere fact that the limitation is aimed at a particular situation does not of itself invalidate the general and permanent nature of the principle. Such concrete applications may indicate that what is being invoked is an abiding law. Paul applied the immutable rule in his day; we must apply it in ours. The proper procedure, then, would be not to invalidate the principle but to exercise scrupulous care in seeing that current applications are in keeping with the apostle's intent.

As has been partially noted above, the exceptions to the general rule, both the prophesying in public church assemblies and the function of teaching in the homes on the part of women, can be explained without subverting the basic principle. The prophesying was by way of exception, to be granted only to those women who had a special charismatic gift from the Holy Spirit and to be exercised in such a way as still to respect the headship of man. And even such charismatically endowed women were apparently barred from the public ministry. Imparting religious instructions in the homes was another matter and a function permissible to the female sex. Perhaps 1 Tim. 2:12 does not forbid a woman to instruct her husband if she is better trained than he, but she ought not to use this opportunity to arrogate to herself authority over her husband.

The excited egalitarian thinking of the present age must not be permitted to blur nor erase the limits indicated by the New Testament. The broad outline must be kept constantly and clearly in mind. There is a hierarchical differentiation between male and female established by God in the distinction of the sexes, and this hierarchy, properly understood in its Biblical explication and context, is to be permanently respected.

An unbiased reading of 1 Tim. 2:11 ff. and related texts makes it inescapably clear that the author is opposed to such emancipation of women as would subvert the role to which God has assigned them by virtue of their very femininity. This role involves Christian recognition of the headship of man, and this principle

63

in turn must be reflected in church regulations. It is another question whether church tradition has accurately seen what limitations should be made and whether these insights have been faithfully applied in the ordering of congregational functions. And yet it remains evident that repudiation of woman's subordination to man means rejection of Paul. If changes in ecclesiastical restrictions in effect abolish such subordination, Paul has been unwittingly misrepresented or deliberately defied. What is permanent is the principle. The application may change, but never so as to invalidate the principle.

Having discussed the questions of Law and Gospel, prayer in the congregation, and the place of women, Paul now addresses himself to the problem of supplying the proper leaders for the church.

Qualifications for Church Officers   *3:1-13*

Bishops   *3:1-7*

¹ **The saying is sure: If any one aspires to the office of bishop, he desires a noble task. ² Now a bishop must be above reproach, the husband of one wife, temperate, sensible, dignified, hospitable, an apt teacher, ³ no drunkard, not violent but gentle, not quarrelsome, and no lover of money. ⁴ He must manage his own household well, keeping his children submissive and respectful in every way; ⁵ for if a man does not know how to manage his own household, how can he care for God's church? ⁶ He must not be a recent convert, or he may be puffed up with conceit and fall into the condemnation of the devil;ᶠ ⁷ more-**

ᶠ Or *slanderer*

64

over he must be well thought of by outsiders, or he
may fall into reproach and the snare of the devil.*

The term "bishop" calls for some clarification.
The Greek word in the original really means an overseer. Usage of the Greek term for varied supervisory
offices in the secular world of the New Testament
period; the designation of leaders of Jewish religious
groups with a parallel Hebrew word; the close linking
of the deacons to the bishops (v. 8); the apparent inter-
changeability of bishop and presbyter (cf. Acts 20:17,
28; Titus 1:5, 7; 1 Tim. 5:17, where the same verb is used
to describe the function of the presbyters as is employed
in reference to the bishops in 3:5) are some of the factors
conspiring to make it impossible to define precisely what
the specific functions of this office were. At all events, it
is unwarranted to set up a series of levels in congregational service and to think of the bishop as the highest
officer. In the light of Phil. 1:1-2 it is even evident that
there were several bishops in one congregation. It is
therefore most accurate to think of the bishop in terms
of congregational leader, or simply, pastor. Because
the designation "bishop" tends to be misleading, some
prefer the simple translation "overseer," thus avoiding
contemporary hierarchical connotations of "bishop"
and leaving the range of duties properly broad and un-
defined. These are hinted at as involving the manage-
ment of the congregation (note the allusion to the family,
vv. 4-5), teaching (v. 2 – "an apt teacher"), involvement in
the congregation's finances (v. 3 – "no lover of money"),
and public relations (v. 2 – "hospitable"; v. 7 – "well
thought of by outsiders"). The closest parallel to this
usage is not to be found in the contemporary Greek
world, where the designation described a variety of

offices, but rather in the Qumran community, with its "overseers" who also had broad duties.

However the functions and duties of this congregational leader might vary according to the circumstances of different periods in church history, the one constant concern is that the Gospel of Christ be faithfully and accurately proclaimed. (Light is also shed on the New Testament understanding of bishop in 1 Peter 2:25; 5:1 ff.)

1 Some ancient manuscripts substitute "popular" for "sure." This is apparently an attempted correction by some copyist who was fearful that the word "sure" would mean Paul was encouraging people to an ambitious grasping for the pastoral office, something certainly irreconcilable with his purpose. But the glory and glamor later associated with the office of bishop was not yet present. There were no milling crowds eagerly aspiring to the pastoral office. Quite the contrary. It was necessary to encourage and recruit suitable candidates. Paul must stress that the pastoral office is a noble task because there were so many who despised it as ignoble. Those who grandiosely conceived of themselves as initiated into the deeper realms of wisdom and knowledge, as acquainted with the lore of myths and genealogies, would likely despise the humble service of the pastoral office. This is not to rule out as impossible that there may have been some who were basely motivated to seek the office of bishop just because it did have some prominence all the same. Also, the responsibilities of leadership may have been avoided by some out of reluctance to assume the burdens of office, preferring to exercise their Christianity in a more relaxed, unofficial status. And then there were probably also those who frivolously thought of the ministry as an easy livelihood.

2 In the form of a catalog of virtues, Paul lists the qualities requisite for the bishop or pastor. So far as Christian ethics and morality are concerned, there is nothing especially striking among the qualities enumerated. They are such as would be required of any good Christian. Against any sacerdotal pretensions, they posit a single ethic, leaving no justification for a distinction of moral requirements between clergy and laity in the history of the church.

Lists of virtues required for various positions and stations in life were common in Hellenistic times. Some of these ethical catalogs reveal striking similarities to the qualifications Paul seeks in the candidate for church office. For instance, the Stoic sage was to be married, not inflated with pride, temperate in the use of wine, chaste, prudent, and the like. A list of qualifications sought in a general in 55 B. C., a description of priests in Egypt, and other parallels suggest that the paradigms of qualifications were a kind of stereotyped scheme. Such lists may well have provided a pattern for the apostle in drawing up his own catalog. And yet, there are evidences of purposeful adaptation by Paul. The very humble nature of the qualifications seem to be a deliberate contrast to the brilliance and dash the contemporary environment adulated in its rhetoricians and sophists. It is also noteworthy that Paul avoids extremes such as the demand for total abstinence from strong drink or the requirement of celibacy. It is basic morality that is called for. Some would see evidence here for a late date of composition, arguing that these prosaic requirements agree better with a relaxed later church rather than with the zest and fervor of an earlier period. However, such an inference fails to give due weight to the historical situation. Since the background of many converts was so low, virtues which to the enlightened seem too obvious for mention cannot be taken for granted.

These requirements for the pastoral office are deserving of individual analysis. A bishop is to be "above reproach." To exercise this office effectively, the leader of the congregation will need to enjoy a good reputation. He is to be of good report because he deserves it. He is to be above reproach both before and after elevation to office, since his work requires that he enjoy the confidence and trust of his people.

He is to be "the husband of one wife." The meaning of the original has been much debated. There are basically three possible interpretations: (1) Married to one wife, as if a prohibition of polygamy; (2) Married only once, meaning the prohibition of remarriage after the death of the first wife; (3) Faithful to his one wife (NEB), implying that the entire moral life of the pastor must be in order. Quite literally the text says "a one-woman man." But the interpretations have varied all the way from the contention that Paul unconditionally demands that bishops be married to the view that only second marriages are proscribed. Without entering into the intricacies of the long and complicated debate, we may note the following salient points:

1. The problem resolves itself into the basic questions of whether Paul here forbids polygamy, whether he rules out second marriages for the bishops, or whether the phrase has the wider connotation that the bishop's marital and moral life must be marked by fidelity and purity.

2. Any interpretation that intrudes ascetic or sacerdotal connotations into the text must be rejected as conflicting with the non-ascetic tone of the Pastoral Epis-

tles and the general nature of the other virtues listed in this catalog.

The interpretation that Paul is here moving toward an ideal of a celibate priesthood is beset with serious difficulties. It cannot be denied that the apostle concedes the basic right of ministers to marry. Also, the contention that second marriages are prohibited, thus marking a stage on the way toward the celibate ideal, is at best shaky, for, as Melanchthon says very simply: "Also he, who after the death of his first wife married another, is the husband of one wife." Furthermore, the celibate interpretation clashes with the thoroughly affirmative attitude of these letters toward matrimony. To the younger widows remarriage is actually commended (5:14). Forbidding marriage is a mark of the degenerate errorist (4:3). Some would argue for celibacy on the grounds that if pagan priests bring this sacrifice to the service of their false gods, could the Christian minister do less in the service of the true God? However, such argumentation and the examples of praise for refraining from second marriages found in secular sources corroborate the suspicion that a negative view toward priestly marriages is not a Biblical thought at all but of pagan provenance. Therefore the argument of the old church father Jerome that it would be a disgrace for Christians if pagan priests could be celibate for their gods but not Christian priests for their God is unconvincing. It is hardly in order to accept the form that heathen willingness to sacrifice may take. Otherwise we should have to introduce human sacrifice and even the castration of priests.

Neither is there any insuperable difficulty in understanding the parallel usage of the term in reference to widows (5:9) in a broader sense than "married only once." Some of the ancient church fathers so understood it. One of them commented: "If she lived chastely with her husband, whether she had only one or was married a second time . . ." There is an interesting dilemma within the realm of possibility. Suppose a young widow were to follow the advice of the apostle (5:14) and remarry, only to be widowed a second time. Is it conceivable that Paul would have her excluded from the official list?

All of this is not to deny that there may also be a special area of service for the unmarried, but it is to dispute that Paul is here taking the first steps toward the requirement of a celibate ministry. It is evident in the text that Paul regards the married man as best qualified for the pastorate that will be bringing him into intimate contact with people, also the women and girls. The depreciatory view of married ministers which sees some kind of friction between family and parish duties is in conflict with the text (vv. 4-5), which regards the good family man as the one with the training and experience qualifying him for effective work as a congregational leader. The rendering of the New English Bible, "faithful to his one wife," is general and yet free from ambiguity. This translation does justice to the wider sweep of the original, obliquely and quietly ruling out polygamy (also veiled polygamy; cf. Matt. 5:32; Mark 10:11) and more directly and emphatically demanding marital fidelity and moral impeccability. If Christianity was to renovate marriage and elevate moral standards in the Greco-Roman world, there could be no shadow over the leaders' own marriages.

"Temperate": Indulgence in wine must be within proper limits. The use of the same word in its verb form in 2 Tim. 4:5 suggests here the wider implications of

70

sobriety in judgment and emotions, vigilance in keeping one's conduct free from excesses.

"Sensible": The literal meaning is "of a sound mind." This quality means that one knows and desires the right things in the right way at the right time.

"Dignified": Being decorous, he will not heedlessly defy convention.

"Hospitable": Hospitality was a noted virtue in antiquity, prominent already in Homer. In the Christian mission it was important that traveling messengers of the churches as well as those in need should find refuge in the homes of believers.

"An apt teacher": Since his work will be inculcating the truth and defending it against error, the candidate must have a special talent for teaching. All that goes on in the church must be kept under the authority of the Word. Hence the centrality of teaching.

3 The bishop is to be "No drunkard": Alcoholism was also an ancient problem. If Christianity was to contribute towards its solution, the leader of the flock himself dare not imbibe too freely. Let him be

"Not violent but gentle": Where he can, he yields, and he does not blast his way through to his objective but is adept at calmer, persuasive techniques. And yet this meekness is not incompatible with the fighting spirit called for in 6:12: "Fight the good fight of the faith." A lover of peace, a good bishop is

"Not quarrelsome": The notorious haggling and quibbling becomes only more bitter and raucous if the pastor is not the source from which a different spirit flows.

"No lover of money": Love of money is a mark of selfishness, a vice that will corrupt effective pastoral work. Selfish clutching for money on the part of the

71

pastor would be as reprehensible as the greed of the father who squanders money on himself in callous disregard of the other members of the family. Commercial concern poisons not only pastors personally but the whole life of the congregation.

4-5 Serious family troubles never occur without some degree of guilt on the part of the head of the house. In the domestic situation with all its pitfalls, the candidate must prove himself. This linking of the task of the overseer to the functions of the head of a family indicates the comprehensive responsibility the bishop has for the total life and welfare of the congregation. He may be assisted in various areas, but he is not so replaced that his concern and accountability cease.

6 The neophyte is not to be immediately inducted into the pastoral office of bishop, for sudden elevation to a position of importance may puff him up with vanity and, inflated with pride, he will never fit into the spot God assigns him. The devil knows how to turn the head of the man who is not preconditioned to the rarefied atmosphere of high position. If the grace experienced by the convert becomes an occasion for pride, then the devil has a telling accusation to lodge against him before God the Judge. Here the concern is for the neophyte himself, though the congregation is also involved.

7 It is also important that the bishop have a good reputation among those outside the Christian fellowship. Though past sin could disqualify him from public office in the church, this is not to question whether his sins were fully forgiven. Before God every believer's sins are remitted for the sake of Christ. However, leadership in the congregation would likely be seriously impaired if the overseer were subject to the jibes of unbelievers because of past sins. There is, moreover, the danger of relapse into old sin, which, if it should reoccur in a leader, would be doubly damaging to the Gospel cause.

For bishops and congregations it is worthy of note what Paul does *not* require. He does not call for organizational ability or oratorical finesse. Here is a clue to guide the congregation in defining its expectations and demands, as well as to help the pastor assign the correct comparative values to all the activities and concerns that clamor for his time and energies. Furthermore, there is no call for remarkable spiritual experiences, no intimation that a sensitive, aesthetic, mystical nature is requisite nor desirable. The laudable but not scintillating virtues enumerated indicate that the office calls for a sturdy character that can inflexibly stand up to human opposition and yet be easily pliant to the breath of God's will.

Deacons   *3:8-13*

8 Deacons likewise must be serious, not double-tongued, not addicted to much wine, not greedy for gain; 9 they must hold the mystery of the faith with a clear conscience. 10 And let them also be tested first; then if they prove themselves blameless let them serve as deacons. 11 The women likewise must be serious, no slanderers, but temperate, faithful in all things. 12 Let deacons be the husband of one wife, and let them manage their children and their households well; 13 for those who serve well as deacons gain a good standing for themselves and also great confidence in the faith which is in Christ Jesus.

Diakonein, the Greek verb from which "deacon" is derived, means basically to wait on tables, to perform some menial task. It is the kind of activity the Greeks tended to designate as undeserving of a freeborn man. By contrast Christ so sanctifies the term that it becomes broadly descriptive of the service to one's followman that marks the true disciple. It is a comprehensive concept involving physical and spiritual ministrations.

8 Although it is not possible to define precisely the duties of deacons, there are several helpful hints in the text. The name itself, meaning "servant," indicates an office somehow below that of bishop (overseer) though linked with it. In the list of qualifications for the office of deacon, "apt teacher" is omitted. The strong term, "not greedy for gain" (different from "no lover of money" in the case of the bishop, v. 3), hints at access to congregational funds. In view of all this it seems safe to conclude that the deacon served in some supervisory, executive position in caring for the poor and probably the sick. A service of such a type is nothing to be despised. Jesus proposes Himself as a model of serving (Mark 10:45; John 13:1 ff.). Therefore it is no surprise that spiritual as well as practical qualifications are requisite for those who would serve as deacons. Besides being "serious" (NEB: "of high principle"), men of their word, and moderate in their use of alcohol, they are to be men of transparent motives who hold on to the Gospel.

9 The Gospel in all its implications is "the mystery of the faith" (cf. v. 16) because it was hidden until God spoke and was not more fully unveiled until the coming of Jesus (cf. Rom. 16:25 ff.; Col. 1:26 ff.). But even after the advent of God's Son, the mystery of faith is not entirely dissipated. It is the continuing nature of faith that it is bold in the certainty of sharing in God's glory, which it cannot see, and of working in the strength of God's might, which it cannot manipulate. Really, but invisibly, faith reaches up to heaven and touches God.

This intangible reality is the abiding mystery of faith.

10 So important was the office of deacon that a probationary period should precede anyone's election to it. And yet, the very possibility of functioning as a trial deacon shows that the office was under that of the bishop, whose work with the Word as pastoral overseer must have an authority from the very outset. Preaching, administering the sacraments, guiding the congregation in the acceptance and exclusion of members are functions not to be discharged by one on probation. Here trial and error are too precarious.

11 There is no agreement on who is meant by "women." Two possibilities suggest themselves: (1) deaconesses, the female counterparts to deacons; (2) wives of the deacons. Against the understanding of "women" as wives of the deacons it has been urged that it would have been more natural for Paul to say "their women (wives)," and also that there is no parallel list of qualifications for the bishop's wife. However, the suggestion that the virtues here demanded would be irrelevant if only the wives of deacons were meant is unconvincing, since the wives' activities and influence would not be limited to the kitchen and nursery. As for deaconesses, it should be kept in mind that Paul's designation of Phoebe as a deaconess (Rom. 16:1) does not prove the existence of a definite order of deaconesses, since the term may simply describe her as one who characteristically rendered conspicuous service in the congregation. (See comments on the "order of widows," 5:3 ff.)

12 As in the case of the bishops, the deacons are to be beyond reproach in their moral life and to have proved themselves in their ability to be competent fathers in their own household.

13 The high qualifications are in order because the office of deacon puts one on a high plane. It involves responsibility before God and influence in the congregation. It would be erroneous to interpret the "good standing" the deacons might achieve for themselves as personal prestige, for this would conflict with the modesty that must characterize any servant of Jesus Christ. Conceivably the meaning might be that the deacon who has acquitted himself well thereby qualifies for the more responsible position of bishop. The "good standing" here would then correspond to "noble task" used in 3:1 to describe the office of bishop.

But perhaps it is better to think in terms of the Old Testament picture of a ladder leading to heaven (Gen. 28). The word for "standing" in the original literally means "step." As he faithfully exercises the duties of his office, the deacon feels himself graciously elevated closer to God, and in His nearer presence a bolder confidence pervades his soul, inspiring him to more fearless testimony and enabling him to look forward without terror to the Day of Judgment. All thoughts of human merit are excluded by the phrase "in the faith which is in Christ Jesus." It is noteworthy that one rises to this high level through humble service, not by clambering from one lofty speculation to another. It is characteristic of loving service to Christ that there is the experience of a joy that increases confidence. Only the wicked servant (Matt. 25:24), the reluctant worker, finds Jesus a harshly exacting master.

Concluding Remarks on Church Order and the
Hymn to Christ   *3:14-16*

14 I hope to come to you soon, but I am writing these instructions to you so that, 15 if I am delayed,

you may know how one ought to behave in the household of God, which is the church of the living God,
the pillar and bulwark of the truth. ¹⁶ Great indeed,
we confess, is the mystery of our religion:
    He ʰ was manifested in the flesh,
    vindicatedⁱ in the Spirit,
        seen by angels,
    preached among the nations,
    believed on in the world,
        taken up in glory.

ʰ Greek *Who;* other ancient authorities read *God;* others, *Which*
ⁱ Or *justified*

14 Looking back to 2:1, Paul explains why he has
elaborated on these practical aspects of church order
even though he hopes to come to Ephesus soon. He has
written these directives in the awareness that his hopes
soon to visit Timothy personally may be upset. Since the
situation is critical, he cannot postpone his instructions
to an uncertain future. The affairs of the church dare not
be lightly handled. Christ, whose praises are sung in the
last verse of this chapter, is the head of the church, and
His work merits careful and conscientious attention not
only to doctrine but also to practical details. But precisely
here there is an instructive silence. Paul does not rigidly
prescribe minute points as to the number of deacons, the
division of functions so as to prevent overlapping and
friction, and specific procedure in electing officers, and
the like. Rather, his insistence on spiritual qualifications
shows where the primary emphasis must lie even in the
most practical of congregational affairs. Where this spirituality is present, Paul is content to leave details to Timothy and his associates, who will proceed in the spirit of

love to order the affairs of the church in Ephesus.

15 When Paul refers to the church as the "household of God," it is reminiscent of his insistence that the public servant of the congregation must first have proved himself in the smaller but crucial realm of his own private household. In the household of God it is the "living" God who rules, an adjective suggested perhaps by Hos. 1:10 (cf. Rom. 9:26) and serving as a reminder that the church of the living God differs from a pagan temple in which is located some speechless and impotent idol.

Moving on from a consideration of the church at Ephesus, Paul speaks in broader terms of the church as "the pillar and bulwark of the truth." As pillars support the superstructure and the foundation in turn sustains the whole mass of a building, so the church upholds the truth. Paradoxically the church, which supports the truth, rests on the truth. However, "church" must not be understood in an institutionalizing sense, as if this verse were ascribing infallibility to the visible organization. That Jesus is the only foundation (1 Cor. 3:11) and that the foundation of the apostles and prophets still rests on the chief Cornerstone, Jesus Christ, are basic facts never to be lost from sight. The church is not mistress but servant of the truth. By believing, proclaiming, and defending the doctrines of the Bible, yes, by purging itself from errors, the church is a pillar and bulwark of the truth. As the visible organization continues faithful to Jesus Christ and the prophetic as well as the apostolic testimony to Him, as it combats the heresies that threaten the content of the Christian faith, it stands firm as the pillar and bulwark of the truth. But the mission of the church is not to build high protective walls around the truth and thus assure its continued purity by sealing it off from the defiling touch of sinners. The church does not have the truth unless it proclaims it.

16 The content of the hymn is anticipated by the summary characterization "great mystery." As will become evident upon closer analysis, the truth celebrated in this Christological doxology is the Incarnation, namely, that the eternal Son of God became a human being (cf. v. 9, "the mystery of faith"). Here the characteristic of New Testament mystery as *revealed* mystery is evident. Whatever incomprehensibility may yet shroud God in His majesty and essence, His gracious purpose in Christ has been made manifest.

There is a question whether the translation "religion" may not impoverish the meaning of the original. The element of piety should perhaps be stressed. Christian piety (AV: "godliness") is a mystery both in what it does and why it does it. The baffling dare of Christian faith controlling the conduct of life derives from the mystery of the incarnate Christ.

When Paul considers the mystery of Christ, he does not call attention to the dim backgrounds in eternity that are veiled in the omniscience of God. His concern is not with the hidden but the revealed God. And precisely this God, who revealed Himself in the Man Jesus, is a mystery. The mysterious miracle is that God could have and did reveal Himself by becoming man, when it would seem that a body would veil rather than unveil God. If the mystery of His appearance in the flesh is to be penetrated by faith, the Holy Spirit must be present with His power to bring insight into God's vindication of His Son by the Resurrection. Jesus, who living among sinners took upon Himself their sins, was "vindicated in the Spirit." Whether this disputed term "Spirit" is understood as indicating divine elements in Christ as opposed to human elements (flesh) or as referring to the Holy Spirit, the point is equally clear in either instance. Flesh of itself cannot rise; divine power effected the miracle of the Resurrection. Neither does mention of the Spirit intimate in any way that the Resurrection is to be understood spiritually rather than literally. Compare Rom. 1:4; 1 Peter 3:18; John 6:63. The resurrected Son, who was made flesh, is now seen by the angels, who worship Him. He is proclaimed among the nations, also the Gentiles, who are invited to join the ranks of those who by believing on Him in the world are linked with Him in glory. The series of events celebrated in this hymn are: (1) the Incarnation; (2) the Resurrection; (3) the appearance to angels, good and bad (cf. Phil. 2:9 ff.); (4) the proclamation of the Gospel; (5) the Ascension.

That the theme of this hymn is the Incarnation is indicated also by the artistic structure. The three pairs of statements each contain one line referring to the heavenly and another to the earthly. The lesson thus inculcated is that the gap between God and man has been closed; in Christ heaven and earth are linked.

The abruptness with which Paul introduces this doxology becomes understandable when one accepts the suggestion that he is quoting from a hymn that was familiar to the congregation. The bumpy linking of the introductory statement, "Great indeed, we confess, is the mystery of our religion," to the hymn is felt in the connective pronoun. "The mystery" is neuter gender, but the masculine connective "who" is found in the best manuscripts. This leaves the entire hymn an incomplete relative clause. In an apparent attempt to smooth out the difficulty, some manuscripts have substituted "which," and others "God," perhaps misled by the similarity of "God" and "who" when written in Greek uncials (large, or capital letters). Following the generally sound principle of preferring the more difficult reading, one must accept that "who" is correct. However, the RSV is justified in translating "He" since in the sudden transition to the hymn Paul simply omits to say explicitly what he obviously means, namely, that the mystery is not a thing but a person, Jesus Christ. In a painfully prosaic paraphrase one might explain the verse thus: Great indeed, we confess, is the mystery of our religion. "This mystery is Jesus, who was manifested in the flesh, etc." The simple substitution of "He" for "who" makes this clumsy expansion unnecessary.

There are various other passages that New Testament scholars have tried to identify as hymns, such as Eph. 5:14; Phil. 2:6-11; Col. 1:15-20; 1 Peter 1:3 ff. Though there is considerable doubt about some of these references, 1 Tim. 3:16 does seem to be a fragment of early Christian hymnody. The difficulties experienced in the attempt to bring logical coherence into an analysis of this passage strengthens the conviction that it is indeed the product of exuberant worship.

HERETICS AND HOW TO OPPOSE THEM   4:1-16

In Chapter 4 Paul returns to the battle Timothy has to wage against errorists. Here Paul concentrates on the false ascetic demands of these errorists. Capable ministers must be at work with the pure Word to bring the church through these dangerous times.

Ascetic Demands of Errorists   *4:1-5*

¹ Now the Spirit expressly says that in later times some will depart from the faith by giving heed

81

to deceitful spirits and doctrines of demons, ² through the pretensions of liars whose consciences are seared, ³ who forbid marriage and enjoin abstinence from foods which God created to be received with thanksgiving by those who believe and know the truth. ⁴ For everything created by God is good, and nothing is to be rejected if it is received with thanksgiving; ⁵ for then it is consecrated by the word of God and prayer.

1 There is no excuse for not seeing through the error of the innovators, for the Holy Spirit had issued advance warning of apostasy and delusive error as characterizing the times through which the believers would later have to pass. Just where and how the Spirit gave these express warnings is not stated. It may have been through special visions (cf. Acts 11:27 ff.; 13:1 ff.; 20: 29-31; 1 Cor. 14). Or there may be an allusion to some written admonition (cf. 2 Thess. 2:3, 11-12). It is also conceivable that a traditional word of Jesus is involved (cf. Mark 13:22-23). Even as Peter on Pentecost interpreted the last days as "the Pentecostal now" (Acts 2:16-17), so the church at Ephesus was to understand the "later times" as the present period. Likewise the church today is to regard the assaults and temptations of the contemporary world as being for it the later times, and is not to become drowsy and inefficient by speculating about a vague, indeterminate future. Thus God spoke once to and through the apostles who put the message in the fixed, definitive form of the New Testament Scriptures. But this revelation is not something static in the past. The message comes alive in the present through the power of the Holy Spirit, who still speaks in that fixed revelation. Despite their deceptively pious appearance,

the errors are called "doctrines of demons." There is a demonic background to false doctrine. Faith comes to be by the almighty power of God's Holy Spirit, with man not sharing the credit. On the other hand, the unbelief furthered by the malevolent power of the devil finds man culpable, for he participates. It is not an unsuccessful part of the devil's wiles that he fights the faith by offering a more pretentious faith. Religion is perverted not only by irreligion but also by new religion.

It is the very "faith" (that which is believed) which is at stake. Although this objective understanding of faith as orthodoxy is unusual in the admittedly Pauline letters, it is not without its parallels (see Gal. 1:23; Phil. 1:27). The failure of the Pastorals to mention the well-known "faith-works" contrast is understandable and natural, for this was not the problem plaguing the addressees of the Pastorals. Moreover, the omission of this characteristic Pauline antithesis argues against an imitator; he would almost certainly have included it.

Personal convictions about Christ and the profession of a common body of doctrine about Christ are complementary, not antithetical. It is therefore not a glaring departure from Pauline usage but rather a natural extension of meaning when "faith" is used to designate orthodoxy. Compare 1 Tim. 6:21; Titus 1:4, 13. Although the verb "will depart" may intimate a participation of the will in apostasy, it still remains true that the faith need not be violently flung away to be lost; it can also slip from the relaxed grasp. (Compare 1 Tim. 1:19, "certain persons have made shipwreck of their faith." See also 1 Tim. 6:21; 2 Tim. 2:18.)

2 The denounced propagandists are really vicious. As tools of the devil they work with specious lies, and yet they bear the trademark of the devil in their con-

sciences. Branding was a Greek form of punishment particularly for runaway slaves. The branded conscience of these errorists therefore indicates that they are enslaved to the aberrations of their false ascetic teachings. (Another understanding stressing the translation "seared" would be that the conscience is benumbed and without sensitivity.) But because the stamp of the devil tends to be hidden, more than superficial examination is required to see the propagandists for what they really are. And yet, to the perceptive eye it is clear that the restlessness of guilt motivates their zealous hypocrisy, which is intended to hide their disturbed conscience.

"Doctrines of demons": The denunciation of false doctrine could hardly be more vehement and harsh, but the severe judgment is warranted because any scheme of self-saving is an affront to the sole Saviorhood of Jesus. And even though the sincerity of the false teachers need not be impugned (they were, after all, making painful sacrifices), sincerity alone is not enough. Obedience is necessary, and to obey properly one must know the will of God. This knowledge must come through the revelation in God's Word and not rise out of the misty speculations of the human heart.

3 The description of the errorists makes it clear that they taught a scheme of salvation by forgoing marriage and by abstaining from certain foods, a twofold ascetic demand. It also appears likely that the twofold error derives from a double source. (1) The ascetic requirements relative to food (perhaps vegetarianism; cf. Rom. 14:1 ff.) would likely have been inspired by Old Testament laws pertaining to clean and unclean foods. (2) The prohibition of marriage, however, is alien to Judaism and indicates the intrusion of a type of late Greek

religious philosophy (Gnostic-Hellentistic thought) into the belief and practice of the errorists. This philosophy with its basic dualism distinguished sharply between the material and the spiritual, so that salvation was to be achieved by extricating the soul from the imprisonment and defiling embrace of all that is material. But the creaturely cannot be inherently evil. Look at the Creator! "And God saw everything that he had made, and behold, it was very good" (Gen. 1:31). And even though a curse rests on the creation since the Fall (Gen. 3:17) so that it groans "in travail" (Rom. 8:22), dualism is wrong in limiting the corruption to the physical, in failing to understand the cosmic sweep of Christ's redemption (Phil. 2:9 ff.), and in supposing that the rift between God and man can be closed by ascetic efforts. Instead of confessing his guilt and blaming himself, man, with an evasion characteristic since the Fall, shifts the responsibility for his abject condition onto nature, God's creation, thus brazenly accusing God (cf. Gen. 3:12). Hence comes the attempt to escape guilt by man's effort to extricate himself from the demands of his physical nature. Contrariwise, faith believes the body is God's creation and is to be sustained by the produce of God's creation. Rather than interposing a barrier between God and man, this acceptance of the physical creation finds a new link to God. This is the point of the emphasis on thanksgiving and prayer. Those who have been led to see how God has provided for their souls in Christ are also able to behold the physical in its true dimensions.

The subtlety of the ascetic heresy is that it is so splendidly decked out in seductive trappings of concerned and earnest spirituality. The deadliness of the error—the inevitable implication of this misleading dualism—consists in the fact that it makes Christ super-

85

fluous. The soul does not need to be purified in the Savior's cleansing blood; it needs only to be sprung from prison so that it can flutter back to its proper clime, the presence of God.

Over against such a fundamental misunderstanding, Paul stresses the goodness of God's creation and the propriety of man's grateful enjoyment of it. God alone is to be worshiped, but God's creation is to be respected. God is not only the Redeemer; He is also the Creator.

4 The cramped and sour approach to the physical world is out of harmony with the freedom that is ours in Christ. (Peter had to be taught this same lesson by a vision, Acts 10:9-16.) By faith in the redemption wrought by Jesus Christ the believer has been rescued from the passions that tangle the unbeliever in helpless bondage to the world. He shares in the kingship of the triumphant Christ. Therefore he may enjoy the world in regal bearing. However, the believer's enjoyment of things created dare never dim his perception of the Creator. "Thanksgiving," so prominent in Jewish custom (cf. the example of Jesus, Mark 6:41; 8:6), will safeguard the believer from sodden absorption in the exclusively physical.

5 The Word of God and prayer are both a *corrective* against the perverse misunderstanding that heaven can be stormed by legalistic observances and a *restraint* holding man back from wantonly plunging into enjoyment of the physical world. Instead of despising God's creation, God's people are to pray for it. They know that the physical was created by God and that man's relation to the physical is set forth in the Word of Scripture. Hence the right use of the creaturely is holy. However, there is a proper place in the exercise of Christian piety for self-limitation and even self-denial. The selfish

clutching of the creaturely is not here condoned. As soon as one's motive or aspiration is to acquire merit and to render oneself more pleasing to God, asceticism becomes a deadly device of the devil.

"Consecrated" means to have put something to pure rather than profane use. There is no change in what is consecrated but rather in the one who uses the creaturely. Of themselves things are not desecrated and in need of consecration. It is fallen man who needs purification. Thanksgiving — the Word of God, and prayer — will save man from sinful forgetfulness of the Giver and will deliver him from selfish exploitation of all that he has received. Having been transformed into a child of God, he will use what he receives of God's creation also for the service of others.

Proper Christian Piety 4:6-10

6 If you put these instructions before the brethren, you will be a good minister of Christ Jesus, nourished on the words of the faith and of the good doctrine which you have followed. 7 Have nothing to do with godless and silly myths. Train yourself in godliness; 8 for while bodily training is of some value, godliness is of value in every way, as it holds promise for the present life and also for the life to come. 9 The saying is sure and worthy of full acceptance. 10 For to this end we toil and strive,*j* because we have our hope set on the living God, who is the Savior of all men, especially of those who believe.

j Other ancient authorities read *suffer reproach*

6 Timothy's task is to transmit to the people those doctrines and principles which Paul has just expounded. So he will be a faithful "minister" ("deacon" is here used in its basic, nontechnical sense) of Christ Jesus. There is no position, or office, in the congregation that brings with it the prestige and prerogatives of lordship. Service is the keyword. Such readiness to be nothing more — and nothing less — than a servant of Christ Jesus will demonstrate that the source of Timothy's strength is the Christian truth. And that Timothy has done this, Paul can testify. In Rom. 10:8 "the word of faith" that Paul preaches is the means whereby God kindles faith in the hearers. Such faith-kindling words must be in accord with "the good doctrine" that makes Christ central. Although the term "good doctrine" means orthodoxy, there is nothing dead about an orthodoxy that has things straight about Jesus Christ. It is a living orthodoxy.

7 Clinging to the truth means rejecting falsehood. Condemned once more are the myths referred to in 1:4, but here they are characterized as godless and silly. The seriousness of doctrinal aberrations is apparent in these condemnatory adjectives. Not only are the errors absurd, so that one might laugh; they are godless, so that one must fight. Sometimes, as in this instance, the error is not deserving of debate and refutation but is best rejected in haughty disdain. There is a double meaning in "fight" that must be carefully noted. To fight others, we must fight ourselves. One cannot fight God's battle against outside opponents of the truth unless one fights against himself. Compare on the one hand John 18:36 ("fight" is the same word translated "strive" in 1 Tim. 4:10) with 1 Cor. 9:25 (again, "every athlete" is literally "every one who strives"). On the other hand Luke 13:24; Col. 1:29; 1 Tim. 6:12; and 2 Tim. 4:7 may well imply both the successful struggle to train oneself and the victory in combating heresy.

The metaphor has connotations both from competition in sports and contest on the field of battle. Therefore he who would pay attention to others must pay attention to himself. To fight heresy one must train himself in the truth. Such training will be necessary if Timothy is to carry out his rigorous assignment.

8 In obvious allusion to the misguided efforts of false asceticism, Paul stresses that spiritual sturdiness is built up only to a small degree by external, bodily exercises. He is not condemning athletic fitness. The sickliness of extreme asceticism, which sometimes seems to regard physical health as a sin and feebleness as a virtue, is irreconcilable with the healthy affirmation of the creaturely in v. 4.

This again is not to deny that there is a place for abstinence and physical self-discipline in the Christian life. Animal desires do threaten to dominate planning and action. The powerful pulsations of good health can deceive one into forgetfulness of dependence on God and into reliance on self. However, the remedy is not to dissipate bodily vigor nor deliberately to weaken God's gift of physical health. When man throws the blessing of health away, this is irresponsible ingratitude; when God takes it away, this is the divine imposition of a cross. Man's deliberate manipulation of the physical gifts of God must, however, be conditioned also by the awareness that asceticism has a relative value, subordinate indeed, but valuable nonetheless. Paul does not view the body in terms of the Greek philosophical dichotomy, which views man as split (rather than united) in body and soul and also regards the body as an impediment to the soul or even the prison of the soul. Man is body and soul, a psychosomatic unity. And yet for man, who is a body-soul entity, to achieve his divinely appointed goal, it will be necessary to tame the desires of the body in the name of higher, spiritual concerns. There is a certain limited value resulting from ascetic training (for instance, the teetotaler is not in immediate danger of becoming an alcoholic; the single man has no worries about providing for a family; the man who fasts is more prepared for privation). By contrast the benefits of true Christian piety extend over all of life — the life given to us here and now in this physical world and that which is to come as the crowning fulfillment. Repudiation of false asceticism does not mean blurring the distinction between the now and the hereafter, but rather seeing them in their true perspectives.

9 There is some dispute as to whether the formula of this verse (cf. 1:15; Titus 3:8) should be referred to the preceding or the following verse. In favor of looking backward is the epigrammatic quality of v. 8, which gives it the appearance of a citation, and the fact that v. 10 seems to be only a practical application of the thought expressed in v. 8.

10 Because their hope in God is so real and their belief in a life to come so confident, believers in Jesus Christ are willing to "toil and strive." This is possible, for they know indeed that God is the Creator and Preserver of all. But they also know that they are the objects of God's special concern and that they may confidently look forward to God's protection all their life and at the end to the gift of eternal life.

Timothy as Exemplar   *4:11-16*

¹¹ **Command and teach these things.** ¹² **Let no one despise your youth, but set the believers an example in speech and conduct, in love, in faith, in purity.** ¹³ **Till I come, attend to the public reading of scrip-**

ture, to preaching, to teaching. ¹⁴ Do not neglect
the gift you have, which was given you by prophetic
utterance when the elders laid their hands upon
you. ¹⁵ Practice these duties, devote yourself to them,
so that all may see your progress. ¹⁶ Take heed to yourself and to your teaching; hold to that, for by so doing
you will save both yourself and your hearers.

11-12 His "youth" (likely in his thirties; Paul perhaps
sixty) is not to deter Timothy from commanding and
teaching all people what Paul has been telling him. In
the assembly it was ordinarily older men who spoke. If
in their company Timothy was to speak the decisive
word, there could easily be those who, struck by his
youth, would bring up the question of his competency.
But Timothy is not to be intimidated; authority is not
something to be demanded in a vacuum. By setting
an example of Christian virtue, Timothy will merit
the respect he needs to function as an efficient servant
of Jesus Christ. Let not his youth become a temptation
for some to discount his admonitions and to despise
his exhortations. Neither age nor youth are finally
normative, but only the truth. Timothy is to be an
example. In order to impress the likeness to Christ on
others, one must first have received the impress himself.
In many and varied areas Timothy is to be such an
example: in the words that he speaks (preaching), in
his total demeanor and behavior, in the evident control
that love exercises over his whole life, in the faith
from which that love derives, and in the moral purity
of his life.

13 The youthful minister who is to prove himself
worthy of respect by his personal virtues must also be
faithful in the discharge of his official duties. There is

to be no gap between belief and life, between faith and conduct. Timothy is to be a living example of faith in action.

This verse provides an incidental insight into some of the ingredients of early Christian worship. There was the "reading" from the Old Testament (a custom taken over from Judaism; cf. Luke 4:16 ff.; Acts 13:15), and to it readings from the apostolic writings and the Gospels were soon added. (Compare 1 Thess. 5:27; Col. 4:16; Rev. 1:3. See also Justin Martyr, *Apology* I, 67.) "Preaching," that is, exhortation with encouragement, was based on such selections as were read. Also included was instruction.

The recurrence of the word "teaching" in v. 16 (and, indeed, throughout the Pastoral Epistles) is a reminder of the importance attaching to this term. Faith in the New Testament is not just pious credulity, a ready willingness to believe something or other that seems edifying, even about Jesus Christ. Faith is based on definite facts about Jesus Christ that one must get straight. This is not to make faith sterile nor static, for it is only as one is taught the correct facts that faith is purified and energized. Impurities in the teaching mean heresy, and it is against heresy that Timothy is to fight.

14 Furthermore, Timothy is not to neglect the gift he received. This gift is called by the same term (*charisma*) that is used in 1 Cor. 12 – 14 for striking but temporary manifestations of the Holy Spirit in such phenomena as the gift of tongues and miraculous healings. What is the gift Timothy has and how did it come to him? Those who believe in some form of apostolic succession interpret this verse (and 2 Tim. 1:6) as proving that the special gift of the ministry is bestowed by ordination through a bishop in the line of episcopal descent or through a presbytery functioning in an episcopal capacity.

One must keep the context in mind. With his qualifications called in question by reason of his youth, Timothy might be overwhelmed by misgivings. To reassure him that he had not brashly intruded himself into a position of authority, Paul reminds Timothy how the qualifications for the ministry and his call into it came from outside of himself: such qualifications and such a call exist in fact, not in fancy. In a solemn service a brother with the gift of prophecy declared that God had given him the equipment he needed to do the work of the ministry. (The expression "given you by prophetic utterance" is rendered "given you under the guidance of prophecy" by the New English Bible. See also 1 Tim. 1:18, where prophetic utterances are said to have pointed to Timothy, and 2 Tim. 1:6, where Paul states that he took part in the ceremony of the laying on of hands. Some commentators believe this last reference refers to a separate occasion.) Further to certify this fact, the testimony of the elders was given by the laying on of hands.

This interpretation regards 2 Tim. 1:7 ("for God did not give us a spirit of timidity but a spirit of power and love and self-control") as descriptive of what the gift basically is, and 2 Tim. 1:8 ("Do not be ashamed then of testifying to our Lord, nor of me his prisoner, but take your share of suffering for the Gospel in the power of God") as showing the effect the gift is to have in those to whom it has come. Paul wishes to reassure Timothy in the face of any doubts that may assault him. He does this not by telling him that through ordination he has been transposed into an order where he has a special gift he cannot lose (the exhortation implies that the neglected gift can be lost) but by making clear that the Spirit God bestows on His own makes them equal to their tasks, also the rigorous tasks of the ministry.

15 Timothy has a gift. He is to use it in a way that will be profitable to others and to himself. Faithful endeavor and robust effort will mean evident progress. By leading others forward in the faith, he himself will advance. Such progress does not need to be paraded; it is evident simply by being present.

16 Concern for the congregation necessarily involves concern for himself. With his own spiritual life in order, Timothy is to give scrupulous attention to setting forth to the congregation the will and ways of God. "Take heed to your teaching" means particularly "Be careful what it is you teach, that it is uncontaminated truth." In this task perseverance is required. Moreover, his personal fate and that of the congregation are intertwined. Man is not saved in isolation. They who proclaim and they who hear find that their lives constantly intersect, for progress or retrogression, for judgment or salvation.

Against any misunderstanding of the phrase "you will save yourself" it is to be emphatically remarked that all the imperatives (e. g. "train yourself," "set the believers an example") are based on a prior gift: the bestowal of faith, the gracious creation of the new man within. At the end there can be the gift of salvation only because at the beginning there is the gift of faith. Faith at the outset is the gift of God's mercy; continuance in faith is the gift of God's mercy; dying in the faith is the gift of God's mercy. Therefore, though grace does not exclude but includes the striving and the battling, it is grace alone that saves.

94

EXTENDED NOTE:
THE PROBLEM OF ORDINATION

It is doubtless far-fetched to identify the *charisma* "gift" of 1 Tim. 4:14 with the gift of tongues or the transitory gifts described in 1 Cor. 12 – 14. The special endowment in the present context obviously has to do with the work of the ministry. Calvin comments: "The meaning is that Timothy – having been called to the ministry by the voice of the prophets and having afterwards been solemnly ordained – was at the same time endued with the grace of the Holy Spirit for the discharge of his office."

In this verse, therefore, there seems to be an intensifying of the general sense of *charisma* as a special gift of the Spirit for carrying out some function in the Christian community. (See also Rom. 12:6 ff.; 1 Cor. 12:4 ff.) The gift of the Gospel ministry, which had been conferred on Timothy, is a special *charisma* including the grace of teaching, exhorting, interpreting the Scriptures, and of confuting objectors. Such a gift cannot be summarily identified with any indelible character imprinted by the external rite of the imposition of hands.

It is thus necessary to ask: When was the gift received? How was it conferred? In answer to the first question two possibilities suggest themselves: Either when Timothy was first enrolled as a co-worker with the apostle in Lystra (Acts 16:1 ff.) or at a consecration in Ephesus. A further refining of the "when" blends into the "how." Are the "prophetic utterance" and the laying on of hands to be understood as simultaneous? It seems preferable to interpret the designation of Timothy by prophets in the congregation as having preceded

95

any deputizing service with the laying on of hands. If this understanding is correct, then the laying on of hands did not so much confer the gift as certify its presence and reality. In response to the prayers of the assembled Christian community, the gift is increased, expanded, intensified. The Holy Spirit confers all gifts (1 Cor. 12:8), and the laying on of hands, rather than being a quasi-magic effective cause, is the time-honored attendant gesture. The gift came by the gracious will of God "under the guidance of prophecy" and was externally certified by the imposition of hands.

Since the imposition of hands was employed in various instances, it is precarious to read too much specialized significance into the ceremony on the occasion of Timothy's ordination. (Other references include the laying on of hands as a gesture: in blessing—Gen. 48; Lev. 9:22; Matt. 19:13-15; in healing—Mark 5:23; 6:5; Acts 5:12; in imparting the Holy Spirit—Acts 8:17; 9:17; 19:6; in deputizing for a special mission—Acts 13:3.) When assistants for the apostles in caring for the daily ministrations to the widows were to be selected, the brethren were to choose men who were already full of the Holy Spirit. The imposition of hands *followed* —did not precede—the bestowal of the Spirit (Acts 6:1 ff.). In Acts 13:3 Saul and Barnabas do not receive the official gift (the Holy Spirit has already marked them out) but are certified and commissioned, as it were, for their assignment by the laying on of hands. Furthermore, if 2 Tim. 1:6 refers to some occasion other than that of 1 Tim. 4:14 (as some interpreters believe), the attempt to link a once-for-all bestowal of the ministerial *charisma* to the imposition of hands is weakened. The ceremony was substantially repeated too often to have this unique, abiding significance.

Another interpretation of "when the elders laid their hands upon you" must be noted. It has been argued that the Greek original in question is simply parallel to a technical Hebrew expression meaning the laying on of hands *for ordination as an elder.* Hands were laid on to make an elder rather than bespeak an act done by the elders. Although this view has been convincingly elaborated in modern times, even Calvin, who thought that "presbytery" here means college of presbyters, or elders, was willing to concede: "I acknowledge that a different meaning is not inapplicable, that is, that *presbytery,* or *eldership,* is the name of an office."

However that may be, a tentative assembling of the evidence would seem to indicate that the following were elements included in ordination:

1. Prophetic direction—Acts 13:2; 1 Tim. 1:18; 4:14

2. Confession by the candidate before the assembled congregation—2 Tim. 2:2

3. Committing a sacred deposit to the ordinand for guarding—1 Tim. 6:20; 2 Tim. 1:14

4. Laying on of hands to the accompaniment of prayer—Acts 6:6; 13:3; 1 Tim. 4:14; 5:22; 2 Tim. 1:6

The external and the internal elements must be kept in proper balance. Ordination always has the same import: to give expression in the visible life of the church to that which, in its invisible life, God has bestowed upon it as a gift of grace. For the understanding of the church of the New Testament it is of great significance to understand that this visible act also belongs to the life of the church, even as the invisible bestowal by God.

A further question concerns the nature and extent of the authority exercised by Timothy. Since Timothy is a special emissary of the apostle, it is scarcely permissible to disregard his unique position and consider him the antetype of the later monarchial episcopate (the bishop in charge of a see). But even if the specialized nature of Timothy's mission is left out of account, his authority must not be magnified beyond the probabilities of the evidence. It is true that Timothy, like Titus (1:5), was to handle the appointment of bishops. (This is evidently the meaning of 1 Tim. 5:22 and 2 Tim. 2:2.) And yet, by enumerating qualifications for office that necessarily involved approbation on the part of the congregation (3:2 ff., esp. v. 7; cf. Titus 1:5 ff.), Paul makes it clear that his emissary is not invested with autocratic power. Melanchthon comments on the Titus passage: "These statements manifestly show that the command is given to the church to elect ministers. Therefore Paul gives orders concerning qualifications for election, because he wants the election, which is effected by the voice of the church, to be valid." Melanchthon's argumentation is reminiscent of Luther's line of thought in the treatise "That a Christian Assembly or Congregation Has the Right and Power to Judge All Doctrine, to Call Teachers, to Induct and to Depose Them: Basis and Proof from the Scriptures." In specific reference to Timothy and Titus Luther affirms: "For neither Titus nor Timothy — nor Paul — ever inducted a priest without the choice and call of the congregation. This is clearly proved by the fact that in Titus 1:7 and 1 Tim. 3:2 he says: 'A bishop must be above reproach.' Likewise the deacon must first be tested. Now, Titus would never have known who were above reproach, but such a reputation had to derive from the congregation, which had to indicate who they were."

THE PROPER ATTITUDES TOWARD
VARIOUS GROUPS IN THE CHURCH 5:1 — 6:2

Whereas in the earlier sections of his letter Paul speaks of duties toward all, he now describes more exactly the special considerations due the various groups in the church. There is specific advice for specific needs. Every group has its particular dangers and its special tasks.

Attitude Toward Age Groups 5:1-2

¹ **Do not rebuke an older man but exhort him as you would a father; treat younger men like brothers,** ² **older women like mothers, younger women like sisters, in all purity.**

1-2 If Timothy will but remember to view his congregation as a family, he will find reliable guidance in his contacts with various age groups of both sexes. (The concept of believers as a family is found also in the Gospels. Compare Mark 3:31-35; 10:29 ff.; and parallels.) The dignity attaching to old age does not bring immunity from deserved rebuke but does temper the tone of the admonition. Neither is there to be any harshness in dealing with the younger members. They are brothers and sisters in Christ. And in the case of the latter, Paul adds a special admonition to purity. Pastoral dealings with younger women, which may be of an intimate nature, must always be pure and chaste.

Attitude Toward Widows 5:3-16

³ **Honor widows who are real widows.** ⁴ **If a widow has children or grandchildren, let them first learn**

99

their religious duty to their own family and make some return to their parents; for this is acceptable in the sight of God. [5] She who is a real widow, and is left all alone, has set her hope on God and continues in supplications and prayers night and day; [6] whereas she who is self-indulgent is dead even while she lives. [7] Command this, so that they may be without reproach. [8] If any one does not provide for his relatives, and especially for his own family, he has disowned the faith and is worse than an unbeliever.

[9] Let a widow be enrolled if she is not less than sixty years of age, having been the wife of one husband; [10] and she must be well attested for her good deeds, as one who has brought up children, shown hospitality, washed the feet of the saints, relieved the afflicted, and devoted herself to doing good in every way. [11] But refuse to enrol younger widows; for when they grow wanton against Christ they desire to marry, [12] and so they incur condemnation for having violated their first pledge. [13] Besides that, they learn to be idlers, gadding about from house to house, and not only idlers but gossips and busybodies, saying what they should not. [14] So I would have younger widows marry, bear children, rule their households, and give the enemy no occasion to revile us. [15] For some have already strayed after Satan. [16] If any believing woman[l] has relatives who are widows, let her assist them; let the church not be burdened, so that it may assist those who are real widows.

[l] Other ancient authorities read *man or woman;* others, simply *man*

This section contains two parts, the first (vv. 3-8) concerned more exclusively with the care of widows, the second (vv. 9-16) speaking more specifically of what may be regarded as a special order of widows. The care of widows was a concern to the Christian community from the beginning. Compare Acts 6:1 ff.

3 The "honor" Paul seeks for widows is not merely an attitude of respect; he means honor by actual support. And such support given in love to those truly in need is not degrading. The potential of charity is uncertain, for it can either help or harm. Therefore pastoral discretion of the highest order is needed if the administration of charity is to be properly adapted to individual needs. Thus Paul immediately makes a distinction between "real widows" and those with relatives whose duty it is to provide for them. It takes more than the loss of a husband to make a real widow. Widows without relatives are particularly helpless and in need of support from the congregation. Here is the area for the exercise of true piety. Compare James 1:27.

4 "If a widow has children or grandchildren," they should assume the responsibilities of providing for her needs so that the congregation as such need not be burdened. In supplying the needs of the widowed mother or grandmother, the children will express gratitude for benefits they themselves have received. This is pleasing to God. One of the Ten Commandments makes God's will on this point inescapably clear. (Ex. 20:12)

5 But there are also widows bereft of relatives, lacking means of support. In their lonely sorrow they have learned to fix their hope on heaven and therefore to devote their days and nights with prayer. They are to receive the special support of the congregation. Prayer can be an occupation that fills vacant hours with meaningful activity, provided such prayer is not interminable pious chatter nor merely disjointed, peevish sighs.

101

6 However, bereavement and sorrow do not automatically beget spirituality. There are some who turn in the wrong direction for solace. They seek to fill the vacuum in their life with luxury. It is not that they turn to licentiousness (though this is also a temptation) but that in a selfish, materialistic way they seek to enrich their impoverished lives with pampering indulgence. But to mollycoddle self instead of serving others is to be as good as dead. Thus they cut themselves off from God. If they are severed from God, they have also excluded themselves from any claim on the church's loving support. Financial aid will only lubricate their slide into sloth and sin. Charity is not to be squandered on those whom it will not help.

7 The earnestness of his concern prompts Paul to call on Timothy to emphasize strongly the points he has just made. Like the bishops (3:2) who hold a congregational position, the widows who enjoy congregational support should be above reproach.

8 The duty to provide for one's own family and relatives is not unknown to the pagan. This natural awareness and native impulse is quickened and sharpened by the Christian faith. Therefore the believer, who has had the opportunity to learn the deeper meaning of love in his associations with the Savior, places himself on a level beneath that of the unprivileged unbeliever if he fails to practice this fundamental demand of love. Christ is confessed or denied also by deeds.

Is Paul in vv. 9-16 describing another category of widows? It is a moot question whether the previous section (vv. 3-8) refers to widows in general and vv. 9-16 to a special order of widows. A widow is not to be enrolled unless she is at least 60 years of age. Enrolled into what category? A widow entitled to support or a widow to be a member of an order of "deaconesses"? (Clear uses of the term to indicate a special order are somewhat later than the Pastorals.) It seems reasonable to assume that here Paul is referring to a special order, a kind of female presbytery. Otherwise how can one account for the expanded presentation including further requirements and the repetition of the basic requirement that the candidate be a real widow, which would otherwise be a redundancy? Those not meeting the added requirements were not refused physical support; they were merely excluded from the female presbytery. The objection that at 60 years or more a woman could not be of much service is unconvincing, for Titus 2:3-5 shows that a special position of honor was accorded the older widows who were to supervise and train the younger women in their maternal and Christian duties. (However, this is not to concur in the exuberant interpretation that the believing woman of v. 16 is a well-to-do Christian supporting widows in her house and supervising them as a kind of prioress, an arrangement that would be the precursor of the later cloister. Apparently the female diaconate [cf. Rom. 16: 1 ff.] is extended to include an order of widows.)

9 Two requirements are immediately stated. The candidate must be at least 60 years old, and the requirement relative to marriage, which in 3:2 was made of bishops, is here extended to the widow-deaconess. (For the meaning compare comments on 3:2.) Since v. 14 recommends the remarriage of younger widows, it is plain that Paul does not regard the remarriage of widows as reprehensible in any way. Remarriage of the divorced is culpable; remarriage of the widowed is permissible but disqualifies from eligibility for the special order.

10 The candidate must also have a reputation for good deeds, and these are forthwith defined. If she is to practice love in the congregation, she must have proved herself in the rearing of her own children (or perhaps also orphans). Her genuine concern for itinerant missionaries must have been apparent in her generous "hospitality." The washing of feet may well have been literally involved. It is also symbolical of the demand for humble self-effacing service (cf. John 13:1 ff.). In fact the acceptable candidate must be marked by a readiness to relieve any and all need and by dedication to every form of good work. The saints are not only the heroes of the faith but rather "God's people" (NEB) more generally.

11 Younger widows are not qualified since physical and emotional desires will likely assert themselves so that they will forsake the order and remarry.

12 Remarriage is not objectionable in itself. However, since entering the "order of widow-deaconesses" involves a pledge (not a formal vow), forsaking the order means breaking that pledge. The pledge is to be understood as a resolve to live on as a widow dedicated to congregational service in the strength that God supplies. Withdrawal would mean breaking the resolution, thus betraying a vacillating spirit. Such wavering, irresolute behavior is spiritually dangerous. Compare Rom. 14:5.

13 In making the rounds from house to house where the Word is proclaimed and menial service rendered, the young widows deflect their attention to trivialities and gossip. When the Word of God is used only to delight aesthetically or even to thrill emotionally but is not allowed to impel to appropriate action, spiritual deterioration is sure to result. It is sadly not unknown that people can still attend church faithfully for gossip rather than Gospel.

14 Therefore it would be better for the "younger widows" to marry and be engrossed in household and family duties. Without careful attention to these considerations there might well be developments that would give "the enemy" occasion to mock. Even though the definite article and singular number ("the adversary") may hint that the apostle has the devil in mind, he surely includes his agents, those satanically inspired opponents of the church, who relish and exploit scandal in an effort to discredit the church.

15 In fact, it has already occurred that some have fallen away, perhaps marrying a pagan and returning to the old ways of heathenism.

16 Once again Paul calls on the individual to support widowed relatives, perhaps widening the circle. At first it may seem strange that just the believing *woman* should be singled out as responsible. Several manuscripts have attempted to smooth out the difficulty by introducing the reading "If any believing man or believing woman." However, since the direct burden of caring for the widow will be the task of the housewife, the reading of the text is perfectly understandable. The congregation is to be challenged to charitable endeavor but not to be crushed by needless overburdening.

An important feature of this section on the female presbytery is that it teaches a lesson about charity. Christian charity does not degrade but honors the recipient. This is achieved not only because of the loving, ungrudging generosity of the giver but also by affording the recipient an opportunity for service. Therefore true charity does not only put money into the receiver's hands but tools for service as well.

Attitude Toward the Presbyters 5:17-25

¹⁷ Let the elders who rule well be considered worthy of double honor, especially those who labor in preaching and teaching; ¹⁸ for the scripture says, "You shall not muzzle an ox when it is treading out the grain," and, "The laborer deserves his wages." ¹⁹ Never admit any charge against an elder except on the evidence of two or three witnesses. ²⁰ As for those who persist in sin, rebuke them in the presence of all, so that the rest may stand in fear. ²¹ In the presence of God and of Christ Jesus and of the elect angels I charge you to keep those rules without favor, doing nothing from partiality. ²² Do not be hasty in the laying on of hands, nor participate in another man's sin; keep yourself pure.

²³ No longer drink only water, but use a little wine for the sake of your stomach and your frequent ailments.

²⁴ The sins of some men are conspicuous, pointing to judgment, but the sins of others appear later. ²⁵ So also good deeds are conspicuous; and even when they are not, they cannot remain hidden.

EXTENDED NOTE: WHO ARE THE PRESBYTERS?

The Greek word translated "elders" is "presbyters." The term originally meant elder in terms of age. However, the precise meaning of the four occurrences (1 Tim. 5:1; 5:17; 5:19; Titus 1:5) is much disputed. Who is meant, an age group or an official group without chronological connotations? It is apparently beyond controversy that in 5:1 the term means simply an "older man." It has recently been maintained that in every instance the Pastorals use the word in this chronological sense of "older man." The chief concern is to demonstrate that the Pastorals know only a twofold form of ministry, elders and deacons, which is early. The nonchronological use of presbyter to denote an office, it is held, is late, and since this usage is not found in the Pastorals, they are to be dated early.

However, against this interpretation serious objections may be raised. If presbyters are only older men, it is difficult to understand the call for double pay ("honor") in v. 17 and to comprehend the meaning of Titus 1:5, with its directive that Titus "appoint elders (presbyters) in every town." Occurrences of the same term elsewhere in the New Testament seem to support the view that "elder" designates an official position that has lost virtually all connotation of age. See, for instance, Acts 15:4, 6, 23; 20:17. Perhaps following the precedent of the Jewish synogogs with their board of elders, Paul regularly placed presbyters at the head of the congregations he founded. Compare Acts 14:23.

If one accepts that the elders were officials, they are difficult to distinguish neatly from bishops (cf. Titus 1:5, 7). Again, it is to be noted that the imprecise usage precludes the possibility of reproducing the early Christian structures of the ministry in the church of today (cf. above, at 3:1). The widely varied distribution of official functions met in the Pastorals would seem to warrant a flexibility that can legitimately mold offices to fit new situations.

17 Elders who have done a commendable job are entitled to special honor. "Double" may mean more than other elders or more than the widows. Here again (cf. 5:3) "honor" means the concrete expression of esteem by increased pay. This recommendation is particularly pertinent to those who preach and teach the

Word, a function in which not all elders were engaged. Not mere physiological aging is to be especially honored, but particularly the willingness to turn the experience of age to practical advantage for the congregation. The term "labor" dispels any romanticizing to which some may be tempted when they think of spiritual activity. Preaching and teaching are labor (the term in the original is heavy with connotations of weariness and exhaustion) and so deserving of pay.

18 The duty of providing adequate recompense is corroborated by the Old Testament (Deut. 25:4; cf. 1 Cor. 9:9) prohibition against muzzling the ox that snatched up a few mouthfuls of grain while threshing and by the statement from Jesus (Luke 10:7) that the laborer is deserving of his pay. (Cf. 1 Cor. 9:9-14)

The formula of quotation is instructive since an Old Testament and a New Testament reference are conjoined under the rubric "Scripture." Whether Paul knew this quotation as a detached, traditional saying of Jesus, as part of some collection, or even as from the Gospel of Luke cannot be determined with finality. If it is assumed that we here have a direct quotation from the Gospel of Luke, the dating and hence the authorship of the epistle will be affected. At all events, the proverbial statement, though not directly ascribed to Jesus here, seems to be designated as authoritative Scripture along with the Old Testament citation.

Having thus established the general principle of the duty to support the church workers, Paul makes no further specific recommendations. Love and respect will make adequate adjustments to varied and particular circumstances.

19 To be in a prominent position is to be exposed not only to criticisms but also to unjust accusations.

108

This is particularly true of the faithful minister who is often a victim of the malice of underhanded and slanderous people. Therefore Timothy is not to accept accusations hastily. Only the evidence of several unimpeachable witnesses can establish charges worth investigating (cf. Deut. 19:15; Matt. 18:16). Timothy is not here invested with some type of dictatorial power. Rather, his position is detached from that of the elders so that he stands over against them as a third party in a special kind of independence as the emissary of the apostle.

20 However, if there really is a sin, even in the case of an elder, his office and the honor due him do not render him immune from rebuke and discipline. Public discipline will instill salutary fear in the others. Tranquility is not to be preserved by tolerating or glossing over sins that have really been committed. Properly exposing and reprimanding the sin of others is not an occasion for gloating but for fear — fear at this demonstration of the power and craft of sin and the devil, fear that will impel to Christ as one despairs of his own resources.

21 So important is the exercise of unprejudiced but unflinching discipline that Paul employs an earnest formula of invocation in exacting of Timothy that he proceed with necessary censure undeterred by the status of the offender and unbiased by personal feelings of sympathy or antipathy. Evangelical practice does not discard the rules but follows them without fear or partiality.

22 The "laying on of hands" apparently refers to ordination. (It has also been argued that the laying on of hands here refers to the restoration of the penitent offender.) Precipitate ordination and uncritical admission to the teaching presbytery could have disas-

109

trous consequences. If a candidate whom Timothy has not adequately investigated turns out to be a failure, Timothy implicates himself in the sin of the misfit who has disgraced the office. But if Timothy is to demand a blameless life to the elders, he must himself be pure. Purity and discipline can thrive in the congregation only if there is purity and discipline in the lives of its leaders.

23 However, the purity Timothy needs is not to be sought in observing rigorous rules of abstinence. (Compare 4:3, which, combined with this verse, makes it a likely assumption that total abstinence from wine was demanded by the ascetics. Whatever place self-discipline may have in the believer's life, it is not ever to impair health. Another motive for abstinence may have been the desire to avoid offense. Since wine was used in pagan rituals and ceremonies, abstinence could be conceived of as a protest against heathenism and withdrawal from its contaminations.

Of course, this verse is not a condemnation of every temperance crusade. Neither does the sentiment here warrant the conclusion that one may indulge in alcoholic beverages only for medicinal reasons. Whether one drinks or does not drink must be determined by circumstances and motives. Out of considerations of love Paul pronounced himself ready to forego the eating of meat entirely (cf. 1 Cor. 8:13). The paramount concern for Timothy must be to maintain his physical health for vigorous service in his ministry.

24 Paul now returns to a more direct concern with the theme of v. 22. In selecting candidates for the office of elder, Timothy is to be assured that sins will betray themselves, though in some instances they may not be immediately apparent. Therefore notorious sinners are to be rejected out of hand. But because sin can be elusive, Timothy is never to be carelessly hasty. Perhaps the last statement of the verse is meant to encourage Timothy in case he has disillusioning experiences. In the event that despite his most scrupulous efforts he miscalculates, he is not to be overwhelmed. Sin is an evil not always perceptible even upon close inspection.

25 In a corresponding manner good works will come to light to witness that the applicant is suitable. For a while the good may be obscured. But God knows, and eventually virtue must be revealed.

Attitude of Slaves Toward Masters

6:1-2a

¹ Let all who are under the yoke of slavery regard their masters as worthy of all honor, so that the name of God and the teaching may not be defamed. ² Those who have believing masters must not be disrespectful on the ground that they are brethren; rather they must serve all the better since those who benefit by their service are believers and beloved.

It is apparent that among Christian converts were many slaves. But even slaves could complicate or facilitate the Christian witness to unbelievers. Should his master be an unbeliever, the behavior of the slave would determine to a large degree the attitude of the master toward the Christian faith. There might be the temptation for the believing slave to despise the unbelieving master. But the slave is reminded that finally a master is to be obeyed because he is a master, not because he has certain amiable characteristics nor even because he shares the faith. In the event that the master himself had become a Christian, there was the further temptation to conclude that religious equality meant the

111

obliteration of social distinctions. Was the slave still to obey the master who had become Christian? Not only was he to obey, but his service should be the more zealous and dedicated just because the master, too, was now one of the beloved of Christ. All classes are to fret less about their personal comfort and concentrate on their concern to preserve the Christian teaching from defamation and disrepute. How Christianity slowly dissolves the foundations on which a system of slavery is based may be best seen in the Letter to Philemon. (For further reference to slaves see Col. 3:22 — 4:1; Eph. 6:5-9; 1 Peter 2:18-25.)

GENERAL ADMONITIONS 6:3-19

Now that Paul is about to conclude his letter, he is concerned to add to the urgency of his warnings against the dangers threatening those who serve in official capacities in the church. Though the admonitions concern primarily those who occupy some office, the warnings may be fittingly extended to the Christian life generally. (The words of 6:2b, "Teach and urge these duties," may refer to the directives concerning slaves and masters in vv. 1 and 2, but serving as a transition they are also to be regarded as a superscription of what follows in vv. 3 ff.)

Heresy and Greed 6:2b-10

Teach and urge these duties. ³ If any one teaches otherwise and does not agree with the sound words of our Lord Jesus Christ and the teaching which accords with godliness, ⁴ he is puffed up with conceit, he knows nothing; he has a morbid craving for controversy and for disputes about words, which produce

envy, dissension, slander, base suspicions, ⁵ and wrangling among men who are depraved in mind and bereft of the truth, imagining that godliness is a means of gain. ⁶ There is great gain in godliness with contentment; ⁷ for we brought nothing into the world, and^m we cannot take anything out of the world; ⁸ but if we have food and clothing, with these we shall be content. ⁹ But those who desire to be rich fall into temptation, into a snare, into many senseless and hurtful desires that plunge men into ruin and destruction. ¹⁰ For the love of money is the root of all evils; it is through this craving that some have wandered away from the faith and pierced their hearts with many pangs.

^m Other ancient authorities insert *it is certain that*

3 Paul is much concerned with heresy. It is no insignificant matter to be dismissed with a wave of the hand that the propagandists for a supposedly loftier religion advocate a piety that looks down on the routine household duties in which the remarrying widow will involve herself. It is deadly serious to give the blundering advice to the slave that he should assert his equality with his master by sullen service. The hardened heretic is not to be dealt with patiently as a humble searcher for the truth. Only the words of Jesus can maintain spiritual health, and it is these which the errorist poisons. "Sound" in the original means "healthy." The "morbid craving for controversy" of v. 4 literally reads "sick concerning controversy."

4 In the inflation of his own conceit, the errorist spews out pretentious but controversial "words." The importance of words must not be minimized. Both the

malady and the remedy have to do with words. Coupled with a vain desire for novelty is a morbid fascination with controversy. If logical argumentation is wanting, name-calling is substituted. Permeating and vitiating the mind of the errorist is a haunting suspicion of his opponent.

5 But heresy is not only a result of pride. The perverter of the truth has blackened his soul with another vice — greed. Sin is not only wicked; it is also stupid. Greed can so distort the mind of the errorist that he actually thinks the truth of God is to be used as a means of gain. As a gift of grace, the truth is freely given, and if abused, it is deservedly withdrawn. The abuse of grace means the loss of grace. The false propagandists are punished by being denied the very thing they seek. Pretending to have deep insights, they really understand nothing.

6-7 The heretic is right in supposing that godliness brings "gain" (cf. 4:8). The trouble is that he does not understand the true nature of gain. Purporting to be spiritual, he is really so materialistic that he can see profit only in terms of coin and currency. He is blind to the blessings of contentment. And yet, the perversion of making godliness into a means of gain is more subtly expansive. Anyone who uses godliness as a means of advancing himself, of asserting himself, even spiritually, in the presence of God, is guilty of making egoistic profit out of the faith. The selfishness which is the essence of greed is also the root for all manner of sinful concentration on the ego. Godliness is not profitable as a means of realizing the aspirations of the selfish ego. Only when there is "contentment" that renounces all claims and knows no greed is godliness a great gain. Here is the paradox of this epistle: Godliness is profitable only when

114

it seeks no profit. Contentment, a favorite word of the Stoic philosophers, which for them meant a way of mastering the world, has a deeper significance here. The Christian does not so much become master as find his happiness in submission to God as his loving Master whose dispensations he trusts. There is a difference between trusting contentment and indolent or despairing indifference. The man who lives contentedly within the limits God has drawn in his life is happy. This is gain.

8 Therefore material possessions, which are of value only during the limited period between birth and death, ought not to be valued too highly. If the basic needs for food and clothing are met, there should be no complaint, no envy.

9 Merely being rich involves one in special temptations. But when being rich is the intent and aspiration of the individual, soul-destroying forces are unleashed. As the ability to satisfy material desires increases, the desires themselves grow. Desire outstrips the ability to satisfy desire. It is therefore inevitable, if one enters the mad chase after riches, that he will tumble into disaster.

10 Paul is not saying that all evil can finally be traced to love of money. This is evident because the definite article before "root" is wanting in the original. Phillips translates: "For loving money leads to all kinds of evil." Kelly's rendering manages to use the definite article and yet avoid any undue restrictiveness: "For evils of every kind are rooted in the love of money." Love of money can make a man capable of any crime, even murder. The accursed craving for wealth so tyrannizes a man's life that he plunges himself into all manner of vice until faith is lost. There remains only the bleeding conscience painfully pierced through with vain regrets.

115

Timothy as a Man of God   *6:11-16*

¹¹ **But as for you, man of God, shun all this; aim at righteousness, godliness, faith, love, steadfastness, gentleness.** ¹² **Fight the good fight of the faith; take hold of the eternal life to which you were called when you made the good confession in the presence of many witnesses.** ¹³ **In the presence of God who gives life to all things, and of Christ Jesus who in his testimony before Pontius Pilate made the good confession,** ¹⁴ **I charge you to keep the commandment unstained and free from reproach until the appearing of our Lord Jesus Christ;** ¹⁵ **and this will be made manifest at the proper time by the blessed and only Sovereign, the King of kings and Lord of lords,** ¹⁶ **who alone has immortality and dwells in unapproachable light, whom no man has ever seen or can see. To him be honor and eternal dominion. Amen.**

11 Timothy is different. He is a "man of God," God's possession and God's servant. Though the man who has made the ministry his life's calling is particularly a "man of God," the title is appropriate for every believer. (Compare 2 Tim. 3:17. For the Old Testament precedent for applying the designation to a prophet, see 1 Kings 12:22; 13:1 ff.) Fleeing from greed, Timothy is to pursue characteristic Christian virtues. The Christian life is strenuous, involving both flight and pursuit, the avoidance of evil and the following after of the good. The virtues to be cultivated are six in number. "Righteousness" is conduct in keeping with the commandments of God on the part of those who have been declared righteous in Jesus' name. "Godliness" properly comes first, since submissive humbling of self before God will

116

control the selfish ego. "Faith" and "love" are the two pillars on which a life free from greed must rest. Faith is not merely theory; it affects practical life. "Steadfastness" is the proof of faith. The man of God needs the power to oppose evil unflinchingly. He must be able to endure so as not to be unnerved by the revelations of sin he will see and combat. In the encounter with wickedness, he must yet have a tender, forgiving heart. Mindful of his own imperfections, he must not flare up at the guilt he discovers in others. This is the "gentleness" which proves his love.

12 The Christian is not meekly passive. He must "fight." But not every fight deserves the designation "good." The noble struggle in which Timothy is engaged is the one to which he committed himself at his ordination. (Other possible interpretations for the "good confession" are that it refers to Baptism or even to bold testimony when Timothy was on trial, a kind of parallel to Jesus before Pilate.) To be victorious in the good fight and to retain a firm hold on eternal life are possibilities because of the call of God. We can take what God gives.

13-14 In solemn tones Paul recalls to Timothy's memory the occasion of his confession of Christ. Whether we are to think of Timothy's baptism or ordination or another occasion is not decisive. But it is of great moment to keep in mind that the confession was made and is to be followed in the presence of God, who bestows physical and spiritual life, as well as in the presence of Christ Jesus, who Himself witnessed a good confession before Pontius Pilate (Luke 23:3; John 18:30 ff.; Rev. 1:5). Confession involves commitment. Therefore it is for Timothy now to prove himself. Keeping vividly in mind the Christ of the *via dolorosa*, he is to discharge the obligation assumed in ordination until the Lord returns in glory.

15-16 It is the sovereign God, who alone has times and seasons in His authority (cf. Acts 1:7), who will determine the day of the Second Coming, early or late. The elevated style in which Paul expresses his confident expectation of Jesus' return in glory seems to indicate that he is quoting from a hymn. There are also Old Testament echoes. By nature "immortality" belongs only to God. But terms which the Greeks used to describe a god who is majestically elevated above the world are here employed to delineate the God who in sovereign power penetrates and controls all earthly life and historical events. Two errors are quietly condemned. The emphasis on the sole lordship of the one God seems to imply a condemnation of emperor worship (compare the comment at Titus 2:11 ff.), and the description of God as dwelling in an unapproachable light is apparently aimed at the pretensions of the Gnostics to penetrate through to a special insight of God. To us in this life God reveals Himself only in Jesus Christ. And even in the life to come, seeing God is not a natural capability but must be supernaturally bestowed by God (Matt. 5:8; 1 John 3:2). Not only is man's reason incapable of fathoming God, but his sin necessarily keeps him at a distance from God. Only the triumphant Christ can close the gap.

Advice to the Wealthy   *6:17-19*

[17] As for the rich in this world, charge them not to be haughty, nor to set their hopes on uncertain riches but on God who richly furnishes us with everything to enjoy. [18] They are to do good, to be rich in good deeds, liberal and generous, [19] thus laying up for themselves a good foundation for the future, so that they may take hold of the life which is life indeed.

118

17 Earlier (6:9) Paul had warned "those who desire to be rich" against cupidity. Now he cautions those who *are* rich against their special temptation: haughty confidence in the power and prestige that wealth confers in the present temporal order. In reality, however, the man who is rich only in this aeon and not for eternity is really destitute. Here is incidental evidence that though in the earliest years most converts came from the poorer classes, the Gospel also claimed adherents from among the more affluent. Since the durability of wealth is notoriously uncertain, it is sinful folly to build hope on earthly possessions (Luke 12:20). There is, however, a richness the apostle can commend, namely, that of God, who provides abundantly. St. Augustine makes an interesting distinction between using and enjoying. Temporal benefits are given for our use, the means whereby we can do good; eternal benefits are given for our enjoyment, the means whereby we are made good.

18 The wealthy are not to fling away their riches as if the mere touch of gold were contaminating, but they are to employ them carefully in doing good. The happy and full enjoyment of possessions is realized only when they are shared.

19 Moreover, by God's power earthly riches can be transmuted into heavenly riches. The sinful attitude toward wealth makes the possessor revel in his independence from his fellowman. Contrariwise, the Christian who understands the privilege of property recognizes the joyful obligation of establishing closer ties with others. He comes to recognize their needs and lends help. Such conduct lays a solid foundation which not only survives the corrosions of time but endures into eternity. A superficial view suggests that here merit is ascribed to works, a thought that would conflict with the doctrine

119

of grace alone (2 Tim. 1:9). There is no clash between the statements that God in His grace rewards good works and that we are not saved by works, unless the untenable claim is made that works are meritorious. Every temptation to clamor for a reward on the basis of good performance must sputter into silence in view of the fact that we are still unworthy servants who have only done our duty (Luke 17:10). The reward comes because God is generous, not because we are good.

Concluding Admonition   *6:20-21*

20 O Timothy, guard what has been entrusted to you. Avoid the godless chatter and contradictions of what is falsely called knowledge, 21 for by professing it some have missed the mark as regards the faith.
Grace be with you.

20 The insidious appeal of false doctrine is so great that Paul once more warns Timothy. Christian doctrine is a precious deposit to be guarded against the corruptive contradictions of supposed knowledge. This deposit is to be transmitted and proclaimed without falsifying additions (cf. 2 Tim. 2:2). The recommendation is to avoid rather than to fight these heresies, although the latter implication cannot be utterly excluded. The point then is that some errors are so pestilential that the best way to escape contagion is to avoid contact. Empty words are not far removed from wrong words. Paul's counsel is to avoid not only the full-blown heresy but also the heresy latent in godless chatter.

21 The sad example of some who have dallied with the antitheses to God's truth should add urgency to the warning. Whatever promises knowledge falsely so called might make, if the result misses the mark as regards the

faith, the grandiloquent claims are all exposed as godless twaddle.

For the accomplishment of the intricate and yet massive task assigned to Timothy, only the enabling grace of God is adequate. Surprisingly the "you" is plural. Though Timothy is specifically addressed, a wider circle of readers is envisioned, and they will all need the grace of God if they are to fulfill their respective tasks.

The term for "knowledge" *(gnosis)* seems to indicate that the opponents' pretensions to esoteric knowledge, if not directly related to the heresies of later Gnosticism, at least bore some germinal resemblance to them. In part the basic error, which became explicit in the later Gnostic systems, was the arrogant assumption that man's knowledge of God rather than God's knowledge of man brings salvation. (For the passive form compare 1 Cor. 13:12.)

2 Timothy

OUTLINE

Commentary on Second Timothy

INTRODUCTION: GREETING AND
SALUTATION   1:1-2

¹ Paul, an apostle of Christ Jesus by the will of
God according to the promise of the life which is in
Christ Jesus.

² To Timothy, my beloved child:

Grace, mercy, and peace from God the Father and
Christ Jesus our Lord.

The solemnity and much of the sentiment in the
greeting are familiar from First Timothy. However circumstances may change, the source of strength remains
grace, mercy, and peace from God. What stands out with
special emphasis here is the phrase "according to the
promise of life which is in Christ Jesus." Confronted by
the grim prospect of execution, Paul, finding the darkness of death dispelled by the light of the Gospel (1:10),
sees with precise clarity that his apostolate — any apostolate — has its basis and meaning in the message that

promises life in Christ Jesus. If the pessimist is right and there is only death as the destroyer, then the Gospel is not good news but false rumor; if the optimist is right and death is only a friend in disguise, then the Gospel is good but not news. However, Paul knows that death is real, the "last enemy" (1 Cor. 15:26), but the last enemy destroyed by Christ, so that there is a mission for the apostle and a message to be proclaimed. An imminent sword threatens to cut off Paul's time of privileged service. Co-laborers like Timothy must continue the work. In the other letters Paul calls Timothy (1 Tim. 1:2) and Titus (1:4) *true* children; here he uses a term of endearment, "beloved," which fits the tone of his tender but insistent plea that Timothy should hurry to visit him in Rome before it is too late.

EXHORTATION TO SHARE IN FAITHFUL WITNESSING   1:3 — 2:13

Timothy's Faith: An Occasion for Gratitude and Exhortation   *1:3-7*

³ I thank God whom I serve with a clear conscience, as did my fathers, when I remember you constantly in my prayers. ⁴ As I remember your tears, I long night and day to see you, that I may be filled with joy. ⁵ I am reminded of your sincere faith, a faith that dwelt first in your grandmother Lo'is and your mother Eunice and now, I am sure, dwells in you. ⁶ Hence I remind you to rekindle the gift of God that is within you through the laying on of my hands; ⁷ for God did not give us a spirit of timidity but a spirit of power and love and self-control.

128

3 Though his religious activities have landed him in jail, the apostle protests that he has "a clear conscience" (cf. Acts 24:14-16; 1 Tim. 1:13 ff.). Before his conversion Paul was wrong in rejecting Jesus, but he was not a deceiver. He could have a good conscience as far as his sincerity was concerned. And yet this did not excuse him, as he himself was painfully aware. Only the intervention of God in His mercy could halt the mad course of persecution and set him on the way of a Christian missionary. Conversion meant a break with his past but not a rejection of the Old Testament and of the God of the Old Testament. Hence Paul can praise his "fathers" as servants of God. But after the coming of Christ those who served the God of the Old Testament must acknowledge Jesus as the promised Savior. The Christian faith is the continuation of the Old Testament faith, but continuation as fulfillment. Since God has advanced from the Old Testament to the New, it is wrong for man to refuse to follow. However, to advance is not to forsake the Old but rather to acknowledge and accept the fulfillment God has wrought and thus to see both Old and New Testaments in interlocking harmony. And now, Paul being what he is and Timothy being what he is, the apostle can thankfully remember his younger colleague in his prayers.

4 Even the valiant in faith need the fellowship of the brethren. On the occasion of their parting (when and where we do not know), Timothy's affection was evidenced by his "tears." In the darkness of his dungeon, though there is the light of faith, Paul now longs incessantly for the joy Timothy's presence could bring him (cf. the plea of 4:9, 21). Paul's work has been to bring men into the intimate fellowship of Christ's love. The presence of Timothy will be a warm reminder to the im-

prisoned apostle that his life's work has not been in vain, that he and the churches he established are so much one in Christ Jesus that dungeon bars cannot destroy the fellowship.

5 In his own way Timothy, too, had enjoyed the blessings of a pious home. There is no mention of the father, who was a Greek and not a believer (Acts 16:1). The advantages of a devout "grandmother" and "mother" are evident in Timothy's "sincere faith," which has been called to Paul's attention, possibly by Onesiphoros (cf. vv. 16-17). This reminder makes the prisoner long so poignantly for a final visit. Since faith "inhabits" (the literal meaning of the verb "dwelt") the believer, it is not his achievement but God's gift, and even though its presence is not only known but deliberately cultivated, it is still of God's grace. Whatever the advantages of a pious home, faith is not hereditary; it must be conferred as a special gift of God.

6 Paul's prayer at the time of Timothy's ordination was not ineffectual. As a believer upon whom hands were laid and for whom intercessions were made, Timothy entered upon his work with a particular blessing of God. (See the comment on 1 Tim. 4:14.) The "gift" is, as it were, fire from the Holy Spirit. But even the Spirit's gift can be smothered under the ashes of neglect. In the work of the ministry there are routine days and there are periods of crisis. (Concerning ordination see comment on 1 Tim. 4:14.)

7 There is no place for "timidity" in the life and work of those in whom God's Spirit dwells with His gifts. This is not to say that they are unaware of the problems and dangers. They see clearly. But in this awareness they are neither anxious nor do they in blind panic rush to foolish extremes. Together with "power" which over-

comes cowardice, there is bestowed "love" which is considerate of the brethren, and "self-control" which restrains from rash, thoughtless acts. The gift of this spirit is conferred not only on the ordained clergy but also on the whole congregation. (Cf. Rom. 8:15)

Testimony Without Shame   *1:8-14*

8 Do not be ashamed then of testifying to our Lord, nor of me his prisoner, but take your share of suffering for the gospel in the power of God, 9 who saved us and called us with a holy calling, not in virtue of our works but in virtue of his own purpose and the grace which he gave us in Christ Jesus ages ago, 10 and now has manifested through the appearing of our Savior Christ Jesus, who abolished death and brought life and immortality to light through the gospel. 11 For this gospel I was appointed a preacher and apostle and teacher, 12 and therefore I suffer as I do. But I am not ashamed, for I know whom I have believed, and I am sure that he is able to guard until that Day what has been entrusted to me.[a] **13 Follow the pattern of the sound words which you have heard from me, in the faith and love which are in Christ Jesus; 14 guard the truth that has been entrusted to you by the Holy Spirit who dwells within us.**

[a] Or *what I have entrusted to him*

8 If Timothy is intimidated by the apparent disgrace of Paul's imprisonment, the special gifts God has conferred upon him will be in vain. Testimony to the Gospel in this specific situation means willingness to "share" in the "suffering" that regularly attends the proclamation of the Good News. Let Timothy not be ashamed to acknowledge both the crucified Christ and

131

His imprisoned ambassador. However, not of human origin is the readiness to enter upon a way of suffering that might lead to violent death under Nero. Such readiness would be impossible if Timothy is cast back on his own resources. Instead he may count on the "power of God." Not only does the might of God triumph over every injury man inflicts, but it is even God's power that has imprisoned Paul. The apostle can call himself "His [the Lord's] prisoner," not only because it is His witness to the Gospel that brought him to a narrow cell, but also because it is only by the will of the Lord and somehow in fulfillment of His purposes for him that the apostle is now in jail. It is a mighty and not a weak God who brings His message and messengers to triumph through torment and tribulation. (Cf. Mark 8:38; Rom. 1:16)

9 The God who exercises this power is now characterized. The tone of the descriptive phrases is solemnly liturgical. Some scholars regard this and the following verse as part of an early Christian hymn. Another suggestion is that Paul may be adapting semistereotyped catechetical material. This mighty God is the saving God. He has turned to the individual with a call to the holy life. Now there follows a typically Pauline emphasis. If God called on the basis of man's love for God instead of God's love for man, the whole would be on a shaking foundation. But if God's love is His own sovereign choice, unmotivated by qualities in man, it has an eternal origin and an eternal future. Therefore this love cannot be lost in the swirl of persecutions and sufferings. The ruling out of human "works" means that even the affirmative response, when the call comes, is of divine "grace" and not of human achievement. Being gracious, God's "purpose," though sovereign, is not arbitrary. The only place to contemplate the mystery is at Calvary's cross.

Here the intention of God's eternal decree is revealed. His desire is that all the world might behold His love and believe.

10 What the invisible God does is easier to grasp because His acts became visible. In the appearing of Jesus, the Son of God, on earth it became possible for man to see the invisible. ("Appearing" is the word otherwise reserved for the Second Coming of Jesus.) What a loving God has accomplished for sinful man is the conquest of death and the gift of life. These are remarkable words coming from one in the midst of mortality and marked for early execution. (On the use of Hellenistic terms such as "appearing" and "Savior" see comment at 1 Tim. 1:1 and Titus 2:11 ff.)

11 What a remarkable audacity, that a man whose hold on life is slipping dares to introduce himself into the discussion right after a description of the Lord of life! But really he does not introduce himself; God does. Note the passive. Paul "was appointed"; he did not intrude himself. The invisible acts of God that became visible in Christ Jesus are of necessity and by the will of God to be proclaimed. Three terms are used to describe Paul's function in God's plan:

1. As a "preacher" (herald) he is to proclaim the message.
2. As an "apostle" he is to transmit the message.
3. As a "teacher" he is to inculcate the message.

12 Since his apostolate is of such importance, how can he be "ashamed" just because he is in prison? The shamelessness Paul demands of Timothy (v. 8) he himself exemplifies.

It is difficult to decide between the translation in the text and that of the margin. At issue is the question whether "what has been entrusted" (literally, "de-

133

posit") is something God has committed to Paul or something Paul has committed to God. Favoring the first interpretation is the fact that in v. 14 the word "deposit" unquestionably refers to something God entrusts to man. The same is true for the occurrence of the term in 1 Tim. 6:20. However, the literal translation "my deposit" could mean either my deposit *to* God or my deposit *from* God. In the two usages where "deposit" must mean what God has committed to men, the possessive pronoun "my" is not used, as is the case here. This, plus the fact that here it is God who does the guarding and not man, makes the alternate translation a reasonable possibility. If one prefers to understand "deposit" as made by Paul to God, the meaning is that Paul confidently turns over his soul (Cf. 1 Peter 4:19) to God for assured safekeeping even through martyrdom. If the translation of the text is favored, "deposit" will mean the Gospel and the ministry of the Gospel committed to Paul. The truth of the Gospel, the special gifts of God to those who proclaim its truth, will even be under the protective shadow of the Almighty. Guarded by God, Paul is apprehensive of nothing, not even "that Day," the day of the Final Judgment.

13 The "sound words" are the words of the Lord Jesus Christ (cf. 1 Tim. 6:3). What Jesus witnessed concerning Himself Paul also taught, and it is this healthy norm that Timothy is to follow in his life and teaching. That healthy ("sound") teaching must indeed produce healthy spiritual life is evidenced by the stress on "faith *and* love."

14 To "guard the truth" is no easy task. The exhortations, admonitions, and warnings of the Pastorals are ample evidence for that. But the difficult becomes possible in the power of God's Holy Spirit, who dwells not only in the preachers but in all who come to know the Lord. Guarding the truth will mean primarily protecting it from contamination by falsehood. But it will also mean the constant demonstration that faith and love, the themes of the Gospel, are a unified power that changes lives.

Timidity and Courage Exemplified   1:15-18

15 You are aware that all who are in Asia turned away from me, and among them Phy'gelus and Hermog'enes. 16 May the Lord grant mercy to the household of Onesiph'orus, for he often refreshed me; he was not ashamed of my chains, 17 but when he arrived in Rome he searched for me eagerly and found me — 18 may the Lord grant him to find mercy from the Lord on that Day — and you well know all the service he rendered at Ephesus.

15 Paul had spent much time and energy preaching the Gospel "in Asia" (that is, Asia Minor, the Roman province) and so quite naturally had high expectations. But now when he is imprisoned in Rome, his Asian friends have failed him. The verse does not say that they fell from faith but seems rather to imply only that they refused to visit him in Rome, perhaps when it was desirable for them to testify at his trial. Possibly they were fearful of being regarded as accomplices of Paul. Their timidity grieves the apostle. Two men in particular, "Phygelus and Hermogenes," otherwise unknown to us, had previously enjoyed the confidence of Paul. Their turning away from him in the loneliness of his imprisonment is especially disillusioning. The poignancy of the apostle's appeal that Timothy should not neglect to visit him is heightened by mentioning this painful

memory. There are no recriminations. The miserable
examples of timidity are mentioned not to scold nor to
indulge in self-pity but to encourage Timothy to remain
faithful and brave.

16 The unhappy memory of infidelity on the part
of some is assuaged by the experience of the bold friend-
ship of "Onesiphorus," who had "often refreshed"
Paul, perhaps ministering to his physical needs in prison
as far as possible and doubtless encouraging the apostle's heart by his constancy. The form of the prayer for
God's blessing the household of Onesiphorus seems to
indicate that he may have died. Whether his assumed
death resulted from disturbances and persecutions in
Rome is not stated.

17 Even though the prison where Paul was under
arrest was not known, Onesiphorus was not to be turned
aside from his intention to visit the apostle. So great
was his devotion that no effort was spared to search out
the whereabouts of the prisoner.

18 The double use of the word "Lord" seems awk-
ward. Evidently what is meant may be clarified by two
simple bracketed insertions, thus: "May the Lord
[Jesus Christ] grant him to find mercy from the Lord
[God] on that Day." The brackets may be reversed.

Timothy well knows all that Onesiphorus did for
the church in Ephesus. In fact, since Timothy likely
worked with him longer than Paul, he was in a position
to be even better acquainted with the facts firsthand.
Therefore the comparative form "better" instead of
"well" may be appropriately retained in the translation.
"You know better," that is, "even better than I."

The attempt to wring Biblical warrant for prayer in
behalf of the dead from these verses is misguided. It
is not even certain that Onesiphorus was dead (see

4:19 and the comment there). But even if it is conceded that the inescapable implication is that Onesiphorus has died, the pious wish of this verse and v. 16, which commends the deceased and those who mourn his departure to the mercy of God, is overinterpreted when the claim is made that there is Biblical proof for prayer in behalf of the dead. "That Day," as noted, is the day of the Final Judgment, and when it comes, the household of Onesiphorus and Onesiphorus himself, together with Paul, will, despite their faithful service and exemplary devotion, all be utterly dependent on the Lord's "mercy." For a happy verdict there is need of God's mercy even when the believer's deeds of mercy are on display. Prayers purporting to elicit the mercy of God and guide it to specific souls in the afterlife are in conflict with the basic nature of mercy as sovereign and unmotivated. God bestows mercy because He is merciful. The living and the dead are appropriately commended to God's mercy, but it is presumptuous to undertake the manipulation of mercy.

The Need for Strength   2:1-7

¹ You then, my son, be strong in the grace that is in Christ Jesus, ² and what you have heard from me before many witnesses entrust to faithful men who will be able to teach others also. ³ Take your share of suffering as a good soldier of Christ Jesus. ⁴ No soldier on service gets entangled in civilian pursuits, since his aim is to satisfy the one who enlisted him. ⁵ An athlete is not crowned unless he competes according to the rules. ⁶ It is the hard-working farmer who ought to have the first share of the crops. ⁷ Think over what I say, for the Lord will grant you understanding in everything.

1 In order to be like faithful Onesiphorus and unlike timid Phygelus and Hermogenes (cf. 1:15), Timothy will need to "be strong." Since he is a spiritual "son" of the apostle who is now in prison, the same zeal in the Gospel cause will naturally expose Timothy to similar hardships. These would break the weak. The source of strength is God's "grace." The unmerited love of God, which forgives sinners for Christ's sake, does not desert them once they are transposed from the way of death to the way of life. Instead it accompanies them to stimulate and to strengthen for the special tasks and problems that inevitably arise. Strength is found in taking seriously what God has conferred in the gift of His grace.

2 If Timothy heeds the plea of Paul to come to visit him in prison, it will be at the risk of his own life. From such a risk many will shrink and thus fail to follow in the apostle's footsteps. The general need to provide for worthy successors to the pastoral office is therefore particularly acute. The word "entrust" is the verb from which the term "entrusted truth," or "deposit" (1:12, 14), has been derived. Thus the thought suggested is that the apostolic witness to Jesus is a fixed truth to be protected against the assault and corrosion of false teaching, but not by remote storage in safety deposit. The entrusted truth ("deposit") must in turn be deposited with successors who will neither dilute it by additions nor weaken it by subtractions but commit it to the fiercely competitive battle for men's loyalties and lives. The doctrine Timothy heard from Paul was certified not only by the "witnesses" at his ordination (cf. 1 Tim. 6:12) but by many others in whose presence Paul spoke of Jesus and who were in a position to confirm or deny what Paul was saying. Unlike Gnosticism, Christianity had no secret tradition. Though Paul had a distinct

apostolic mission that may have called for particular emphases, the teaching he brought was not peculiarly his own but one and the same as that of the other apostles. To keep it the same and thus insure both its purity and its proclamation, Timothy is to search out carefully "faithful men" to whom the work may be confidently committed. Their qualifications will be the familiar virtues of fidelity and aptitude for teaching (cf. 1 Tim. 3:1 ff.; Titus 1:6 ff.). Paul is concerned that the deposit of Christian truth be preserved and proclaimed. The Gospel had come to him as something handed down (see 1 Cor. 11:23; 15:1 ff.) that is to be handed on. Though there is deep concern for faithful teachers, there is no doctrine of an apostolic succession. Kelly correctly observes: "There is no suggestion of apostles as such passing on the faith to bishops and deacons, but we simply have Paul himself charging Timothy, and his interest is in the reliability rather than the status of the men Timothy will select."

3 When one enters the military, he must be prepared to accept the total life of the fighting man. He will need to endure not only routine drill but the hardships of battle. And so it is with the "soldier of Christ Jesus." He may be granted some pleasant times as a kind of furlough, but he cannot expect to be exempted from service in bitterly contested campaigns. Christ is engaged in combat with a world that not only foolishly flees His loving ministrations but also madly rebels against His sovereignty. Those who take their stand with Him must also be prepared to take their "share of suffering."

4 The comparison of the pastor to a soldier suggests a further point: He must be free from alien entanglements. There must be a singleness of purpose, the total intent to please the Lord "who enlisted him," which dare

not be compromised by any conflict of interests. (The suggestion that clerical celibacy is implied is in jarring conflict with 1 Tim. 3:2 and Titus 1:6.) The necessary renunciations will be determined by individual circumstances and the specific situation. This will mean that the ministers should be set free from worldly distractions which may interfere with total dedication to their proper task. A full-time ministry supported by contributions from the faithful seems to be emerging as the ideal. Paul's refusal to accept support was therefore an exception (cf. Acts 18:3; 1 Cor. 9:4 ff.). For Timothy the implication of this comparison would also seem to be that whatever threatened to impede his visit to Paul ought to be critically questioned, even such pious considerations as concern for his own apparently irreplaceable importance for the work where he is.

5 If the boxer is to be accorded the prize of victory, he cannot make things easy for himself by finishing off his opponent with a foul blow. The runner does not win by allowing himself a head start contrary to the rules of the sport. If "according to the rules" means the rules of preliminary training, the sense is not materially changed, for also these were rigidly prescribed. In the Olympic games competing athletes had to certify under oath before the statue of Zeus that they had trained for ten months. Similarly the minister of Christ cannot set up his own convenient standards for Gospel proclamation. The rules are not of human choosing but of divine ordering. Evangelical practice is therefore not always to be identified with the more convenient, the more pleasant way of discharging pastoral duties. Timothy might easily persuade himself that the call of duty was to remain faithfully (and comfortably!) where he was and to continue his work there rather than to hazard his elim-

ination from the ranks of active laborers by a foolhardy trip to Rome.

6 Now comes a comparison designed to instill encouragement. Only "the hard-working farmer" will have a good harvest. And that is as it should be. There is a blessing in laboring and suffering as a witness to Jesus. There is the blessing of fruitful labors in the Lord's vineyards, and at last there is a reward, a certain reward, not because the service was perfectly dedicated and beyond reproach, for it never is, but because the reward comes as a beneficent gift from a loving and forgiving Master. It is also possible that this verse implies that Timothy is entitled to financial support from those for whom he labors (cf. 1 Cor. 9:8 ff.). The three comparisons of vv. 3-6 are commonplaces in moral exhortations of the time, usually referred to as "diatribes." (See also 1 Cor. 9:7, 24.)

7 Significantly, Paul does not spell out exactly how Timothy should apply what has been said. There have been implications of that, but nothing more. If the basic relationship to Jesus, the sovereign Lord, is in order, divine guidance will direct Timothy toward the right decisions. Timothy has it within his power to ponder the facts, and into his devout consideration God will send the enlightenment of His Spirit, so that the path of duty will be clearly illumined.

Suffering and Triumphing with Christ   2:8-13

8 **Remember Jesus Christ, risen from the dead, descended from David, as preached in my gospel,** 9 **the gospel for which I am suffering and wearing fetters like a criminal. But the word of God is not fettered.** 10 **Therefore I endure everything for the sake of the elect, that they also may obtain the salvation**

which in Christ Jesus goes with eternal glory. [11] The saying is sure:
If we have died with him, we shall also live with him;
[12] if we endure, we shall also reign with him;
if we deny him, he also will deny us;
[13] if we are faithless, he remains faithful—
for he cannot deny himself.

8 Paul began the exhortation to be strong with an explicit reference to divine grace in the Savior (2:1), and he now returns to Christ in his message of joy. In his exertions and amid the privations he will inescapably be called upon to endure, Timothy is so to remember Jesus Christ as to be enabled to follow Him through hardship and suffering. The ringing emphasis on the resurrection of Jesus is to remind Timothy that Gospel proclamation is not a lost cause. The One whom he follows has demonstrated His power over death. He who has vanquished the ultimate foe will not be baffled by lesser obstacles. The victory of Christ is not some ethereal, escapist dream, for this Jesus, "risen from the dead," is also "descended from David." This Davidic descent (the one genealogy that is important; (cf. 1 Tim. 1:4; Titus 3:9) thus stresses two facts about Jesus: (1) He is the promised Messiah; (2) Though He is a heavenly figure, He belongs to this earthly situation, and it is man's terrestrial existence into which He has brought the glory of celestial power and the light of heavenly conquest. The solemnity of the terms seem to echo an early creed. (For the same twofold emphasis, compare Rom. 1:3-4.)

9 So marvelous is the Gospel of the risen Christ that even though the herald is chained, the message es-

capes all "fetters." Imprisonment is no pleasure, for Paul plainly states that he is suffering and that not only physically. To his bodily pain is added the more painful anguish of disgrace: He is a preacher of the Gospel and yet is abused like a criminal. (The term "criminal" may be an indication of the technical legal charge against Paul, as if preaching the Christian faith were regarded as a criminal act by the Roman authorities. However, it seems more likely that the apostle means only to compare his ignominy with that of a common criminal.) And still his cry is not a whine but a shout of joy. Perhaps in this imprisonment Paul was not able to bear witness personally as he had been able to do when jailed before (cf. Phil. 1:12 ff.; 2 Tim. 4:17). And yet the Gospel cannot be halted, for God will fill the ranks with new warriors.

10 Since neither suffering nor chains nor prison can arrest the Gospel, Paul joyfully endures his imprisonment. Ball and chain may anchor the evangelist to the spot, but the Gospel is still running. More than that, his suffering has a positive value; it is not sterile but productive of the highest good (cf. Phil. 1:12; Col. 1:24). In the sovereign plans of God there is a measure of suffering and hardship still to be endured before the glorious return of Jesus at the Last Day, and Paul is glad to endure whatever pain and distress God may assign in order that the elect may be gathered in.

11 The familiar formula "the saying is sure (cf. 1 Tim. 1:15; 3:1; 4:9; Titus 3:8) now introduces further thoughts on the topic of triumph in and through suffering. The four sets of double lines give the impression that a hymn is being quoted. Since the style of these verses is non-Greek, and because the sentiment of the first pair of lines is Pauline (cf. Rom. 6:8), the possibility has been suggested that Paul himself may have

143

composed the hymn. One might expect that Paul, who is prepared to endure everything, would surely be thinking of martyrdom when he now mentions dying. Perhaps he is. But it is to be noted that he speaks of *having* died with Jesus (past tense), so that the primary emphasis (cf. Rom. 6:8; 2 Cor. 5:14; Gal. 2:19) is on the believer's sharing in the benefits of Christ's death, with whom he is now identified through Baptism and faith. Therefore the one who has died is immune to death. Martyrdom has no terrors for Paul because when he died with Christ, he was also made to share in the triumphs which that death won, namely, the certainty of living with Jesus forever.

12 The dying with Christ may be past, but the patient endurance is going on now. In order to strengthen those who are in danger of breaking under the pressures of persecution, the life with Christ is more specifically defined as having the promise that believers shall rule with Him. Let the believer be fully aware of the possibility and consequences of desertion. Is it a worthwhile exchange to dodge sufferings now by denying Christ, only to be forever repudiated by Him at last? (Compare Matt. 10:33.) Christian comfort is realistic; it also warns.

13 As the struggling Christian feels himself shake and tremble in weakness, he is not to panic and collapse. His sturdiness can, and indeed must, be nourished by the reliability of God. The pattern of the preceding lines, in which God responds in kind, is broken in this verse by citing the startling nature of God's love. "If we are faithless" (unlike Him), He does not become faithless (like us), but remains true to Himself as the God of grace. Our weakness does not make God weak, but His strength does make us strong. Obviously this verse does not condone weakness, for which it offers a remedy,

not a veil. Still less does it excuse the treachery of denial. It would be difficult to concoct a more blatant perversion of the text than to reason: Since God is faithful, since He cannot deny Himself, we may with impunity deny Him.

COMBATING FALSE TEACHERS 2:14 – 4:8

The Need to Avoid Godless Chatter *2:14-19*

¹⁴ **Remind them of this, and charge them before the Lord**[b] **to avoid disputing about words, which does no good, but only ruins the hearers. ¹⁵ Do your best to present yourself to God as one approved, a workman who has no need to be ashamed, rightly handling the word of truth. ¹⁶ Avoid such godless chatter, for it will lead people into more and more ungodliness, ¹⁷ and their talk will eat its way like gangrene. Among them are Hymenae′us and Phile′tus, ¹⁸ who have swerved from the truth by holding that the resurrection is past already. They are upsetting the faith of some. ¹⁹ But God's firm foundation stands, bearing this seal: "The Lord knows those who are his," and, "Let every one who names the name of the Lord depart from iniquity."**

[b] Other ancient authorities read *God*

Before his anticipated execution Paul wishes to warn his protégé emphatically and explicitly about heresies plaguing the church at the moment and likely to continue as a source of difficulty after the apostle's death.

14 Just as the saving act of Jesus was precisely that – a deed and not "words" – so must the life of His

145

followers be one of acts and deeds, not mere rhetoric and oratory. To be sure, the witness to Jesus requires both a Christlike life and sound words of testimony. But herein lies a great temptation: to substitute verbiage for deeds and to insist obstinately on one's own pet pattern of words. Such folly might be dismissed as childish trifling, except that the damage done is no trifle. Not only is such quibbling useless; it is harmful. In combating heresy, Timothy will need to do more than exchange words with the errorists if he is to defend the Gospel and reclaim the erring.

15 Both the importance and the treachery inherent in words are of concern to Paul. Timothy is reminded that he is not to be a deft juggler of words but a "workman" who does his duty as an evangelist aware of his accountability to God. If he has done his work faithfully, he will not blush in shame when God comes to inspect. "Do your best" is an exhortation that reminds the youthful worker that this difficult task demands dedication and zeal. "The Word of truth" means simply the message of the Gospel. (Cf. Eph. 1:13)

There is considerable uncertainty about the expression "rightly handling." The original Greek term means literally "cutting straight." To some the picture suggested is that taken from Paul's trade as a tentmaker. Carelessness with the Word of truth would then be comparable to the clumsy and destructive cuttings an inept child might make in costly material. Conscientious skill is requisite if the Word of truth is to be parceled out to individuals in accord with their needs and understanding so that they may be led to do God's will.

However, a majority of commentators seem to agree that the emphasis is on the "rightly" part of the verb and that the metaphor of "cutting" has all but disappeared. The compound word itself does not occur at all in classical Greek and is found only here in the New Testament. The Greek Old Testament (Septuagint) uses the term twice (Prov. 3:6 and 11:5), both times in reference to "way." Classical Greek does speak of "cutting a way," meaning simply to lay out or prepare a road. The Hebrew of Prov. 3:6 and 11:5 lacks any reference to cutting and means merely to make straight. Thus the compound Greek term of the Septuagint seems to stress the "rightly" part of the verb and to use the "cutting" without its metaphorical sense, signifying nothing more colorful than "preparing."

The problem of the usage by Paul in the present passage may therefore be reduced to the question: Does Paul mean primarily to exhort Timothy to right teaching (rightly cutting and apportioning) or to right living (rightly handling)? The contrast obvious in the context is between "disputing about words" and "rightly handling the Word of truth." There is no doubt but that one of the best answers to the empty wordiness of the heretics will be Timothy's irrefutably Christian conduct. And yet the answer to the abuse of words is not only Christian life but also the proper use of words. Although the metaphor is different, speaking (teaching) and living seem to be combined in something of a parallel in 2 Cor. 2:17: "For we are not, like so many, peddlers of God's Word; but as men of sincerity, as commissioned by God, in the sight of God we speak in Christ." After the new Testament period an ancient church father (Clement of Alexandria, 150? – 213?) used the noun form of the term "rightly cutting" for "orthodoxy." Though the emphasis is again on "rightly," the teaching (cutting) cannot be omitted, and it is scarcely justifiable to think of orthodoxy in terms of teaching by example to the exclusion of teaching by verbal proclamation.

The attempt therefore to equate the "rightly cutting" of the present verse with the "walking rightly according to the truth" (RSV: "that they were not straightforward about the truth of the Gospel") of Gal. 2:14 appears to be too audacious. The New English Bible cannot be faulted for choosing one of the possible lively metaphors in its rendering: "driving a straight furrow in your proclamation of the truth." As a final comment, to make of the "cutting" a division into Law and Gospel has no explicit warrant in the text.

16 There are times when it is better to "avoid" the errorist than to debate with him (cf. 1 Tim. 4:7; 6:20). Horrible perversions of the truth are to be combated, deadly errors refuted, and ugly sins dealt with. Yet, if the disputing is simply vain theologizing and not the anguished search of a struggling heart, there comes a time when it is wiser to avoid further discussion. There are no mechanical means for determining this point. Experience, prayer, and evangelical sensitivity will supply the necessary guidance.

17 The need to avoid "godless chatter" is emphasized by the comparison to "gangrene" which spreads to infect sound parts of the body. This destructive process occurs both in the individual and in the congregation. When error corrupts one area of the individual's Christian thought and commitment, it is not apt to stop there but tends to spread. Likewise, if heresy embeds itself in the Christian community, the contamination seeps and oozes in all directions, befouling and poisoning. Two names serve to illustrate.

"Hymenaeus," after his expulsion from the church (cf. 1 Tim. 1:20), is now engaged in the full-time service of heresy. Of "Philetus" nothing further is known. 18 These two propound a doctrine which for all of its evident conflict with the basic facts of the Gospel succeeds in winning adherents. Their error results from an attempt to accommodate the Biblical doctrine of the resurrection of the body to human thinking. Since the bodily resurrection seemed preposterous, not only to the Greeks (cf. 1 Cor. 15:35; Acts 17:32) but also to the Sadducees, who went even further (cf. Matt. 22:23; Acts 23:8), and indeed to the rationalists of all times, some undertook to adjust divine doctrine to human thought and in the process inevitably corrupted Christian truth. The deadliness of the error may well have been disguised by an appeal to Paul's description of Baptism as a dying and rising again with Christ (cf. Rom. 6:4; Col. 2:12; 3:1-4). The heretics were likely not intent on being heretical at all. Their purpose was only to make Christianity more palatable to people imbued with Platonic philosophy, which regarded the physical body as evil, as a prison of the pure soul. Such a low opinion of the body must inevitably lead people to be offended at the doctrine of the physical resurrection. The errorists apparently limited the resurrection to a supposedly more purified, spiritualized conception, describing it as an inward renewal of man. But the attempt to trim Biblical teaching to fit human thought patterns results in mutilation.

The heresy inflicts damage on the Christian faith at several points. (1) It creates pride and overconfidence. If the resurrection has already taken place, then the anticipation of it and the struggle of the Christian life to achieve it is over. The goal has already been reached. (2) Again, if the physical part of man is the source and basis of evil, the way of asceticism with its fastings and chastisings of the body offers a technique for self-saving (cf. 1 Tim. 4:3). (3) Or, instead of the ascetic pummeling of the body, there might be the libertine's wanton indulgence with the specious defense: Since the body is of no account, what harm could there be in indiscriminately satisfying its appetites? (Cf. 1 Cor. 6:12 ff.)

It has been suggested that the nature of the heresy here described yields important evidence for the early dating of the Pastorals. A later Gnosticism (associated with the name of Cerinthus; cf. 1 and 2 John) attempted to remove the stumbling block of Christ's crucifixion by contending that it was not the Son of God but the man Jesus who died on the cross or that it was a phantom body (Docetism) which hung on the accursed tree. The absence of these later features, plus the presence of Judaizing aspects in the heresy combated, witness to an early date of composition for the Pastoral Epistles. (For a general description of Gnosticism see the Introduction.)

19 Realism does not mean pessimism. Paul knows the sad facts about heresy—how readily it deludes the unstable. But in faith he knows something more, something higher, something more certain. Like a sturdy temple stands the structure reared by God. Jesus Christ is its "foundation" (cf. 1 Cor. 3:11). All that God has associated with Jesus Christ in the divinely commissioned proclamation is part of the foundation that cannot be subverted. (See also 1 Cor. 3:10; Rom. 15:20; Eph. 2:20; Heb. 6:1.) It is as if two inscriptions were carved into the foundation for all to read. The one is a promise from God. He knows His own, that is, He has His eye on them to protect them against danger. (cf. Num. 16:5). The other is an exhortation which, because it is a divine imperative, confers the power to do what it demands. To "name the name of the Lord" is to express loyalty to the Lord. (See Is. 26:13, where the Septuagint, the Greek translation of the Old Testament, uses the expression "to name the name of the Lord.") Such loyalty cannot be harmonized with "iniquity" (cf. Num. 16:26; Is. 52:11). Indeed, prior to the winnowing on the Day of Judgment the pretenders are commingled with genuine believers. But as St. Augustine points out, even now the situation is not static: "How many that are not ours are yet, as it were, within; and how many that are ours are still, as it were, without. And they that are not ours, who are within, when they find their opportunities, go out, and they that are ours, who are without, when they find opportunities, return" (on Ps. 106:14). But all of this movement does not shake God's sure foundation.

Avoiding and Converting the Errorist   2:20-26

20 In a great house there are not only vessels of gold and silver but also of wood and earthenware, and some for noble use, some for ignoble. 21 If any one purifies himself from what is ignoble, then he will be a vessel for noble use, consecrated and useful to the master of the house, ready for any good work. 22 So shun youthful passions and aim at righteousness, faith, love, and peace, along with those who call upon the Lord from a pure heart. 23 Have nothing to do with stupid, senseless controversies; you know that they breed quarrels. 24 And the Lord's servant must not be quarrelsome but kindly to every one, an apt teacher, forbearing, 25 correcting his opponents with gentleness. God may perhaps grant that they will repent and come to know the truth, 26 and they may escape from the snare of the devil, after being captured by him to do his will.*c**

c Or *by him, to do his* (that is, God's) *will*

151

20 The description of the church just given in v. 19 might seem poetic and unreal, not quite in harmony with the harsh fact that errorists arise in its midst to disturb and confuse. In a kind of parable Paul illustrates the point that in the church, prior to the Last Judgment, there will coexist the "noble" and the "ignoble." (Compare Mark 4:1 ff.; Matt. 13:36 ff.) Not all the "vessels" in the church of God as it struggles in this world are "gold and silver." And though God can overrule even the ignoble and compel it to serve His purposes, this does not make the fact of being noble or ignoble a matter of little or no consequence. The following verses plead for separation and purity. Not everything within the sacred precincts of the church is holy. The impure and the abominable will slip in and cannot be fully purged out until the Day of Judgment. In the meantime, therefore, the Christian must be on the alert. The inescapable coexistence of good and evil in the church dare not become an excuse for not escaping from the defiling touch of evil where this is both necessary and possible (for instance, Hymenaeus and Philetus).

21 When the ignoble asserts itself, the faithful are to demonstrate their decision. They are to separate themselves from heretics and thus be vessels available to God for use toward noble ends. This self-purification must not be misunderstood in a synergistic sense, as if man were able to shake off sin by his own vigorous efforts and thus become acceptable to God. The cleansing from sin comes only through the Savior's blood. Those forgiven and purged wish to stand ready for service to God. The purification of this verse consists in withdrawal from persistent errorists, not from the weak, not from those whose gifts are meager or whose talents are not lustrous. And yet, even when this separation has taken place, man is still only a vessel waiting for God in His sovereign grace to use him as He sees fit.

22 There is more to "youthful passions" than errant sexual desires, as is evident from the virtues to which Timothy is directed (cf. 1 Tim. 6:11). The exuberant vitality of youth must be carefully guided. The surge of energy in the immature can easily impel to ambition, pride, and haughtiness. Youthful passion trusts the vitality of its own throbbing energy. If self-trust is basically the vice condemned, the virtue commended is God-trust, that is, simply faith. The mere advance in years will not automatically bring dedication to the higher, spiritual ideals. Here conscious effort is necessary. After cutting himself off from the errorist, the dedicated believer is not isolated. He is to pursue Christian virtues in the company of others who "call upon the Lord" and who do so "from a pure heart." There may be those (Hymenaeus and Philetus, v. 17, among them) who call upon the name of the Lord and yet must be avoided. The pure heart will show itself in giving up all false teaching and by an honest effort to depart from evil. Again it is to be noted that the pure heart is a gift rather than an attainment, a gift in the strength of which the believer is to live vigorously and strenuously for God. The pure heart is not inherently innocent (Matt. 15:19) nor purged by its own efforts (Ps. 51:17) but purified by grace (Acts 15:9) through the Savior's blood (1 John 1:7). And if "heart" is virtually synonymous with "conscience" (cf. 1 John 3:19 ff.), then there is the reminder that a really good conscience comes only through the continual forgiveness of the sin that inevitably slithers in to corrupt it. An undisturbed conscience apart from Christ is not "good" but deluded.

23 "Youthful passion" can also mean a proneness

to argue irrelevancies. This is a form of immaturity. That the servant of God must contend for the truth is an emphatic theme of the Pastorals (1 Tim. 1:18; 6:12; 6:20; Titus 2:1; 3:10). However, readiness to defend the truth dare not deteriorate into a pugnacious delight in debate. **24** The apt teacher is "not quarrelsome" but rather one who, though he cannot tolerate any injury to God's truth, can yet endure personal abuse patiently as he strives in love to win the erring opponent. It requires nothing less than the dexterity of love learned at the cross to be able to fight for the truth without becoming quarrelsome.

25 This "gentleness" of loving concern rather than skill in acrimonious disputation is designed to overwhelm an opponent and recall him to the truth, for God is love, and human harshness cannot readily bear witness to divine love. The way of love is not to dodge the encounter with falsehood but to come to the battle in the right armor. The repeated emphasis on knowledge (Greek, *gnosis*; cf. 1 Tim. 2:4; 2 Tim. 3:7; Titus 1:1) is apparently aimed at the pretensions of the Gnostics to possess and be able to impart knowledge superior to that of Paul's Gospel. Love includes hope; it does not despair of the possibility that God may convert the opponent.

26 The Greek word translated "escape" has a good deal more color, meaning literally "to become sober again." The NEB translates: "that they may come to their senses and escape." Error is highly intoxicating. Snared by the "devil" (cf. 1 Tim. 3:7), men are too drunk even to realize that they are being led about in Satan's noose and are subject to his will. Reclaimed by love and having regained his senses through repentance, the errorist is turned from the stupor of his servitude to the wakefulness of liberty under God. The alternate translation suggested by RSV footnote c is both linguistically possible and doctrinally acceptable, since the will is dominated either by God or Satan, but with this tremendous difference: The will captured by the devil is really enslaved, whereas the will captured by God is truly free.

Demoralization in the Last Times   3:1-9

¹ But understand this, that in the last days there will come times of stress. ² For men will be lovers of self, lovers of money, proud, arrogant, abusive, disobedient to their parents, ungrateful, unholy, ³ inhuman, implacable, slanderers, profligates, fierce, haters of good, ⁴ treacherous, reckless, swollen with conceit, lovers of pleasure rather than lovers of God, ⁵ holding the form of religion but denying the power of it. Avoid such people. ⁶ For among them are those who make their way into households and capture weak women, burdened with sins and swayed by various impulses, ⁷ who will listen to anybody and can never arrive at a knowledge of the truth. ⁸ As Jannes and Jambres opposed Moses, so these men also oppose the truth, men of corrupt mind and counterfeit faith; ⁹ but they will not get very far, for their folly will be plain to all, as was that of those two men.

1 Though Paul speaks of the future, he sees it as beginning in the present and having lessons for the present. After describing the demoralized types of men who will characterize the coming and last times, he exhorts to avoidance of such people *now* (cf. v. 5; see also 1 Tim. 4:1 ff.). Those who deny Pauline authorship suggest that the writer is describing a situation contemporary with himself but future for Paul. However, the com-

mingling of future and present is not unusual in the Biblical perspective and serves both to warn and encourage the faithful. "The last days" are not always easy to define precisely because this and related terminology undergoes subtle variations, depending on the context (cf. 1 Tim. 4:1; Is. 2:2; Acts 2:17; 2 Peter 3:3; Heb. 1:2). Here Paul is chronologically imprecise but spiritually emphatic. If evil developments that will reach a peak at an indeterminate time are already in ferment, his forewarning is all the more intensified. There is no time for drowsy relaxation. The man of God must be constantly alert, always ready for appropriate action. That the last times would be difficult is repeatedly and emphatically stated in the New Testament (see, for instance, Mark 13:1 ff. and parallels). Here the urgency of the warning and exhortation is intensified by the fact that the opposition and deterioration develop not only in the world but also within the Christian community. The attack is apparently not launched from the outside (see v. 6). The vices (vv. 2-5) besetting the masses in the last days will also be evident in the subversive activities of traitors within the church. (Contrast Rom. 1:29 ff., where vices of the heathen are enumerated.)

2-5 The tumult of the last days is now made vivid by listing the immoral traits that will prevail. Such a catalog of vices has parallels in the lists both of Greek moralists and the Jewish writer Philo (30 B. C. – A. D. 50). It is therefore difficult to determine whether the ultimate source was Jewish tradition or the Greek diatribe. At all events, the writer shows a genius for adapting these lists to his purposes. The catalog of vices runs to 19 descriptive terms, some of which are too self-explanatory to require special comment. The following features, however, are noteworthy. There are two sources in the murky depths of unconverted human nature from which the foul flood bubbles up, namely, love of self and love of money. But even these two are really one, for love of money is basically love of self, whose desire for comfort, prestige, and power money is to serve (see also 1 Tim. 6:10). Another interesting aspect of this list is that various vices may be conjoined and that even these clusters are not isolated. (However, the attempt of some commentators to set up a neat schema has the appearance of being forced and artificial.) Thus "lovers of self" and "lovers of money" are twins. Pride and arrogance mean a haughtiness that defies God and abuses man, even parents. For those consumed by self-love all the contacts with their fellowmen are inflamed with passion and violence until even God becomes boring and only pleasure is exciting enough to be loved. Thus sin is not an isolated weakness, nor does it consist of fragmented vices. Rather sin is a tangle of evil which, when unscrambled, points back to a selfish, loveless heart. Self-love and heresy, closely related, combine to bring about the moral collapse of individual lives. False doctrine has a way of perverting ethics.

The warning of v. 5 shows that the unhappy developments are not all reserved for the future but are already under way. It is bewildering that those addicted to such violent passions and degrading vices should yet parade an external claim to the Christian faith. Timothy is not to be fooled. However pious the words and however saintly the customs, if that transforming power which works deep in the recesses of man's inner being and effects changes that cannot remain hidden is lacking, then Timothy is confronted by despicable hypocrisy. His reaction is to be clear and decisive. The spread of this deterioration must be halted by breaking off fellowship with the errorists (cf. 2 John 10; Titus 3:10). By avoiding these impostors Timothy will witness emphatically that such pretended piety is a hollow fraud and has nothing to do with the Gospel of Christ proclaimed by Paul and himself.

6 The impostors betray themselves by the prey they seek. Slinking into households, they concentrate their unholy efforts on unstable women. (In the original a diminutive form is used for "women" to express contempt, which the translation brings out by inserting the adjective "weak." These are women with a past. Their sense of sin impels them to religion, being attracted by the easy escape offered by such errorists who prefer forms and appearances of piety without the painful uprooting of sin. But the pleasant promise of effortless freedom is a cruel hoax. Instead of being freed, these pitiable victims are captured and enslaved; they are made dupes of the heretics. They are deluded by passions of body and mind. 7 In the confusion of sin and guilt, these weak women are incapable of solid, abiding convictions. It is fatally easy for them to interpret their willingness to learn from every teacher as evidence of genuine piety. Paul rejects the perpetual search for the truth which never arrives at sturdy knowledge. He sees it for what it is: not so much inability to learn as reluctance to repent. This is not to deny that continued study of the truth reveals facets before unknown. However, the new knowledge never subverts the old but rather corroborates and expands it.

8 Paul now illustrates the problem by an episode from the Old Testament. In order that Moses and Aaron might impress the Pharaoh as being emissaries of the Lord, God equipped them with the power to perform certain miraculous signs as their credentials. When the

Egyptian sorcerers were able to duplicate the miracle, it seemed that their cause was lost. (See Ex. 7:8 ff. The names "Jannes and Jambres" are not given in the Old Testament account but are repeated from Jewish traditional sources.) 9 However disconcerting the duplication of their miracle by Jannes and Jambres may have been, Moses and Aaron triumphed over the Pharaoh in the might of God. The difference between the power of God and the deceit of men cannot remain hidden. The errorists will fail as did those Egyptian sorcerers. This promise does not conflict with 2:16, where it is said that "godless chatter will lead people into more and more ungodliness," for it is one thing to say that those bewitched by godless chatter keep sinking more deeply into their errors and to promise that there is a limit to the success of error and that it will never overcome nor completely obscure the truth.

Following the Apostolic Example   *3:10-17*

10 Now you have observed my teaching, my conduct, my aim in life, my faith, my patience, my love, my steadfastness, 11 my persecutions, my sufferings, what befell me at Antioch, at Ico'nium, and at Lystra, what persecutions I endured; yet from them all the Lord rescued me. 12 Indeed all who desire to live a godly life in Christ Jesus will be persecuted, 13 while evil men and impostors will go on from bad to worse, deceivers and deceived. 14 But as for you, continue in what you have learned and have firmly believed, knowing from whom you learned it 15 and how from childhood you have been acquainted with the sacred writings which are able to instruct you for salvation through faith in Christ Jesus. 16 All scripture is in-

159

spired by God and*d* profitable for teaching, for reproof, for correction, and for training in righteousness, **17** that the man of God may be complete, equipped for every good work.

d Or *Every scripture inspired by God is also*

10 With satisfaction and gratitude the apostle can now turn to Timothy, whose faithfulness is a welcome contrast to the treachery of the errorists. He has "observed" that is, he has not only looked at but followed — set as the guide and standard of his life — what he has learned from Paul through instruction and by example. (Compare NEB: "have followed, step by step.") A detailed list specifies areas in which Timothy has demonstrated fidelity in following the apostle. At the head of the series of terms stands "teaching." But Paul's primary concern with doctrine does not view teaching in isolation from the necessary effect on life, and that in its totality, for the whole aim and direction of life's aspirations are determined by the teaching. Faith and love, the familiar pillars supporting the godly life, are named, and then there is also emphasis on patient steadfastness as indispensable for successful work as a messenger of the Gospel.

11 The need for patience and steadfastness was made evident to Timothy immediately after his conversion by what had happened to the apostle "at Antioch," where Paul and Barnabas were driven out of the district (Acts 13:50); "at Iconium," where they fled just in time to escape from their opponents (Acts 14:5-6); and "at Lystra," where the persecutors caught up with Paul, stoned him, and dragged him out of the city for dead (Acts 14:19). The knowledge of such courageously endured sufferings hardened Timothy in his resolve to follow the apostle. (Timothy enters the narrative in Acts 16:1 ff.) Having received such an introduction to the Christian way, the new disciple was not befuddled, nor did he panic now that the master was imprisoned and under the shadow of the sword. The optimism of both the incarcerated apostle and his free but endangered disciple derived from confidence in God, who had demonstrated His superior might by rescues as many as the desperate plights.

12 Christian optimism is not naiveté, is not hopefulness because of ignorance of the obstacles, is not fearlessness because of blindness to the dangers. Paul blurts it out plainly: To be a Christian means to "be persecuted." And there are no exceptions. All and each must suffer, although of course the persecutions are not always of the same kind nor of identical intensity. The emphasis on the desire "to live a godly life" is a reminder that Christianity as a theory is tolerable, but Christianity as a way of life that is unsparing in its denunciation and avoidance of evil and unswerving in its commitment to the good is insufferable to the opposition.

13 Charlatans will know how to escape the rage of those who would extirpate true Christianity. However, these jugglers are doomed to be fouled up in their own tricks. The proverbial expression "deceivers and deceived" is a warning that the judgment of God on those who set out to snare others in their errors is that they themselves become easy prey for deceivers. The very success of the impostors hardens them in their evil ways, for the noisy applause of the crowd deafens them to the voice of conscience (cf. v. 9). The progress of fraudulent men is an ironical progress, from bad to worse, and besides it is short-lived. Though the fast-dying heresies arise in a rash of new forms, the same process of victory

for the truth goes on, so that the fighter for the Gospel may be optimistic.

14 Whatever others may do, Timothy is to be different. There are compelling reasons why he should be. He is not one who contemplates continuously but never draws firm conclusions; he is not one who learns endlessly but never arrives "at a knowledge of the truth" (v. 7). The revelation of God that Jesus brought to the church is not to be expanded through new and repeated "revelations." Timothy has learned the truth and is fully convinced. Now it remains for him to live by and put into practice what he firmly believes. The doctrine Timothy is to proclaim rests on two pillars. The one is the apostolic Word, the Gospel witness to Jesus as the Messiah, and the other is the Old Testament Scripture as the antecedent, predictive testimony to the Messiah (vv. 15-16). There is no thought here of tradition as a second or auxiliary source of doctrine alongside Scripture.

The challenge to accept the apostolic witness to Jesus is indeed rendered the more overwhelming by considering the character of those who had instructed Timothy. No succession of ministers can be meant, for those involved range from his mother and grandmother (1:5) to the apostle Paul himself (v. 10; cf. 1 Tim. 2:7). But nothing is added to the body of revealed truth because of those who teach it. (On the fixed and limited nature of the revelation compare 2:2; 1 Tim. 6:20.) Paul did not tie Timothy to himself nor to other apostles nor to apostolic successors, but bound him to the apostolic witness to Jesus which was then in the process of becoming fixed in the New Testament Scriptures. After Paul's death, when his apostolic voice was silenced, Timothy was to be even more closely bound to the Written Record.

This, in order that there might be no freewheeling tradition.

15 As noted above, the second pillar of doctrine is the Old Testament. Timothy's instruction in the Law and the Prophets began at an early age. (A rabbinical recommendation from about A. D. 100 suggests that instruction in reading the Scripture should begin at the age of five.) This written Word is not dead but dynamic, for in it is the wisdom that shows the way to "salvation through faith in Christ Jesus." To seek eternal rescue is the proper approach to the Bible, and only to him who comes with this concern are its treasures revealed. Implicit in this verse is the judgment that the Old Testament is misread without the Gospel. If the Old Testament is not understood as witness to Jesus Christ, it is misunderstood as a legal code, and it is in this latter capacity that the Law has lost its significance for the believer. (Cf. 1 Tim. 1:8; Rom. 3:21)

16 Perhaps the temptation to repudiate the Old Testament entirely was particularly acute for young Greek congregations, to whom its difficulties might suggest that it was quite expendable. To forestall any such development, Paul vindicates his praise of the Old Testament with the reminder that all Scripture (Sacred Scripture in all its parts) "is inspired by God" (cf. 2 Peter 1:21). Man cannot reveal God to himself. The revelation of God must be made by God. And this He has done in the totality of the Old Testament. Although Timothy presumably never doubted the inspiration of Scripture, which was accepted by the Jews, some of his converts may have had their problems, so that the reminder is in order both for their sake and to establish the *usefulness* of Scripture as immediately emphasized by Paul. The stress on plenary inspiration is to warn against piecemeal

163

use of the Bible, for such selectivity is based on the individual's whims and, besides impoverishing the vast riches of Scripture, will shrink its fullness and distort its perspectives. To insist that "all Scripture is inspired" is not to deny that there are differences between books and sections of the Bible. However, this concession does not condone the misconception that some parts of the Bible are merely human, lacking in their composition the guidance and approval of God's inspiration. Rather the differences are those of purpose and adaptability to the varying needs and diverse conditions of men.

Its miraculous origin rescues the letter of Holy Scripture from being a dead letter, for, as Bengel puts it: "The Scripture was not only divinely inspired while it was written, God breathing through the writers, but also while it is read, God breathing through the Scripture and the Scripture breathing Him." For Paul the written letter of the inspired Scripture is not dead. Hence for Timothy to continue in what he has learned (v. 14) does not mean stagnating with what he has already mastered but continuing in the fixed but forever rich and multi-faceted truth of God's living Spirit that confronts him in every passage of the Old Testament.

The written Word, being inspired, is therefore designed to serve as the source and proof of Christian doctrine, to convict the erring of the folly of their sin, to straighten out those who want to escape from the oblique ways of sin, and positively, to educate and rear the willing in the requirements of righteousness.

The alternate translation: "Every Scripture inspired by God is also . . ." may be a linguistic possibility, but if it is interpreted to mean that in the conviction of Paul some parts of the Old Testament were not inspired by God's Holy Spirit, it is misleading. Conceivably one could argue that this translation marks out a difference between Old Testament Scripture and secular writings. It is also possible that the broadening implicit in this marginal translation be interpreted to mean that the incipient New Testament is to be included among the authoritative inspired writings. (For Paul's emphasis on the importance of his own letters compare Col. 4:16 and 1 Thess. 5:27. See also 2 Peter 3:15-16.) To urge in favor of this marginal translation that the indefinite term "scripture" requires an adjective before it can be understood as the Old Testament Scripture is unconvincing in the light of 1 Peter 2:6 and 2 Peter 1:20.

It is a natural consequence that such divinely inspired Scripture should possess special qualities making it "profitable." It is profitable in a positive way "for teaching." What is proclaimed and inculcated in Christian instruction is to be drawn from and established on the Sacred Writings. There is also a negative utility of Scripture, namely, "for reproof." In the refutation of false doctrine Timothy is to invoke the authority of Scripture. Paul himself vindicates his teachings by citing the Old Testament, thus supplying a model for a proper proof-text method. Not only the delusions of heresy are to be reproved, but all sin is to feel the lash of Scriptural rebuke. The profitableness of the inspired writings extends also to the moral and ethical field, since they are useful "for correction." The original means literally "to set on one's feet." The taught and reproved sinner confronted by his guilt is knocked off his feet. The restitution can be effected only by God, who works through His inspired Scripture to bring about repentance unto life. After the stumbling or prostrate sinner has been set on his feet, he still needs the inspired writings "for training in righteousness," that is, for spiritual and moral progress. The restored sinner needs the continued guidance of Scripture.

17 The inspired Scripture, which reveals man's weakness, does not leave him weak. He is reconstituted, not to be a mere thinker and theorizer but to be a person ready for action, one who cannot fail to respond to every situation that calls for a "good work." Though the term "man of God" refers specifically to Timothy, any and every Christian is to be a man of God in bringing God's will to realization in all life's complex situations. This assignment is beyond man but not beyond the "man of God."

The Need for a Dutiful Successor to the Apostle   *4:1-8*

¹ **I charge you in the presence of God and of Christ Jesus who is to judge the living and the dead, and by his appearing and his kingdom: ² preach the word, be urgent in season and out of season, convince, rebuke, and exhort, be unfailing in patience and in teaching. ³ For the time is coming when people will not endure sound teaching, but having itching ears they will accumulate for themselves teachers to suit their own likings, ⁴ and will turn away from listening to the truth and wander into myths. ⁵ As for you, always be steady, endure suffering, do the work of an evangelist, fulfil your ministry.**

⁶ **For I am already on the point of being sacrificed; the time of my departure has come. ⁷ I have fought the good fight, I have finished the race, I have kept the faith. ⁸ Henceforth there is laid up for me the crown of righteousness, which the Lord, the righteous judge, will award to me on that Day, and not only to me but also to all who have loved his appearing.**

1 With the weapon of the inspired Scripture Timothy is outfitted for the task of continuing the apostle's mission after Paul's death. To this work Timothy is now summoned with the solemn reminder that all evangelistic labors are carried out in the presence of God and Christ, who will judge Paul, destined soon to die, and Timothy, privileged yet to live and serve. At the last Jesus will return finally and fully to establish "His kingdom."

2 Now the assignment. Timothy is to shout out the Word of the Gospel like a herald. Here is a message the world needs, and shy whispering is ill-designed to get the Good News spread around. Doubtless there are more, and less, appropriate times for witnessing, but when man stops to calculate, many opportunities will likely be missed. Therefore, "Preach the word!" without particular regard to times and seasons, without timidly consulting the convenience of the hearers, and least of all your own. By proclaiming the Word of the Lord, Timothy will break through the sham and pretenses to expose the shame of guilt and the ugliness of sin. And when evil is laid bare, the herald cannot dissemble; he must denounce and "rebuke." This activity, which at first may seem negative, serving only to beat the sinner down, is really positive, for it is only preliminary to the dominant purpose to bring the encouraging news that Christ has conquered sin. In loving "patience" the teaching must go on. If concerned efforts are repulsed, Christian heralds do not withdraw permanently. They return again and again, adopting new forms, attempting other approaches.

3-4 There is need for haste, for future developments will complicate the herald's task. As a faithful preacher Timothy will be drilling his charges in the simple, unpretentious topics of sin and forgiveness, judgment and grace, redemption and sanctification. Some, not willing to probe the inexhaustible depths of these sober themes but lusting for excitement, will fall prey to the more ecstatic titillations of errors and "myths" (cf. 1 Tim. 1:4; 4:7). To add to the seductive plausibility of heresy is the fact that the teachers are impressive and come in droves. Further to complicate matters for the Gospel herald is the appeal of heresy to the likes and desires inherent in human nature. Part of the insidious attraction is man's ingrained preference merely to listen rather than to give heed to hearing *and* doing. Man likes having his ears tickled rather than having his heart shattered, until by the power of God's Holy Spirit he understands that the heart broken in repentance is reassembled and reconstituted in the joy of forgiveness. On "sound doctrine" see the comment at 1 Tim. 1:10.

5 When the unabridged Gospel is proclaimed without anxious regard for propitious timing, the bearer of the Good News may be in for a bad time (cf. 2 Tim. 1:8; 2:3). In sober awareness of the facts ("be steady," literally, "be sober") Timothy is to endure animosities and overcome hindrances so that in all respects his service is complete. The New English Bible rendering of "do the work of an evangelist" as "work to spread the Gospel" rightly emphasizes the missionary impulse. One who bears the Good News of Christ crucified and risen again has motivation to consecrated effort unknown to the one who slinks about with no better wares to offer than myths and genealogies. There is no evidence to indicate that the term "evangelist" had a precise, technical meaning in the vocabulary of the apostolic church (cf. Acts 21:8; Eph. 4:11). An evangelistic aspect was common to all work in the church. Ministry means

168

service, and in this all Christians are engaged, most emphatically the full-time pastor such as Timothy.

6 Zeal and fidelity on the part of Timothy are the more necessary because Paul will soon be dead. In fact, Paul regards his execution as so imminent that he uses the present tense. (In v. 7 the repeated perfect tense stresses the completion and finality of his active life which is now past.) The two terms to describe his death are meaningful. "Being sacrificed," literally, "being poured out as a drink offering," suggests that his martyr's death will be a sacrifice, not meriting forgiveness but doing honor to God, who redeemed him, and to the strengthening of the brethren who will miss him (cf. Phil. 2:17). "Departure" indicates that Paul views his death without fear as a transfer from this world to be with Christ. (Cf. Phil. 1:23)

7 In v. 7 Paul looks back; in v. 8 he looks forward, and what he beholds in either direction leaves him calm and peaceful. Looking back, he sees his life for Christ as one of struggle and strenuous effort. Two pictures from the world of athletics make this clear. His career has been that of one called upon to fight and to run a race. For "fight" compare 1 Tim. 6:12; for "race," Acts 20:24, where "finish the race" (the same word in the original as here) is translated "accomplish my course." The metaphor is frequent. See also 1 Cor. 9:24-25; Gal. 2:2; 5:7; Phil. 2:16; Heb. 12:1. These vigorous comparisons show that Paul viewed his calling as being work for God in which he testified by word and deed what the grace of God in Christ can accomplish. He is not congratulating himself on his achievement but exulting in the power of "the faith" in which he began, which he proclaimed and fought for in the face of adversities, and to which, by the grace of God, he still remains faithful. In the faith God supplied such strength as he needed to continue in the panting race to a victorious conclusion. Thus though "faith" here likely means the doctrinal content of the Christian faith, the sturdy effect of the faith in those who believe it is illustrated.

8 Beyond his death by execution Paul discerns the glorious "crown" awaiting him (cf. James 1:12; Rev. 2:10). The imagery in Paul's mind is apparently taken from the realm of sports (cf. 1 Cor. 9:25). In Greek athletic contests the victor was rewarded with a garland of laurel, ivy, or olive. Though of little intrinsic worth, this wreath was highly prized, for it was the symbol of high achievement. The apostle's death appears under three aspects: as for the past, he has fought; as for the present, a crown is laid up; as for the future, the crown will be awarded. "The crown of righteousness" both confers and recognizes righteousness. By bestowing the crown Christ includes Paul in the number of those righteous through His blood. But at the same time the bestowal of the crown recognizes that in Paul the grace of God has not been in vain (cf. Matt. 25:21). Faith, and faith alone, has saved Paul (cf. Phil. 3:8-9). However, it has not been a slumbering, indolent faith but one active in love and zealous in service. There are no gaps in his faith that his praiseworthy performance must fill in. On the basis of faith alone he was and will be pronounced righteous. They are righteous who in faith, repentance, and obedience "have loved His appearing." As if to preclude any misunderstanding that his apostolic virtues won the crown just for him, Paul calls attention to how others share in the blessing. All those who have loved the first appearing of the Lord, in which the saving grace of God was revealed (2 Tim. 1:10), will also anticipate

His Second Coming in a loving expectation that will sustain believers even through imprisonment and martyrdom.

Personal Notes   *4:9-18*

⁹ Do your best to come to me soon. ¹⁰ For Demas, in love with this present world, has deserted me and gone to Thessaloni'ca; Crescens has gone to Galatia,ᵉ Titus to Dalmatia. ¹¹ Luke alone is with me. Get Mark and bring him with you; for he is very useful in serving me. ¹² Tych'icus I have sent to Ephesus. ¹³ When you come, bring the cloak that I left with Carpus at Tro'- as, also the books, and above all the parchments. ¹⁴ Alexander the coppersmith did me great harm; the Lord will requite him for his deeds. ¹⁵ Beware of him yourself, for he strongly opposed our message. ¹⁶ At my first defense no one took my part; all deserted me. May it not be charged against them! ¹⁷ But the Lord stood by me and gave me strength to proclaim the word fully, that all the Gentiles might hear it. So I was rescued from the lion's mouth. ¹⁸ The Lord will rescue me from every evil and save me for his heavenly kingdom. To him be the glory for ever and ever. Amen.

ᵉ Other ancient authorities read *Gaul*

9 Paul's urgent pleas that Timothy should hurry to Rome (see also v. 21 and 1:4) are free of maudlin sentimentality and self-pity. Not that the apostle does not think of himself. Indeed he does, but as one dedicated to and concerned about the advance of the Gospel, also after his death, and as a servant of Christ who, as he languishes in prison awaiting execution, longs for the strength and refreshment to be found in the visits of

171

faithful friends and co-workers. Knowledge of the conduct of Paul's co-laborers, good and bad, and a vivid awareness of the apostle's desperate plight will also help Timothy to be a more effective witness to Christ.

10 Because he loved this world rather than the appearing of the Lord on the Last Day, "Demas" (cf. Col. 4:14; Philemon 24) deserted Paul for the safety of Thessalonica. This act betokens loss of courage, not necessarily loss of faith. Two other friends have been sent off on special missions, "Crescens" (otherwise unknown) to Galatia and "Titus" to Dalmatia. Some manuscripts read Gaul (France) instead of Galatia. Even if rejected, this variant reading seems to indicate the early spread of the Christian faith to Gaul. (For some Greek writers up to the second century, Gaul was called Galatia.) Paul does not wish to keep Gospel workers at his side even when he especially needs them because of his imprisonment, if the cause requires that they be sent off on special missions.

11 Only Luke, "the beloved physician" (Col. 4:14), is still at the apostle's side. Since Mark was particularly associated with Peter (cf. 1 Peter 5:13) and the work of the church in Jerusalem, it will be a testimony to the unity of the church if he comes to Paul in Rome, and also his background and experience will stand him in good stead in ministering to the Roman Christians with their varied backgrounds. "Useful in serving me" therefore does not mean helpful for Paul's personal comfort but valuable as an assistant in the service of the Gospel.

12 By sending "Tychicus" to Ephesus, Paul is supplying a tried and trusted replacement for Timothy so that he may leave the Ephesian congregation and come to the apostle's side without any misgivings. Tychicus is met on a number of other occasions. He was among those who accompanied Paul to Jerusalem, where the apostle was arrested (Acts 20:4). A "beloved brother and faithful minister and fellow servant in the Lord" (Col. 4:7), he was sent to the Colossians and in a similar capacity to the Ephesians. (6:21)

13 Paul anticipates that the route Timothy will follow to Rome will be from Ephesus up the coast to Troas, shipping over to Macedonia, across Macedonia to Brundisium, and thence to Rome. Since with the approach of winter the prison cell will be damp and chilly, Paul will be glad to have his cloak left behind "with Carpus at Troas," apparently in the expectation of returning soon. Imprisonment upset his plans. But why bring the "books" and "parchments" if execution is imminent? It is only a guess that documents vital to his defense may have been involved. Paul accepts his condemnation as a foregone conclusion, and elaborate preparations for a defense would appear futile. Did some of the parchments contain personal annotations that Paul chose to keep private? Did he wish to turn over these writings, whatever they were, to particular individuals in Rome? Or were they letters to congregations ("books"=papyrus rolls) and Old Testament writings ("parchments")? There is no way of knowing. However, it is apparent that a forger would never have thought of inserting any such request if he were counterfeiting a letter from Paul in prison awaiting early and inevitable execution.

14-15 Mention of Troas, probably the home town of Alexander, reminds Paul of a bitter and dangerous opponent. "Alexander the coppersmith" is likely the same person mentioned 1 Tim. 1:20, who had been admonished and excommunicated without effecting his recall to repentance. (There is apparently no connection

173

with the Alexander of Acts 19:33.) Although Alexander did him much harm, Paul is not peevishly vindictive. He does not invoke God's retaliatory judgment upon his harsh opponent but simply predicts that God's justice will inevitably strike. The reading of some manuscripts, "may the Lord requite him" (though theologically justifiable; for instance, Bengel comments: "The apostle knew that he could not be unpunished. Therefore he subscribes to the judgment of the Lord."), is an obvious attempt of some copyist to bring the text in line with what his own feelings would have been under similar circumstances. Paul's generous spirit is evident in the next verse, where he says of those who deserted him: "May it not be charged against them." Furthermore, Paul does not construe the hostility of Alexander as a purely personal matter. "He strongly opposed our message." It was the cause common to all Christians that was at stake.

Though Timothy must be willing to suffer, he is not heedlessly to plunge himself into dangerous and perhaps painful conflict. Against this incorrigible apostate, Timothy is to be on his guard. There comes, therefore, a time when the opponent of the Gospel reaches such a point of irremediable deterioration that further efforts to restore him are ill-advised. He is simply to be avoided. Man can do nothing more. The case rests in the hand of God, the Judge of all.

16 Another painful memory comes to the apostle's mind. At his "first defense" he was so totally deserted that it seemed he had no friend, no disciple in all Rome. And yet he is not bitter but prays for those who feared to stand at his side. The spirit of this prayer, reminiscent of the word of Jesus: "Father, forgive them, for they know not what they do" (Luke 23:34), and of the plea of

Stephen: "Lord, do not hold this sin against them" (Acts 7:60), indicates that v. 14b is better understood as a statement of fact rather than as an imprecation.

Does "first defense" mean an earlier imprisonment or simply a prior hearing as part of the proceedings in this present arrest? The traditional interpretation sees Paul here in prison for the second time, thinking back to his first imprisonment. The "lion" in the next verse could then be a reference to Nero, and the rescue would mean acquittal and release. The other interpretation considers the meaning to be that "first defense" means part of the present legal proceedings. Paul had already been summoned before his judge where he was to defend himself. Since Paul foresees that the second hearing will be final and fatal, it is intimated that Timothy should lose no time in hurrying to Rome. If this understanding is accepted, the "lion" may mean the hostile imperial power as such from which Paul has escaped by reason of a temporary delay. For the comparison to a wild animal see 1 Cor. 15:32. The Old Testament precedents (Ps. 7:2; 17:12; 22:21) suggest that the metaphor broadly means a violent death and that the "lion" is not to be identified with a specific individual.

Arguments urged in favor of interpreting this verse as referring to a prior hearing in the present captivity include the observation that Timothy would already have known about an earlier imprisonment and that Paul would not call this to his attention as something new to him. The counterargument retorts that Paul is not talking about his first imprisonment as something unknown to Timothy but recalling it to his mind as an encouragement to hasten to Rome now. What happened in a previous arrest should somehow have lessons for the present situation. A more serious objection to the theory of a prior imprisonment is the difficulty of understanding how Paul could have been so totally deserted in his first Roman captivity as to fit the present description. On the other hand, in favor of a first imprisonment it is also argued that the full proclamation of the Word to all Gentiles referred to in v. 17 cannot be harmonized with the limited witness at an earlier hearing without strain and affected interpretation. The meaning would then have to be that through his testimony before Roman officials at a prior hearing the apostle's lifelong mission to the Gentiles reached its climax. By contrast, the natural understanding is said to be that after release from a first imprisonment Paul was able to expand his missionary activities to remote frontiers.

17 The concern to proclaim the Good News constantly dominated the apostle's mood and thought. The failure and timidity of men, even of fellow Christians, could not frustrate the strength God can supply to the forsaken and the success He can confer on the imprisoned.

18 Free from any illusions as to his impending fate, Paul knows that even as the executioner's ax falls, God saves him. Though he will surely die, God will rescue him. His death in the faith will transpose him to a kingdom where no imperial might of Rome can execute or harrass. God's rescue of the faithful is sometimes *from* death and finally *through* death. As is usual (cf. 1 Tim. 1:17), Paul cannot think of God's benefactions without breaking out in a doxology.

Concluding Greetings 4:19-22

19 Greet Prisca and Aquila, and the household of Onesiph'orus. 20 Eras'tus remained at Corinth; Troph'imus I left ill at Mile'tus. 21 Do your best to

come before winter. Eubu'lus sends greetings to you, as do Pudens and Linus and Claudia and all the brethren.

²² The Lord be with your spirit. Grace be with you.

19 Prisca and Aquila were dear to Paul because of their close associations in the work of the Gospel (see Acts 18:2-3, 18, 26; 1 Cor. 16:19). They even risked their lives for Paul (Rom. 16:3-4). Onesiphorus has already been mentioned 1:16 ff., and since Paul's phrase here is "the household of Onesiphorus," it is assumed by some that this is an indication Onesiphorus himself was dead. However, comparison with 1 Cor. 1:16, shows this to be an unconvincing argument.

Jeremias *(Das neue Testament Deutsch)* shows how a comparison of various references indicates that Timothy was still in Ephesus. According to 2 Tim. 1:18 Onesiphorus rendered service in Ephesus. Prisca and Aquila met and instructed Apollos of Alexandria in Ephesus. The first letter was sent to Timothy in Ephesus (1 Tim. 1:3). And even when Paul writes "Ephesus" rather than "to you" in 2 Tim. 4:12, this is no counter-argument, since in the context Paul has been naming other men sent to other places. The mere mention of "Ephesus" does not prevent us from understanding the reference as "to you in Ephesus."

20 The apostle now gives precise information concerning two men who, as Timothy might mistakenly assume, ought to be with Paul. "Erastus," perhaps the city treasurer mentioned in Rom. 16:23 (see also Acts 19:22), is in Corinth. "Trophimus," one of those who had accompanied Paul on his last trip to Jerusalem (Acts 20:4; 21:29), was "left ill in Miletus." This episode obviously does not fit into the narrative of Luke in Acts, since Trophimus did not stay behind ill in Miletus but accompanied the apostle all the way to Jerusalem. The journey here referred to must therefore have taken place shortly before Paul's arrest. If the sequence in which Corinth and Miletus are named in this verse is significant, it may indicate that Paul was on his way to Jerusalem when arrested and brought to Rome.

21 The urgent plea to hurry to Rome before it is too late is repeated (cf. 4:9). With the advent of "winter," shipping across the Adriatic will be closed. According to some this request may be exploited as a clue in dating the letter. Since it is unlikely that Paul would have urged Timothy to hasten to Rome in the fall of 64, when the Neronian persecution was raging, the previous autumn suggests itself as the date of composition. Some of the Roman Christians, though having forsaken Paul in his imprisonment and trial, must have been in sufficiently close contact with him to know that he was writing to Timothy and were bold enough to make the request (which Paul was generous enough to honor) that he include their greetings.

According to a tradition preserved by Irenaeus (*Against the Heresies* 3, 3, 3; written about 180), Peter and Paul, having established the church in Rome, committed the leadership into the hands of one Linus, who is then identified as the "Linus" of Second Timothy. The ancient church historian Eusebius (about 263 – 340) describes the Linus of Second Timothy as the first after Peter to be appointed bishop of Rome (*Ecclesiastical History* 3, 2 and 4). There is no reason to deny this identification of the Linus of Second Timothy with the first bishop of Rome after the apostles. However, the meaning and nature of this episcopate are theological and historical problems not directly related to the interpretation of the present text.

22 A benediction concludes the letter. "The Lord" is to supply strength of spirit for Timothy (cf. Gal. 6:18; Phil. 4:23; Philemon 25). The second part of the benediction is addressed to the entire congregation, the "you" in the original being in the plural. This is also the case with the closing greeting of the other Pastorals. Paul's writings are for the benefit of the entire congregation.

Verses 6-21 in their unadorned presentation of personal items are admittedly one of the strongest arguments that the Pastoral Epistles really came from the hand of Paul himself. (See the introductory remarks.)

Titus

OUTLINE

Commentary on Titus

¹ Paul, a servant*ᵃ* of God and an apostle of Jesus
Christ, to further the faith of God's elect and their
knowledge of the truth which accords with godliness,
² in hope of eternal life which God, who never lies,
promised ages ago ³ and at the proper time manifested in his word through the preaching with which
I have been entrusted by command of God our Savior;
⁴ To Titus, my true child in a common faith:
Grace and peace from God the Father and Christ
Jesus our Savior.

ᵃ Or *slave*

Paul begins his letter with a description of himself,
his mission, and his relationship to Titus, and then wishes
Titus God's blessing. At least two problems arise because
of the elaborate nature of the introductory greeting in
this epistle. (1) Why should the author find it necessary
to expand on his apostolic authority and mission in
writing to a co-worker, who presumably questions none

185

of this? (2) Does the ornate presentation not betray the efforts of a writer other than Paul striving to achieve the maximum authority for his work? In reply to the first difficulty it is suggested that the letter was not purely personal and that therefore emphasis on the apostle's authority would be in order for members of the Christian community. The second question may simply be reversed. Would an imitator be so daring as to depart glaringly from the apostle's characteristic style of greeting?

1 The designation "servant" stresses the factor of obedience. As one obedient to God, Paul is also an apostle, a man sent on a mission, and that mission is to help bring to faith those whom God has elected. In order to be of service to men in bringing them to faith and increasing their faith, he must help them to grow in "knowledge of the truth." (*The New English Bible* prefers to make these phrases descriptive of Paul's person rather than his work: "Paul, servant of God and apostle of Jesus Christ, marked as such by faith and knowledge and hope." But see also the marginal translation in the NEB.) Faith comes to be and continues to be only as it is kindled and sustained by knowledge of the truth. This truth is what God has revealed about Jesus Christ. But the errorists, too, are purportedly concerned with knowledge of the truth. The antithesis to the knowledge described by Paul is that of the opponents, who are apparently Gnostics of a sort. (See the Introduction for a brief description of Gnosticism. On the phrase "knowledge of the truth" compare 1 Tim. 2:4; 2 Tim. 2:25; 3:7.) The descriptive clause Paul adds, "which accords with godliness," signalizes the difference. Whereas the heretics are interested in knowledge that dazzles the mind with

186

brilliant, soaring insights, Paul is inculcating truth which, though indeed it thrills the mind, is glorious chiefly in this, that it molds lives into the shapes and forms of piety set forth by the revealed will of God. Knowledge alone is inadequate. It must be such knowledge as changes lives and controls conduct.

2 The kind of truth Paul proclaims rests on more than a human foundation, namely, on the "hope of eternal life" that God has promised. In 1 Tim. 1:1 Christ Jesus is called our hope. His resurrection is the presupposition and basis for any real hope we may have for eternal life. This hope, though it transcends the world, having been conceived by God in His eternal counsels and drawing men's aspirations to higher horizons than the merely earthly, yet reaches down into the here and now, dispelling shadows and radiating light, the light of everlasting life. Though the full realization of eternal life lies in the future, it is real and operative even now. God, who never lies, gave His Word "ages ago" in the first promises of a Savior. (Cf. 2 Tim. 1:9; Rom. 1:2)

3 At the time set by God in His sovereign reign, there came the further revelation, the clearer "Word," spoken in and by Jesus, the Christ. (How the New Testament applies the Greek term *logos* = "Word" both to Jesus and to the witness by Him and about Him may be seen in a comparison of John 1:1 ff. and Mark 2:2; Acts 4:4.) To the further proclamation of this revelation Paul has been called. In His desire to provide for the dissemination of the Gospel through ambassadors like Paul, God shows himself to be the concerned "Savior" of mankind.

4 The affectionate designation "my true child," applied to Timothy in 1 Tim. 1:1, is here extended also

to Titus. The implication again is that Paul is a spiritual father, for he has been instrumental in bringing another to faith. By calling God "Savior" in v. 3 and Jesus "Savior" in v. 4, Paul puts them on the same divine level. (On the greeting compare the comment on 1 Tim. 1:2.)

THE TRUE CHURCH IN ITS STRUGGLE AGAINST SECTS 1:5-16

The Faithful Minister 1:5-9

5 **This is why I left you in Crete, that you might amend what was defective, and appoint elders in every town as I directed you,** 6 **if any man is blameless, the husband of one wife, and his children are believers and not open to the charge of being profligate or insubordinate.** 7 **For a bishop, as God's steward, must be blameless; he must not be arrogant or quicktempered or a drunkard or violent or greedy for gain,** 8 **but hospitable, a lover of goodness, master of himself, upright, holy, and self-controlled;** 9 **he must hold firm to the sure word as taught, so that he may be able to give instruction in sound doctrine and also to confute those who contradict it.**

The aspect of church organization with which Paul is most concerned is the ministry. If the church is to fulfill its mission, if it is not only to survive but to defeat heresy, then faithful, capable ministers must be at work. (See the comment at 1 Tim. 3:1 ff. for observations on the catalog of virtues.)

5 The establishment and spread of the church is the sovereign achievement of God's Holy Spirit, who works where and when He pleases. But in the course of expan-

188

sion, there is need for external, human ordering and systematizing. Paul himself had been on the island of Crete but apparently not sufficiently long to allow him to establish and organize the church adequately. Perhaps the number of converts had increased significantly since Paul's departure, so that more leaders were necessary. The increased ranks of believers should also have provided a reservoir from which suitable manpower could be drawn to meet the growing demands. It is incorrect to conclude that Paul and Titus are exercising a quasi-dictatorial power over the congregations. In young, inexperienced congregations the selection of leaders would best be undertaken under the close supervision of Titus. There is no reason to assume that elders were forced on congregations contrary to their will or even without their consent. (See the comment and extended note at 1 Tim. 4:14.)

6 The qualifications requisite for the elder are now developed in a way similar to that of 1 Tim. 3:2 ff. The elder must have an unsullied reputation, and his household must be beyond reproach. His children must not only be professing believers, but their lives must also certify the sincerity of their professions. The conduct of the children inevitably gives testimony, good or bad, concerning the father and his aptitude for office.

7 In v. 5 the original for elders is "presbyters." Here in v. 7 the apostle uses the term "bishop" (Greek — *episkopos;* cf. 1 Tim. 3:2). The shift from "presbyters." (plural) to "bishop" (singular) does not mean that in each town there were a *group* of elders and a *single* bishop. To bring out the point that "elder" describes an official and "bishop" describes his function, Barrett paraphrases: "The elders you appoint must have certain qualifications, for a man who exercises oversight must

189

be . . . ." This sudden switch in terms from presbyter to bishop is a clear indication that the designations are to a degree interchangeable and have not at this period in the church's history been distinguished in a way that would indicate any clear-cut hierarchical organization in the church. (Compare the similar interchange of terms in Acts 20:17 and 28.) Since the church is the household (literally, "house") of God (1 Tim. 3:15), the position of the presbyter, or bishop, is appropriately likened to that of a steward whose function it shall be to see that everything proceeds in order according to the will of the master. (Compare 1 Cor. 4:1, where the fullness of apostolic authority is indicated by the phrase "stewards of the mysteries of God," and 1 Peter 4:10, where Peter extends the metaphor, emphasizing that every Christian must be a good steward of God's grace.) If the aspirant to the ministerial office is one who insists on whatever suits his fancy or easily flares up in anger, he is suffering from defects of character which disqualify him.

8 The positive qualities demanded are substantially the same as those of 1 Tim. 3:2 ff. The "lover of goodness" will possess this virtue not merely as a disposition of the mind but as the motive and guiding power in the practical conduct of life. Self-control is to be understood as extending to all the desires and appetites which, if uncritically indulged, sweep one away from fellowship with Christ.

9 In keeping with a repeated emphasis of the Pastoral Epistles (cf. 1 Tim. 4:6; 2 Tim. 3:14), Paul stresses that the minister in God's church must renounce pet ideas, novelties, and eccentricities and follow faithfully and gladly the doctrine he has learned in the apostolic Word of witness to Jesus. In unswerving dedication to this sure Word Titus will be able to discharge his twofold

190

obligation of strengthening those who come to faith and refuting those who presume to contradict the faith. Believers need guidance so that they may conduct their practical life in harmony with God's will. But they can never know God's will if, instead of a clear word of direction, they are enveloped in the haze and fog of fantastic theologies. Because of the perversities of sinful human nature, the presbyter-bishop is also going to encounter opposition to the Christian doctrine. Though he cannot always win the errorist, he can and must "confute" him with the Word.

The Errorists   *1:10-16*

¹⁰ **For there are many insubordinate men, empty talkers and deceivers, especially the circumcision party; ¹¹ they must be silenced, since they are upsetting whole families by teaching for base gain what they have no right to teach. ¹² One of themselves, a prophet of their own, said, "Cretans are always liars, evil beasts, lazy gluttons." ¹³ This testimony is true. Therefore rebuke them sharply, that they may be sound in the faith, ¹⁴ instead of giving heed to Jewish myths or to commands of men who reject the truth. ¹⁵ To the pure all things are pure, but to the corrupt and unbelieving nothing is pure; their very minds and consciences are corrupted. ¹⁶ They profess to know God, but they deny him by their deeds; they are detestable, disobedient, unfit for any good deed.**

¹⁰ The errorists in Crete seem to be basically similar to those in Ephesus. Compare 1 Tim. 1:3-11; 4:1-11; 6:3-10; and 2 Tim. 2:14-18. The proud insubordination that insists on asserting itself is found particularly

among the Jewish converts who could pride themselves on the knowledge they had acquired in a long period of religious instruction. Commendable as religious knowledge is, when it vaunts itself, it is wrong and sure to be a menace that all too easily becomes wordy and deceptive, both to self and to others. Because the errorist can talk impressively on religious topics, he himself may be persuaded that he is a good man. His hearers, too, are in danger of being overwhelmed by his pretentious glibness. The particular offenders in this respect are the members of the "circumcision party," that is, Jewish-Christians, and from them the evil had perhaps spread also to Gentile converts. (Note that v. 12 quotes a Cretan against Cretans. Either the Jews had become so assimilated that they were properly regarded as Cretans, or native Cretans were also involved in the heresy.)

11 Actually, the errorists are vicious persons whose motive is really base gain. Therefore Paul makes the rigorous demand that they be silenced. Their deadly potential has been demonstrated in the subversion of "whole families," for where an individual has been infected, the disease of heresy has often spread to the other members of the family circle. The word for "silenced" in the original is especially strong, meaning to bridle, or gag. And yet this silencing of error is not to be achieved by a kind of police coercion but through the convicting power of God's Word. (Cf. v. 9.)

12 Besides the basic similarity of the perverse human heart in all mankind, there is the danger of particular national characteristics. With a harshness that can be justified only by the dangerous facts as they obtained in Crete, Paul warns the Cretans, invoking the witness of one of their own countrymen. (The verse is probably quoted from the *De Oraculis* of Epimenides, who lived

in the sixth century B. C.) Even as the proverbial immorality of Corinth created the verb "Corinthianize" = "fornicate," so the Cretan disregard for the truth led to the formation of the verb "Cretanize" = "lie." The condemnation is even more extensive, for the comparison to "evil beasts" charges the Cretans with crudeness and brutality, and the term "lazy gluttons" brings the further accusation of indolence.

13 This judgment may sound harsh, but since the plight is real and dangerous, the remedy must be adequate even if painful. This sin is not eliminated by stroking and caressing; it must be violently uprooted. To be sure, severity is not practiced for its own sake, but is designed to heal. Even excommunication from the congregation is an effort to save (cf. 1 Tim. 1:20). "Sound in the faith" could conceivably mean "sturdy in their loyalty to Christ," but this does not seem so likely as the objective sense: "resolutely adhering to the accepted body of doctrine, continuing in orthodoxy." (For this meaning of faith, somewhat exceptional in Paul, see the commentary at 1 Tim. 4:1 and the remarks on "Religious and Thelogical Concepts" in the Introduction.)

14 And then, when sin has been grubbed out and seen in its naked ugliness and when forgiveness and restitution have been found in Jesus, there develops a spiritual health that is immune to the fantastic and pretentious mingling of truth and falsehood. The concoction is recognized as poisonous by the church member who lives in the daily experience of sin and forgiveness. The troubled sinner who has found peace in Christ is impervious to assaults of error, the appeal of "Jewish myths" and genealogies (cf. 1 Tim. 1:4; 4:7), and the impressiveness of ascetic commands to abstain from things considered to be unclean. (Cf. 1 Tim. 4:3)

15 The devious and delusive ways of human understanding can easily misinterpret the Old Testament distinctions between clean and unclean as implying that there is an inherent goodness or badness in things. Reaffirming the principle enunciated by Jesus (cf. Matt. 15:11, 17 ff.), Paul points out that the impurity is in the heart and mind of man until cleansed by faith in Jesus Christ. Where this cleansing has been effected, "all things are pure." Contrariwise, where sin is unforgiven and therefore in control, impurity stains and contaminates everything. Sinful man's use of nature is inescapably selfish and therefore perverse. His is a defiling touch, wherever he reaches. There is a subtle shifting back and forth in the meaning of "pure" between an ethical and a ceremonial signification. To the morally pure all things are ceremonially permissible. (See Rom. 14, where Paul deals with the problem in a different setting.) The frequent citation of this maxim to mean that the morally pure are safe from pollution by anything morally impure is a distortion of its meaning. Those morally pure will not test their immunity by wanton exposure to contamination. The purging and enlightening of their consciences is too costly to admit of such folly. They have been cleansed, not by the ablutions of ceremonial waters but by the washing in the Savior's blood. There are some parallels in contemporary Epicurean and Stoic philosophy suggesting that Paul may be quoting a catch-phrase and turning it against the opponents.

16 Knowledge and every claim to knowledge impose the obligation to see that practical life is in conformity with all that is professed (cf. 1 John 2:4). This crucial and revealing test the errorists fail most miserably. In their stubborn refusal to be set right, they do what is abominable in the eyes of God and inevitably must be "detestable" to Him.

DIRECTING VARIOUS RANKS IN THE WAY OF PIETY   2:1-15

Christian Duty on Various Levels   *2:1-10*

¹ **But as for you, teach what befits sound doctrine.** ² **Bid the older men be temperate, serious, sensible, sound in faith, in love, and in steadfastness.** ³ **Bid the older women likewise to be reverent in behavior, not to be slanderers or slaves to drink; they are to teach what is good,** ⁴ **and so train the young women to love their husbands and children,** ⁵ **to be sensible, chaste, domestic, kind, and submissive to their husbands, that the word of God may not be discredited.** ⁶ **Likewise urge the younger men to control themselves.** ⁷ **Show yourself in all respects a model of good deeds, and in your teaching show integrity, gravity,** ⁸ **and sound speech that cannot be censured, so that an opponent may be put to shame, having nothing evil to say of us.** ⁹ **Bid slaves to be submissive to their masters and to give satisfaction in every respect; they are not to be refractory,** ¹⁰ **nor to pilfer, but to show entire and true fidelity, so that in everything they may adorn the doctrine of God our Savior.**

1 Paul has just shown the sterility of the pretentious errorists. They talk volubly, but nothing good ever really happens. By contrast, Titus is to set forth for various ranks and levels what kind of conduct it is that healthy doctrine requires and promotes. (On "sound doctrine" see the comment at 1 Tim. 1:10.) There is

195

throughout this section a sensitive concern for the outsider's reaction to behavior within the Christian community. Paul would have Titus keep Christians aware that the nonbeliever's estimate of the Gospel is based on the believer's conduct. The unpretentious obviousness of the virtues called for is a reminder that in this world followers of Christ have not arrived at perfection nor reached the haven of security. They are still exposed to dangers and must be admonished to cautiousness; they are still in the battle and must be exhorted to perseverance.

2 The "older men" are a chronological group, not elders in the sense of men occupying some church office. (The term in the original is slightly different from that of 1:5 and 1 Tim. 5:17 and 19.) Their maturity should show itself in temperance, both literally in regard to use of intoxicants and also figuratively (cf. 1 Tim. 3:2, 11) in the sobriety and even temper of their total conduct, as is further developed by the succeeding adjectives.

"Serious": Deserving of respect, of noble bearing. Cf. 1 Tim. 3:8, 11.

"Sensible": Thinking things through.

"Sound in faith": The adjective "sound" literally means healthy. It is difficult — and perhaps wrong — to try to pinpoint the meaning of "faith" here and delimit the significance too narrowly. The immediate context suggests the subjective meaning, that is, confidence and trust in God. Nevertheless, the wider context of the Pastoral Epistles with their sustained concern for pure doctrine makes it appropriate to think of the objective sense, that is, adherence to the revealed truth of God.

"Sound in love": The pattern for healthy love has been marked out by God's love for the unlovely, His concern to rescue fallen man.

196

"Sound in steadfastness": It will require sound spiritual health to be able to bear up under the burdens that a chastening God permits a hostile world to load on those who serve Him. Compare 1 Tim. 6:11; 2 Tim. 3:10. Neither will it be easy to live hopefully in what often appears to be a hopeless situation nor to maintain a sure footing on God's promises in the swirl and crosscurrents of tumultuous times.

Here, too, the virtues have a typical Greek ring. (See above at 1:5 ff. and 1 Tim. 3:2 ff.) However, it must not be overlooked that such lists of personal duties were also frequent in Hellenistic Judaism. It has been suggested that Judaism borrowed and adapted these moral commonplaces from Hellenistic sources as part of its propaganda to gain proselytes. Thus Paul could have found such catalogs in various places. However that may be, it is again apparent that he invests the terms with nuances of Christian meaning. At the end of the chapter (vv. 11-15) he will supply the specific Gospel basis for the ethical requirements he is issuing.

3a In reference to the older women Paul uses an interesting term, "reverent in behavior." Reverent in the original literally and basically means what is fitting in the holy place, that is, the temple. For the Christian, God's presence is to be respected not only in a holy place but everywhere, for one is always in the presence of the holy God. Sins of the tongue are a special temptation and must be avoided. What a tragedy if the gift of speech which elevates man above the animal level is debased and degraded to serve in the place of claw and fang! Drunkenness, a disgrace for any and all, would be especially revolting in an older woman in whom one rightly expects to see dignity exemplified.

3b-4 Though the formal office of teaching is denied

them (cf. 1 Tim. 2:11 ff.), the older women are in a position to impart instruction in a crucial area. To guide the younger women in the complex household duties of a wife and mother is, at least in part, beyond the ability of Titus and the pastors. A woman's insight, an older woman's experience, are priceless qualifications. Although contemporary culture may have been more appreciative of the wisdom available in the aged than is our own, a domineering busybody was likely as obnoxious then as now. Despite sociological differences, our modern age can profit from the Christian experience and counsel of those advanced in years.

5 There are certain Christian virtues which, if exemplified in the conduct of believing wives, will reflect creditably on the Christian faith. The contrast in conduct between unbelieving and believing women will not escape the notice of the outsider, nor will it be without effect. Again it is to be noted that the virtues called for are basically the same as those extolled by heathen moralists. The Christian faith does not eradicate all the best aspirations of man but gives them deeper and more fruitful rooting in Christ.

The specific virtues of the Christian wife are deserving of close attention.

"Sensible" (see above, v. 2): The impulsiveness of youth is to be controlled by prudence learned from the older women.

"Chaste": Where the total person is dedicated to God, there can be no desecration of the body by unfaithfulness or promiscuity.

"Domestic": Literally, working at home. Because of the temptation to be a gadabout (cf. 1 Tim. 5:13), the young wives will need encouragement and direction so that they may dedicate themselves to their proper career of being homemakers. (Cf. Prov. 7:11; 31:10 ff.)

"Kind": The grind of motherly and wifely duties can easily fray the nerves. Assistance and guidance from the elderly can help the young maintain a sweet disposition.

"Submissive": For one individual to submit to another is not easy. And yet, the equality of men and women before Christ (Gal. 3:28) does not conflict with, let alone eliminate, the will of God that the husband should be the head of the family. Needless to say, since Christ is the head of the husband, the husband's position dare not be distorted into one of tyrannical authority.

Honorific inscriptions of the Hellenistic world present many parallels to the qualities the apostle here extols. Pagans tended to believe the same virtues were wifely ornaments. One well-known epitaph praises a wife "devoted to her husband and devoted to her children." Therefore, if the name of God, which believers represent in the midst of an unbelieving environment, is not to be discredited (literally, "blasphemed," that is, criticized and condemned), these wifely virtues *rightly* lauded by the pagans will have to be splendidly exemplified in the Christian community. This is not to say that acclamations of an unconverted environment are to be mechanically reechoed by the community of believers. Only when the values of society coincide with those of God's revelation can they meet with Christian commendation. Neither is this advice an instance of legitimate accommodation to deluded sensitivities. (Note the contrast with Rom. 14.) If there is a conflicting estimate, the church's mission will be to denounce whatever departs from the will of God and to instruct in the way of the truth. Christian wives have a special opportunity to witness to Christ by conforming their lives to the requirements of the Gospel. Here is a sphere in which women can speak convincingly, and though they may not persuade all, they will be doing much to muzzle critical mouths.

The scope of the present passage does not embrace the particular problems of unmarried women. Despite the fact, however, that all our changed sociological conditions and attitudes are not covered by the apostle's observations, there is no reason to believe that new situations would modify the advice Paul does have for the young wife. (See also 1 Cor. 14:35; Eph. 5:22; Col. 3:18. On the position of women compare 1 Tim. 2:12 ff. and the comment there.)

6 The bursting energies of youth are a threat to the balance and moderation of the young, and Titus is therefore to "urge" (note the energy of the term) self-discipline upon the young men. ("In all respects," v. 7, may also be understood as belonging to v. 6: "Control themselves in all respects.")

7 Pastoral example, which will weigh heavily at any time, will be particularly impressive if Titus, as a young man himself, sets an exemplary pattern of self-discipline (cf. 1 Tim. 4:12). If Titus really is a living pattern of the godly life for young men, he at the same time both demonstrates and guarantees that the new life in Christ is no mirage but a possibility and a reality. For Titus the good example necessarily implies faithful proclamation of the Gospel. Proper teaching will be marked by certain definite characteristics.

"Integrity": Purity of motivation without any desire for base gain is meant. This virtue is notably lacking in the errorists, who are motivated by greed. If there is

200

integrity in the teacher, there will be corresponding consequences in the teaching.

"Gravity": Titus is to demonstrate dignity in contrast to flightiness, and yet a dignity which does not assume arrogant airs. (Compare v. 2, where the corresponding adjective is translated "serious.")

8 "Sound speech that cannot be censured": The speech will be healthy if no germs of falsification are mingled in, if purity is maintained by strict conformity to the revelation of God.

When all of this has been faithfully executed, and when all of the requirements enumerated have been met, the perverse opponent may yet censure and speak evil, but not with a good conscience, for deep within he will know that his charges are falsehoods and malicious fabrications.

9 Though they might seem to occupy an insignificant, frustrating position, even slaves can be a powerful influence in the spread of the Gospel. Compare 1 Tim. 6:1, where the presentation is in terms of the negative, that is, slaves are to honor their masters so that God may not be defamed. Here the godly conduct of slaves is a positive ornament to the Christian doctrine. Even the dull life of a slave, if lived in fidelity, can add luster to the Gospel. **10** Since the usual feeling between slave and master was one of antagonism and hostility, the slave would "pilfer" whatever he could. Christian slaves, however, were obligated to strict honesty, giving further evidence that they belonged to a Savior-God (cf. 1 Tim. 1:1) who by saving them had changed them. This aspect of saving grace is developed in the following verses. It is difficult to determine whether "the doctrine of God our Savior" is teaching about God or from God. In either case the meaning is substantially the same, for

201

the teaching about God is from God, and that from God is about God.

Grace for Salvation and the Life of Piety   *2:11-15*

¹¹ For the grace of God has appeared for the salvation of all men, ¹² training us to renounce irreligion and worldly passions, and to live sober, upright, and godly lives in this world, ¹³ awaiting our blessed hope, the appearing of the glory of our great God and Savior^c Jesus Christ, ¹⁴ who gave himself for us to redeem us from all iniquity and to purify for himself a people of his own who are zealous for good deeds.

¹⁵ Declare these things; exhort and reprove with all authority. Let no one disregard you.

   ᶜ Or of the great God and our Savior

This section is an eloquent summation of Pauline theology. The basic facts of the Gospel are clearly stated. It is God's grace alone that saves. But that very saving grace effects moral and ethical changes in the lives of those it touches by transforming their hearts. The connecting particle "for" emphasizes that what now follows supplies the Gospel basis for the ethical action called for in the preceding verses.

11 The translation, though adequate, obscures the fact that "for salvation" is in the original an adjective modifying grace. The Pastorals therefore know of God as the Savior, who rescues man through *saving grace*. It is important that the adjective modifies grace and is not a noun in apposition with God, as mistakenly rendered by the Latin Vulgate. (The change involves only the slighting of a Greek iota.) With this adjective the nature of grace is succinctly defined and at the same time shielded against misinterpretation. Grace is not an

infusion to enable one to assist in saving himself, but it is rather the very gift of salvation itself in the incarnation and subsequent suffering, death, and resurrection of Jesus (cf. 2 Tim. 1:10). This basic saving nature of God's grace is developed in 3:4 ff. The emphatic position of "appeared" in the original suggests the sudden and unexpected nature of the revelation which God has made in the birth and ministry of Jesus and without which man would not know the invisible God.

12 But saving grace is also educative and disciplinary. As it exercises this function in the lives of all who profess to believe in the Christ whom God manifested, the appearance of grace as a power of God operative in a world of sinners is continued in a brilliance that commands attention. Since God's grace is meant for all, no one (note the slaves in the previous section) is to be exempted from its saving power, and neither dare anyone excuse himself from its purifying might. It is the marvel of God's grace that He finds us wallowing happily or helplessly in our sin and nonetheless loves and accepts us in Christ. But having been so accepted, we cannot again be either happy or helpless in sin, for the grace of God which saves us exercises a further twofold effect. The negative aspect is that grace trains us "to renounce irreligion" and strengthens us to resist the lure of the world pulling away from God. The positive feature of disciplinary grace is that it teaches us to live "sober" (self-disciplined), "upright" (just in our dealings with our fellowman), and "godly" (pious before God) lives. Thus these three adverbs (in the original) are designed to cover the whole range of duties in the Christian life: personal, social, and religious. In the description of what grace does, it seems almost to be personified. Here is a reminder that grace is not elusively ethereal but real

and available in Christ Jesus. The virtues themselves
are not unknown to enlightened paganism, but what is
distinctively Christian is the rooting of the "thou shalt"
in the saving grace of God shown forth in Christ Jesus.
Saving grace, which makes every effort at self-saving
illicit, does not eliminate strenuous effort on man's part,
but rather rescues such effort from futility and makes
progress in holy living possible.

Some see in this description of grace as educative
as a clash with regular Pauline usage, which emphasizes
the liberating function of grace. Whatever freshness
there may be in the terminology here, there is no novelty
in the teaching, for Paul consistently bases the holy life
on God's gracious saving of man through Christ. Note,
for instance, how Paul builds the exhortations of Romans
12 ff. on the Gospel of grace, which he has developed
in the 11 preceding chapters. The Gospel of grace and
the holy life are not contradictory; they are inseparable.
The usual terminology describing this relationship has it
that the "imperatives" of the moral life are based on
the "indicatives" of salvation in Christ. Where it serves
the particular purpose of a Biblical author to emphasize
the moral obligations implicit in grace, this preponder-
ance of imperatives is not in conflict with the basic
indicatives. There might be reason to suspect a clash of
thought between this verse and, let us say, Romans
or Galatians, if here in Titus grace merely trained but
did not also and primarily save. Both the gift of heaven
and the holy life of the heavenbound pilgrim are of grace.
Paradoxically, we go forward in holiness of living by
constantly going back to grace.

13 In order that the strain of godly living may not
end in exhaustion and collapse, there is need to keep
in mind the Christian hope of the Lord's return in glory

(cf. 1 Tim. 6:14). The interminable friction with a hostile environment and the wearisome tussle with his own balky nature will weaken the struggling Christian unless his energies are constantly renewed by his confident expectation of the great day of Jesus' final advent. The Christian, having accepted his assignment to live in this world, yet strains forward toward the climactic return of his Lord.

The translation of the text and that of the margin differ significantly. In the rendering of the text, Jesus is called "the great God." Linguistically this translation is entirely acceptable. In fact, the Greek usage of only one article favors this translation. However, in favor of the marginal rendering, which distinguishes between "the great God" and "our Savior," it has been urged that the alternate understanding would rest on a terminology most unusual in the New Testament. But what shall one say of John 1:1, Heb. 1:8, and the marginal rendering of Rom. 9:5? Moreover, in the language of emperor worship the two terms, God and Savior, were often combined, and it is reasonable to assume that Paul here uses this terminology to dispute by implication the claims made for earthly potentates and to protest that such language and the expectations they include are really pertinent only to Jesus Christ. Furthermore, the dominant figure in the Second Advent will be Jesus Christ in His glory, so that it is natural to assume that He alone is meant. Compare below the extended note on "The Source and Interpretation of Hellenistic Terms."

14 This verse explains why Jesus is called Savior. The basic fact is that He "gave Himself" into death for the sake of sinful man. The words "gave Himself" are reminiscent of the words of Jesus at the institution of the Lord's Supper (cf. 1 Cor. 11:24; Mark 14:24). Borrowing

Old Testament terminology (cf. Ps. 130:8; Ezek. 37:23; Ex. 19:5; also Mark 10:45), Paul indicates a twofold rescue: "redeem" and "purify." On the one hand, at the cost of His own blood Jesus has freed man from imprisonment because of his sin, and on the other hand, He has rescued man from enslavement to his sin. Merely to exchange chains or to switch prisons is no advantage; it is only an illusory freedom. But the sacred blood has a redemptive and a purificatory power. No longer is the longing for release from lawlessness unfulfilled, nor is the restless striving for holiness an impractical aspiration. For all orders and ranks (cf. 2:1-10) there is redemption and purgation.

This means that there is a new concept of the "people" of God. The old Jew-Gentile antithesis has been antiquated by the new believer-unbeliever categories. The expansive call of the Gospel is the invitation to all classes and conditions and races to become members of the people of God, who by the cross of Christ are purged of sin and energized for holy living.

15 So important (and so difficult!) is the task of unfolding the meaning and developing the implications of saving grace, which is also purifying grace, that Paul aims a three-pronged admonition at Titus. He is to "declare these things," that is, he is to speak up, to preach, to proclaim. The next term, "exhort," intensifies Paul's directive, adding to the call for exposition the need for fervent pleading. Then, when opposition develops, Titus is not to be intimidated but is to rise above mere coaxing or wheedling and denounce authoritatively, that is, "reprove with all authority." Finally, Titus is not to permit anyone to slow down the urgency of his call by questioning his status, be it because of his youth or because he is not the apostle Paul himself but only his deputy. As a minister of God bearing the message of the Gospel, he is not to be disregarded. (Cf. 1 Tim. 4:12)

EXTENDED NOTE: THE SOURCE AND INTERPRETATION OF HELLENISTIC TERMS

The diction of v. 11-14 is lofty and has a hymn-like quality. This elevated style and terminology may be the echoings of part of an early Christian liturgy. On the other hand, there are parallels that suggest the possibility of adaptations from Hellenistic cultic vocabulary. When stereotyped terms of emperor worship and the characteristic pagan cultic vocabulary are found in the Septuagint and/or in Hellenistic Judaism (for instance, *appearing* — 1 Tim. 6:14; 2 Tim. 1:10; 4:1, 8; Titus 2:13; *goodness and loving kindness* — Titus 3:4) as well as in pagan Hellenistic circles, it is impossible to be sure which is the source for Paul. Expressions and terms typical of the Hellenistic religious vocabulary may well have entered the Christian community via the circuitous route of Judaism. That is to say: When the Jews, scattered about the Mediterranean world in what is known as the *Diaspora,* appropriated and adapted elements of their environmental religious vocabulary, these cultic terms were at hand for ready use by the early Christian movement and could have been taken over secondhand from Jewish sources rather than firsthand from immediate contacts with the Hellenistic milieu.

If the borrowing is directly from pagan sources, there arises the possibility that claims for Christ in opposition to the claims for the emperor are implied. Rather than being merely a naive transference of terms, a deliberate antithesis may be involved (compare the comment at 1 Tim. 1:1). Arthur Darby Nock summarizes his investigation of the Biblical employment of *Soter* ("Savior") with this balanced judgment: "We conclude therefore that the application of the title *Soter* to Jesus is not in origin connected with non-Jewish religious use of the word. At the same time, converts from the Gentile world must have felt in the term something opposed to other appropriations of it" *(Early Gentile Christianity and Its Hellenistic Background).* This conclusion may be appropriately used as a guide in evaluating the implications of other New Testament usages of Hellenistic terminology. Since the clash with paganism came after the beginnings of the Christian movement, the later the occurrence of these terms in the New Testament, the more likely their oppositional intent becomes.

But even if there is no antithetical design clearly detectable in Paul's usage of such terms, to include such an understanding of the apostle's words does not falsify their content but only enriches their interpretation. Thus if Paul does not here consciously set up an opposition between the appearing of the Savior Jesus Christ and that of the deified emperor, the suggested contrast is still a legitimate application and a helpful illumination of his basic thought.

CHRISTIAN PIETY IN A HOSTILE ENVIRONMENT 3:1-11

¹ Remind them to be submissive to rulers and authorities, to be obedient, to be ready for any honest work, ² to speak evil of no one, to avoid quarreling, to be gentle, and to show perfect courtesy toward all men. ³ For we ourselves were once foolish, disobe-

dient, led astray, slaves to various passions and pleasures, passing our days in malice and envy, hated by men and hating one another; ⁴ but when the goodness and loving kindness of God our Savior appeared, ⁵ he saved us, not because of deeds done by us in righteousness, but in virtue of his own mercy, by the washing of regeneration and renewal in the Holy Spirit, ⁶ which he poured out upon us richly through Jesus Christ our Savior, ⁷ so that we might be justified by his grace and become heirs in hope of eternal life. ⁸ The saying is sure.

I desire you to insist on these things, so that those who have believed in God may be careful to apply themselves to good deeds;ᵈ these are excellent and profitable to men. ⁹ But avoid stupid controversies, genealogies, dissensions, and quarrels over the law, for they are unprofitable and futile. ¹⁰ As for a man who is factious, after admonishing him once or twice, have nothing more to do with him, ¹¹ knowing that such a person is perverted and sinful; he is self-condemned.

ᵈ Or *enter honorable occupations*

1 Turning from the separate classes and groups within the Christian community and their reciprocal obligations, Paul now describes their duties toward the pagan society in which they live. These duties are incumbent upon all believers. Though part of the pagan environment, the government is to be respected. This duty must have been regularly stressed in the oral preaching of the apostle. Such emphasis was in keeping with a part of the Gospel tradition as reflected in Matt. 22:15-22 (cf. Rom. 13:1 ff.; 1 Tim. 2:1 ff.; 1 Peter 2:13). For this reason Titus had only to "remind" the Cretans of what they had already been taught. Thus the preacher's

proclamation is not to introduce new truths but often to remind his hearers of what they already know. The ingenuity of the pastor will be taxed as he seeks to present familiar but neglected truths in a fresh and arresting manner.

2 In the daily contacts with Jews and unconverted Gentiles, there was the constant threat that theological disagreement could lead to harsh discourtesy. Without abandoning their testimony to the truth of the Gospel, the believers are to maintain their convictions with kindliness, even when rudely challenged. Even as God's grace is universal (2:11), so must the missionary concern of the believer be universal — and longsuffering, even as God is longsuffering.

3 The convert can best cultivate the humility requisite for such Christian behavior toward the unconverted by remembering his own recent situation and how he escaped from it. The description of man's sinful state begins with the seemingly innocuous word "foolish." But there is nothing clownishly funny about this folly, not when it can blind one to the meaning of Easter (cf. Luke 24:25) or so bewitch one that he cannot see Christ even when vividly portrayed before his eyes (cf. Gal. 3:1). Here foolishness is the first in a series of deadly downward steps. Paul includes himself in this past foolishment that was disfigured by enslavement to various passions. Because tyrannous selfishness prevailed on all sides, a vicious rebounding of hate meeting with hate marked the contacts of men with each other. Sin begins with disintegration of the individual and ends with the dissolution of society.

Now Paul proceeds to explain that it is God's grace and not man's ingenuity that rescues from the swirling passions of malice and envy and hatred. Verses 4-8a

210

appear to be a quotation or adaptation from a hymn thanking and praising God for the grace bestowed in Baptism. That a citation is involved is intimated by the formula "The saying is sure."

4 The grace of God, which was mentioned in 2:11, is here described in the parallel terms "goodness and loving kindness." The term rendered "goodness" is rich in meaning. Literally it means friendliness to man and describes an attitude of respect on the part of man for his fellowman. The noun and its adverbial form are each used once in Acts (27:3; 28:2) in reference to the kindness pagans showed to Paul. Strangely, and yet significantly, the expression is not used in the New Testament to describe the relationship between man and man as the Christian sees and practices it. The Christian respects and loves his fellowman not just because he is his fellowman but because he is his fellow redeemed. The relationship between people is therefore not just one of friendliness of man for man but one of love after the pattern of Him who first loved us and gave Himself for us. The application of the term to God is thus expressive of God's condescension. God does not love man who is on the same divine level with Himself, but He loves man who has debased himself even below the human level on which God had first established him. The variation in wording ("goodness and loving-kindness" instead of "grace") is adapted to fit the new emphasis, namely, that it must be impossible for one to have experienced the love of God and then to react in bitter annoyance when meeting in others the same failings that God forgave in him.

The gracious concern of God "appeared" with the birth of Christ, shone in the glory of the cross, continues forever resplendent in the victory of Easter, and will be made manifest to all at the Second Advent. The special term "appeared" is appropriate. The Greek word was often used for the personal appearance of a sovereign ruler. Thus God has appeared not in speculation or reverie but in the reality of Christ, in whom we are showered with the gifts of God's goodness and loving kindness.

5 Contrasting the irreconcilables, mercy and merit, Paul states the case for salvation by grace alone with characteristic vigor and clarity (cf. 2 Tim. 1:9). Whereas v. 4 describes man at his worst, v. 5 speaks of man at his best, and yet in both instances the verdict is negative. At his worst or at his best, man is equally helpless to establish his own "righteousness," equally dependent on God's "mercy." With this point settled, all self-exaltation collapses, and the virtues of v. 2 are seen to be necessary but at the same time natural for those re-created by God. Since the new qualities are God's creation, they cannot be man's achievement.

Some would see the expressions "deeds done in righteousness" instead of "deeds of the Law," and "washing of regeneration" instead of "buried and raised with Christ," as significant departures from Pauline usage. One may well ask: When the substance of the doctrine is so identical, must the terminology always be rigidly fixed, and if in Gal. 3:27 Paul could shift from "buried and raised" to "put on Christ," why should he not here use the expression "washing of regeneration"?

Elaborating further, Paul explains something of the meaning of Baptism. Baptism gives what it promises; it confers what it symbolizes. The suggestion that the "washing of regeneration" and the "renewal in the Holy Spirit" are two distinct factors in salvation is weak both doctrinally and linguistically. If the water of Baptism is regenerative, the Spirit's power must be present in it. Furthermore, if the two are meant to be separate, one would look for a second "by" preceding "renewal." Verse 6 also seems to unify rather than divide the saving action, the term "poured out" being linked with Baptism in this context.

The word "regeneration" is interesting. In Stoic philosophy it is the technical term for the renewal of the cosmos that supposedly takes place after periodic destruction by fire. Matt. 19:28 invests the term with a distinctively Christian meaning: "Truly, I say to you, in the *new world* [in the original the Greek term for "regeneration"] when the Son of Man shall sit on His glorious throne, you who have followed Me will also sit on twelve thrones, judging the twelve tribes of Israel." In popular usage the term was generalized, and Cicero even speaks of return from exile as "regeneration." Hellenistic Judaism applies the designation to a new life after death. Thus in describing Baptism as "the washing of regeneration," Paul is giving vivid expression to the doctrine that in Baptism the creation of a new being takes place. (Cf. 2 Cor. 5:17; Gal. 6:15; John 3:1 ff.; 1 Peter 1:3, 23)

6 The figurative expression "poured out" does not make of the Holy Spirit an impersonal power but is simply a term familiar already in the Old Testament (cf. Joel 2:28 and the fulfillment, Acts 2:16 ff.). In fact, the entire Trinity is here involved in the baptismal action. God the Father reveals Himself in Christ, whose redemptive mission invests Baptism with saving power, and the Holy Spirit makes Baptism effective.

7 God's salvation in Christ, conferred in the grace of Baptism, has a definite goal. God wills that we shall not be condemned but acquitted. Credited by His mercy

with the righteousness of Jesus Christ, we are to attain to "eternal life." Therefore instead of being dragged down by a burden of guilt, we can confidently hope for the full enjoyment of our inheritance (cf. Gal. 4:7) at the last.

Again we note that all of these benefits are mercifully bestowed by God so that there is reason for hearty thanks but no pretext for pride (cf. v. 2). And in this theme lies the explanation for what at first seems to be the strange failure to mention faith. In this section Paul is concerned to describe God's saving acts toward us in a way that will melt all hardness of heart, so that we shall not be guilty of the harshness condemned in v. 2. Hence the limitation of what he has to say to a description of God's work in man. Faith is sometimes misunderstood as a human achievement rather than a divine gift. So misconstrued, it might become the basis for pride. Perhaps sensing this danger, Paul concentrates his attention on setting forth what God has done and omits any direct reference to man's response. Surely faith is not excluded. In the presence of a God as here described what other response than that of faith can be called for?

8a The transitional phrase "The saying is sure" is probably best understood as belonging to the previous verses, although it can also be used to refer to something following (cf. 1 Tim. 1:15; 3:1; 4:9; 2 Tim. 2:11). This interpretation, if correct, increases the likelihood that the preceding is essentially a quotation.

8b Faith and life must be in harmony. To this fundamental fact Titus must insistently testify. By witnessing clearly to salvation by God's grace alone, he will also be leading people to fruitful lives. Every effort at self-salvation will be productive either of nothing at all or of evil—the evil of deluded self-exaltation which harshly judges others (again cf. v. 2). Contrariwise, acceptance of God's mercy by placing one's confidence in Christ's atoning death will impel to deeds truly helpful to one's fellowman.

9 Because of imperfect spiritual sight and the residual, albeit shrinking, perversity even of the converted Christian's nature, a pointed warning is necessary. Religious zeal must not burn up its energies in what at best is futile, at worst harmful. (The general complexion of these unprofitable "dissensions" has been described before. See 1 Tim. 1:4; 6:4; 2 Tim. 2:23.) Mere mulling over the truth in a kind of prying curiosity will not lead to a more grateful appreciation of grace and a more dedicated life of service; it will rather issue in pride.

10 A false teacher is a menace to the congregation of believers and is not to be tolerated. Although the gropings, even aberrations, of one sincerely desirous of being led into the truth are to be borne in love, the man who creates splits by seeking adherents for his divergent views is a different case. Such propagandizing for heresy is not to be endured. Insufferable perversity and hardness of heart are made evident by the false teacher's refusal to heed repeated admonitions. The term here rendered "factious" is the word that later became our classic expression "heretic." The heretic is the man who arbitrarily and stubbornly makes his own selection of what shall count as the truth. Compare Luther's definition of a heretic: "He deserves to be called a heretic who stubbornly errs in an article of faith and asserts his error." Perhaps there is a bit of a pun between "factious" and "self-condemned" (v. 11). The man who insists on making his own choice (factious) is really choosing and pronouncing his own condemnation.

Disciplinary action is to be conducted according to the principles of Matt. 18:15 ff. This means that the dispute with the errorist is not to be prolonged indefinitely but must be terminated by breaking off fellowship with him. If the factious ones cannot be silenced (1:11), if they disregard sharp rebuke (1:13), then they must be removed from the congregation of the faithful. Expulsion will not prevent the heretic from going off to establish his own clique, but it will protect the Christian community from unsuspected exposure and the hidden danger of contagion.

11 When admonition has failed and the stern discipline of excommunication becomes necessary, Titus is to be reassured that he has done his duty and that the lamentable plight of the heretic is really self-imposed.

CONCLUSION: PERSONAL NOTES 3:12-15

12 When I send Artemas or Tych'icus to you, do your best to come to me at Nicop'olis, for I have decided to spend the winter there. 13 Do your best to speed Zenas the lawyer and Apol'los on their way; see that they lack nothing. 14 And let our people learn to apply themselves to good deeds,*d* so as to help cases of urgent need, and not to be unfruitful.

15 All who are with me send greetings to you. Greet those who love us in the faith.

Grace be with you all.

d Or enter honorable occupations

12 Paul announces that he will send one of two men, Artemas (otherwise unknown) or Tychicus (mentioned Acts 20:4; Eph. 6:21; Col. 4:7-9; 2 Tim. 4:12), to

relieve Titus, so that he and Titus may meet in Epirus on the Adriatic, where Paul will spend the winter waiting for shipping to open up again in the spring. Since Paul is making his own plans, it is evident that he is still a free man and not imprisoned. (For a discussion of the historical problems see the Introduction.) The report in 2 Tim. 4:12 suggests that since Tychicus was sent to Ephesus, Artemas may have been the one finally assigned to Crete.

13 The journey of two men, Zenas and Apollos, to Crete is the immediate occasion for Paul's writing the letter. Apollos is the eloquent Jewish convert from Alexandria (Acts 18:24 ff.; cf. 1 Cor. 1:12; 3:4 ff., 22; 4:6; 16:12). Zenas (otherwise unknown) is described as a "lawyer." The expression is the same as that used in the Gospels for experts in Jewish law, that is, the scribes. But because opposition on the part of the Jews is mentioned (1:10, 14), some feel that a Roman lawyer is likely meant.

14 The practice of Christian hospitality, so vital in helping the missionaries spread the Good News, was an affair of the entire congregation, not merely a responsibility of Titus. Probably Paul is implying a comparison of "our people" to the Jewish communities scattered about the Mediterranean world, who gladly took care of traveling Jewish teachers who might come to them. Or it may be that even pagan hospitality shows up that of the Christians. A third possibility is that the heretics may be enjoying a more loyal support from their followers than Paul's emissaries were receiving from his. Comparisons need not always be odious. Charitable concern in the reception of these two missionaries is then to be a pattern for further good deeds as the need might arise.

217

The footnote offers an alternate translation of the term "to apply themselves to good deeds," which occurs also in v. 8. If the rendering "enter honorable occupations" is adopted, the meaning of the verse is not substantially altered. Honest zeal in an honorable occupation will, with God's blessing, enable one to provide for his own needs and also put him in a position to exercise generous hospitality. Thus Paul's concern for good works in the sense of charitable deeds can be maintained by adopting either translation. The alternate rendering can be understood in the tradition of 1 Thess. 4:11-12: "to work with your hands . . . and be dependent on nobody," and Eph. 4:28: "let him labor . . . so that he may be able to give to those in need." However, the translation "apply themselves to good deeds" seems to accord better with the analogy of 2:14: "zealous for good deeds" and 3:1: "to be ready for any honest work."

15 The concluding greeting is general. Names would be supplied orally by those who were bearers of the letter, or if the circle around Paul was small and limited, Titus would himself know their names. The warmth of the bond between Paul and those whom he dearly loves derives from their common acceptance of Jesus as the Christ. His greetings would not extend to those factious men who disrupted the congregation with their heresies. The Christian greeting is not identical with wishes for good health or happiness but goes farther and includes the prayer that the "grace" of God, the supernatural gift, may be fully enjoyed by all believers.

For Further Reading

Barrett, C. K. *The Pastoral Epistles*. Oxford: University Press, 1963.

The comment is based on the text of The New English Bible. Although there is some allusion to Greek words, the general reader can use this work with profit and ease. The introduction presents the case against Pauline authorship in readily intelligible form.

Calvin, John. *Commentaries on the Epistles to Timothy, Titus and Philemon*. The translation by William Pringle (Grand Rapids, Mich.: Eerdmans, 1959) has been supplanted by that of T. A. Smail (Grand Rapids: Eerdmans, 1964).

There is abiding value in these old studies. Unfortunately the old Lutheran commentaries of Melanchthon and John Gerhard are not available in translation from the Latin.

Easton, Burton Scott. *The Pastoral Epistles*. New York: Charles Scribner's Sons, 1947.

Besides concise commentary, a special feature of this work is the series of word studies in the final section of the book. The sparing use of Greek terms is no serious impediment to profitable use on the part of those without a knowledge of Greek.

Guthrie, Donald. *The Pastoral Epistles, An Introduction and Commentary.* Grand Rapids: Eerdmans, 1957.

Scholarly, conservative comment in nontechnical language makes this a valuable book. An appendix presents an extended criticism of the theories and arguments of P. N. Harrison against Pauline authorship.

Hanson, Anthony Tyrrell, *The Pastoral Letters.* London: Cambridge University Press, 1966.

The text of the New English Bible is elucidated with very brief commentary designed to acquaint the nonspecialist with the results of modern scholarship.

Hanson, Anthony Tyrrell, *Studies in the Pastoral Epistles.* London: S. P. C. K., 1968.

This second book by Hanson is recommended for those who may wish to gain some insight into the nature of the learned discussion concerning special problems in the Pastorals. The article on "Inspired Scripture" is particularly challenging. Although the work is equipped with the usual scholarly apparatus, the language and format are not too forbidding for the general reader.

Kelley, J. N. D. *The Pastoral Epistles.* New York: Harper & Row, 1963.

In his introduction Kelley contends for the Pauline authorship. The commentary is informative and highly readable.

220

Index to Extended Notes

Philemon

INTRODUCTION

(Philemon)

The best introduction to the Letter to Philemon for the average person is a careful reading of the letter itself in translation(s). The writer of this commentary has taken the risk of placing in the Appendix his own somewhat paraphrastic version in contemporary letter form. Every translation is an interpretation. There are a few puzzling passages even in this short letter of only 335 words in the original Greek text. The paraphrase is a convenient way to present the commentator's own understanding of debated passages.

In reading modern English translations of Philemon the reader should be alert to the fact that the pronoun *"you"* is singular in the body of the letter (vv. 2a, 4-22a, 23). The *"you"* is plural only four times, including "Grace to *you*, (v. 3) and "with *your* spirit," (v. 25). This shows that while Philemon is a personal letter it is not strictly a private letter. Although the request made is directed to Philemon, others shall be apprised of Paul's concern.

Luther's Preface to Philemon

The most widely known and justly admired theological introduction to this letter is Luther's Preface to Philemon in his *German New Testament* of September 1522. Twelve years later (1534) William Tyndale translated and employed it in the second edition of his *English New Testament*, strangely omitting the last sentence. Luther says (*LW* 35:390):

> This epistle gives us a masterful and tender illustration of Christian love. For here we see how St. Paul takes the part of poor Onesimus and, to the best of his ability, advocates his cause with his master. He acts exactly as if he were himself Onesimus, who had done wrong.
>
> Yet he does this not with force or compulsion, as lay within his rights; but he empties himself of his rights in order to compel Philemon also to waive his rights. What Christ has done for us with God the Father, that St. Paul does also for Onesimus with Philemon. For Christ emptied himself of His rights [Phil. 2:7] and overcame the Father with love and humility, so that the Father had to put away His wrath and His rights, and receive us into favor for the sake of Christ, who so earnestly advocates our cause and so heartily takes our part. For we are all His Onesimus's if we believe.

Paul's spontaneous demonstration in the case of Onesimus of how love to the God who first loved us is shown in love to the brother held Luther enthralled. On four days in December 1527 Luther lectured in Latin to his university students on this short letter. He underscores the necessary synthesis of faith and love, and shows other insights valuable to the student of this letter in our own day. These lectures have only recently become available in translation. (*LW* 29:93-105)

226

Time, Place, and Purpose of Writing

Discussion of time and place of writing has relatively little importance for the understanding of this letter. The traditional view that the Prison Epistles of Paul were written in Rome during the imprisonment with which Luke's account in Acts closes is not likely to be effectively shaken. Philemon is inseparably connected with Colossians, and both letters were written at the same time and place. On grounds that need not be presented here, we accept Rome as the place of writing, and as for time, a date close to spring of A. D. 63. (For a fuller discussion consult a good New Testament Introduction. See Bibliography.) As to the purpose of writing, this commentary espouses the ancient and widely accepted view that Paul pleads with Philemon, a resident of Colossae (Col. 4:9), to forgive his fugitive slave Onesimus, who by conversion to Christ through the ministry of Paul has become Philemon's spiritual brother.

John Knox's Reconstruction

It is legitimate to reassess traditional positions as to their congruity with language, context, and the historical situation. In 1935 the notable American New Testament scholar John Knox did that with regard to Philemon in his slender book entitled *Philemon Among the Letters of Paul* (see Bibliography). His reassessment resulted in a complete reconstruction of traditional views. His arguments are ingenious and fascinating but highly speculative. He is aware of this speculative character but is quite sure of the probability of his novel views. Most readers of Knox — and there are many — seem to be grateful for the stimulation received but

227

feel that the more or less tenuous possibilities do not add up to a strong probability. In directing interested readers to the book itself or to Knox's commentary on Philemon in *The Interpreter's Bible*, we shall present as briefly as possible the main positions of Knox and also some considerations that make it difficult to accept his reconstruction. Hopefully this discussion will aid the reader to appreciate and better understand this little letter of Paul. (To be able to follow this discussion, the reader would do well first to look closely at Col. 4:7-18, especially vv. 9 and 15-17.)

(1) Basic to the new view of Knox is his argument that not Philemon but the third individual in the greeting, who is addressed as "Archippus our fellow soldier" (v. 2), is the owner of the fugitive slave Onesimus. It is in his house that the members of the Colossian church, included in the greeting, assemble. However, Knox can present only one letter, written in the fourth or fifth century, which has a multiple address (in this case two persons) in which the first individual is not the one with whom the writer is mainly concerned. But on Knox's own showing (p. 58 ff.), this letter is a weak parallel to Philemon. In Paul's letter Philemon, who is mentioned first, receives especial emphasis with two epithets: "Philemon our dearly beloved, and fellow laborer" (v. 1 KJV). And so it has been the universal view until Knox published his book that the superscription "The Letter of Paul to Philemon" is not a misnomer. No early Greek scribe or scholar, as far as we have evidence, ever deviated on this point. These men knew Greek letter forms.

(2) As Knox sees it, Paul in this letter is requesting something for himself. In v. 10 Paul is asking *for* Onesimus, not merely *in his behalf*. He requests the owner

228

to release Onesimus to him for service of the Gospel (Knox, 22 ff.). One may grant that a few examples in late Greek show that *for* in connection with verbs of "asking" may, as in English, designate the object requested. But the whole tenor of this letter is against such interpretation here. Our exposition endeavors to show this. Even the assumption of a double meaning *(in behalf of* as well as *for)* may be a distortion of Paul's real intent and do injustice to this selfless apostle.

(3) To support the foregoing supposition Knox gives a novel interpretation of Col. 4:17: "And say to Archippus, 'See that you fulfill the ministry [*diakonia*] which you have received in the Lord.'" The verb translated "received" is idiomatic for accepting some teaching or custom and for taking over some office. The word for "ministry" as object of "received" suggests some spiritual ministry not specifically defined and that has been previously assigned. Knox strains the language when he applies this "ministry received in the Lord" to a request by Paul that the owner of the slave Onesimus should release him to Paul for spiritual service. The entire congregation, in this view, is to lend its weight to secure Archippus' compliance.

(4) A major point in Paul's "tactics," as argued by Knox, is the part that Philemon is to play. Archippus, in Knox's view, is a complete stranger to Paul. So Paul not only elicits the sympathetic concern of the church which meets in his house but directs this letter "first to someone of whom he had complete knowledge and in whom he felt unreserved confidence" (p. 64), namely, to Philemon "our dearly beloved and fellow laborer." Philemon, so the conjecture goes, was in the absence of Epaphras (Col. 1:7; 4:12; Philemon 23) the overseer of the churches in the valley of the Lycus River. He

was a resident in Laodicea (Col. 4:15), half way between Colossae and Hierapolis (Col. 4:13). As the spiritual leader of these churches, his support is sought by Paul in the delicate matter concerning Onesimus and his master. Hence his name is first in the address (v. 2). This argument, of course, stands or falls with the correctness of the view that Archippus is the owner of the slave in question. The careful reader of the letter will surely question the assertion that the owner is unknown to Paul. The whole letter breathes intimate acquaintance. Indeed, the wording of v. 19, "to say nothing of your owing me even your own self," quite obviously speaks of the addressee as a personal convert of Paul. The attempt of Knox to show that Paul's language of intimacy is adopted for "tactical reasons" is unconvincing (p. 63 ff.) and smacks of special pleading.

(5) Knox is quite assured that our Letter of Paul to Philemon is none other than the letter "to the Laodiceans" referred to in Col. 4:16: "And when this letter [to the *Colossians*] has been read among you, have it read also in the church of the Laodiceans; and see that you read also the letter from Laodicea." There is a wide consensus of scholarship that what Paul intends is an exchange of letters: Our canonical Colossians is to be sent to Laodicea, and a letter to the Laodiceans is to be sent to Colossae. This reference to a Laodicean letter has puzzled Christian scholars for 19 centuries. (For a useful digest of opinions see Hendriksen, 194-197. Scholars may consult Lightfoot, 272-298.) Here we only point out, as counter to Prof. Knox's identification of "To the Laodiceans" with our "To Philemon," that Marcion (about A. D. 140) knew both Philemon and Laodiceans. The latter he however identified with the canonical Ephesians, probably rightly so on the justly

widespread "circular letter" theory with regard to Ephesians. Furthermore, the oldest extant list of New Testament books received by the church *(Canon Muratori)*, composed about A. D. 200 or earlier, likewise distinguishes Philemon from the letter to the Laodiceans. But the latter, in the form then used in some circles, was suspected as a heretical forgery. At any rate, Philemon is never found in early Christian literature as identical with a letter to Laodicea. Some of the best scholars feel that this alone is fatal to Knox's reconstruction.

To the present writer the final refutation of Knox's reconstruction is the blight it puts on the image of the forthright, open-hearted, Gospel-centered Paul. The charm of the Letter to Philemon, which has enthralled every reader, is not only its stylistic beauty but especially Paul's graceful tact and evangelical diplomacy in presenting his request in behalf of Onesimus. Paul expressly waives all authority and desists from all pressure, making his whole plea on the ground of love. In Knox's reconstruction there is pressure upon pressure. We must conclude from Knox's argument that Paul's lieutenant Tychicus (Col. 4:8), in company with Onesimus ("the faithful and beloved brother, who is one of yourselves," Col. 4:9), summons the congregation to a meeting at which presumably the owner of the slave, Archippus, is present. In the letter (our Colossians) written by Paul to this congregation the church members are charged to tell Archippus: "See that you fulfill the ministry which you have received in the Lord." That really puts Archippus on the spot. Such "tactics" on the part of Paul are incredible. Subsequently the letter to the Laodiceans had to be fetched. Was it the next day? Since in Knox's view this letter is our canonical Letter to Philemon, the Laodicean Christians, along with their leader Philemon, are assumed to have read that personal letter. And thus, if Knox's view would be correct, not only the Colossian church but also that of Laodicea, along with the supervisor of all the churches in the Lycus Valley, add their weight to Paul's request, not only to receive the fugitive but also to release him to Paul. Is that what is meant by resting his effort only on the ground of love (Philemon 9) and wanting to do nothing to pressurize the slave owner so that his action would come from his free will (v. 14)? Our answer is a strong no.

Surely the methodologically correct way to handle any piece of writing is first to read it in its own light. If Philemon is so read, the traditional interpretation will stand unshaken. Despite the above strictures we regard Knox's book as very valuable. A few other references to Knox will be made in the commentary. Not the least value of his book is that for its readers Philemon has ceased to be "one of the most neglected writings of the New Testament."

Slavery in the Age of the Early Church

Slavery may be defined as a social-economic system in which one person is the property of another who has the right to all his labor. Most people born and reared in a climate of humane progress, like those of our generation, bristle at the very thought of slavery and its denial of the basic human right to personal freedom. They relegate the monstrous institution of slavery to darker days of the past. They may be startled to learn that in the very year that man first walked on the surface of the moon (1969) there were still slaves walking on our mother earth. This despite the antislavery climate created by a number of significant pronouncements of the last century which influenced people all over the world: the British Emancipation Act of 1833; Lincoln's Emancipation Proclamation of January 1, 1863, with its sequel in the Thirteenth Amendment to the U. S. Constitution adopted two years later, prohibiting slavery or involuntary servitude in the United States. These pronoucements, affecting first the British Empire, then the United States, found a universal echo in the Fourth Article of the Universal Declaration of Human Rights adopted by the General Assembly of the United Nations on December 10, 1948: "No one shall be held in slavery or servitude; slavery and the slave trade shall be prohibited in all their forms."

And yet the evil persists, even in some countries that are signitories of the U. N. Charter. Year after year to the time of this writing, the London-based Anti-Slavery Society of Britain has been prodding the Commission on Human Rights of the United Nations to take more aggressive action against "the crime that the world ignores." Sometimes it is slavery in all but its name; more often it takes analogous forms, such as gruelling peonage, oppressive indenture, inequitable sharecropping, not to speak of the virtual enslavement of whole peoples by ruthless totalitarian regimes.

In view of these facts the reader of Philemon should be forewarned that in interpreting Paul's letter he must not prejudge Paul's plea for a runaway slave on the basis of "unhistorical thinking." One must realize that slavery dates back as far as historical records go and that humane progress is slow and painful, depending on many factors and on the conflux of different movements favorable to radical change of thinking and action.

The institution of slavery, which is sporadic in our civilization and almost universally condemned, was woven into the very warp and woof of society as the early church began its work. And no voices, pagan or Christian, were raised in condemnation of the institution itself. Ancient society rested in the main upon the foundation of slave labor. Slavery could not at that time be abolished at one stroke, if that had been attempted, without precipitating society into chaos.

Many of the early converts of the apostles and evangelists were recruited from the slave class, like Onesimus in the letter before us. Slaves walk side by side with freemen through the pages of the New Testament from Matthew to Revelation. This fact has been obscured for readers of Luther's German Bible, as well as for readers of the English versions following Luther, by Luther's rendition of the Greek word for slave *(doulos)* with the ambiguous word *Knecht* (servant). Tyndale, Coverdale, and the scholars behind the King James Version and its successive editions down to the American Standard Version (1901) followed suit by using the equally ambiguous word *servant*, although the words *Sklave* and *slave* had been commonly used in the German as well as the English language long before Luther and Tyndale. The Revised Standard Version of 1946 finally broke the unfortunate spell which frequently in the past had applied the New Testament injunctions to slaves quite directly to nonslaves, even to free, contractual laborers. (The KJV uses the word *slave* only once, employing it for translating the word *body* in Rev. 18:13.)

The most fruitful source of slaves was war. One might indeed look upon slavery as an advanced stage of humanity in comparison with the times when all prisoners were put to the sword. The Gallic wars of Caesar, for instance, resulted in about 150,000 slaves.

234

Next to wars piracy, kidnapping, exposure of unwanted children rescued into slavery by the finder, slave breeding, and debt were feeders of this monster.

The exact number of the slave population of the Roman Empire cannot be determined, due to lack of census statistics. Edward Gibbon, in the second chapter of his classic *Decline and Fall of the Roman Empire*, estimated the total population of the Empire at 120 million with one half slave, one half free. The later French historian Le Maistre, retaining the proportion, cut down the estimated total population to 60 million. A competent study by the German historian Beloch (1886) on the relative number of slaves to freemen in peninsular Italy close to the beginning of our era arrives at the estimate of three slaves to every five free persons. His proportions curiously stand in quite close relation to "the proportion of slave and free in the slaveholding states of the United States in 1850 when the slaves, as enumerated in the census returns, stood at fifty-one to every hundred free persons." (Westermann, 69)

A few examples will show the vast numbers there must have been. On a single occasion Caesar sold 63,000 Gauls. Trajan caused 10,000 gladiators, mostly slaves, to engage in mutual slaughter to amuse the Roman populace for 123 days (*Dio Cassius* 68:15). Seneca reports that once a motion was presented in the senate that slaves should be distinguished from freemen in dress. This motion was promptly voted down upon the representation that it would be extremely dangerous to the free masters if the slaves could count their noses and thus become aware of their own numerical superiority (*De Clementia* 1:24). Some Roman establishments possessed enormous numbers, amounting in

235

some cases to 20,000. Petronius declared that not a tenth part of the slaves owned by Trimalchio even knew their master (*Satyricon* 37). Many slaves were employed on the country estates, but hundreds were kept in the family residence in the city, where every kind of work was deputed to them. It was the expected thing that every free citizen should have slave attendants. William Ramsay in his *Paul, the Traveler and Roman Citizen* (p. 316) argued with some supporting evidence that when Luke and Aristarchus accompanied Paul the prisoner on his voyage to Rome (Acts 27:2) they must have passed as his slaves. Paul was treated as a gentleman, and a gentleman couldn't have been thought of as without slaves. It is also a plausible hypothesis that when Aristarchus (Col. 4:10) and Epaphras (Philemon 23) are called by Paul "fellow-prisoners" they voluntarily shared his prison and passed as his slave attendants, possibly serving alternately.

The slave had no legal standing. The axiom universally accepted by jurists was that the slave was a "thing" *(res)*, not a "person" *(persona)*, and had no rights. The question indeed was seriously asked: "Is the slave a man?" Aristotle spoke the view that generally prevailed for centuries when he said: "The slave is a living tool, just as a tool is an inanimate slave" (*Nic. Eth.* VIII:11). Both in Greek and Latin, terms in the neuter gender were employed to designate the slave, words meaning "body," "beast of burden," "living machine," "piece of furniture," "tool," and others. The slave was bought at the slave market as if he were a horse and was trained and exploited the same way, and the master was free to sell him off cheaply when he was old and used up. He had the power of life or death over his slaves. He could condemn him to perpetual celibacy,

236

could abuse his male or female slave sexually, could punish him mercilessly. Indeed, self-interest and sometimes humaneness of spirit would prompt the master to kindness and good care of his slaves. But nonetheless, the slaves were ever at the mercy of the passions and caprices of their master and mistress. Crucifying the slave and then leaving the victim hang until vultures left only a bare skeleton on the cross was a frequent punishment. The slave character Sceledrus in Plautus' popular comedy *The Braggart Warrior* illustrates the case, perhaps with some exaggeration, when he replies to the banter of his cronies: "Enough of your threatening! I know the cross will be my tomb. There's where my ancestors rest—father, grandfather, great-grandfather, and great-great-grandfather." (*Miles Glor.* 527 ff.)

Especially fugitive slaves could not reckon on mercy when apprehended. Throughout the Empire the *fugitivarii* were active. These constituted a semiprivate and semigovernmental branch of service whose business and source of income was to hunt down fugitives and have them returned to the owner. When caught, the letter F (*fugitivus*) might be branded on the runaway's forehead or, as a deterrent to the other slaves, the master might throw him into a pond of voracious fish, cut off some member of his body, or hang him on a cross. In most cases the fate of the recaptured runaway was worse than the situation from which he had tried to escape.

Stoic philosophy, with its emphasis on inner freedom and indifference to outward circumstances, aided in some circles to look upon slaves as human and to accord them humane treatment. Manumission, the liberation from slavery, was not infrequent, though regulated by law so as not to upset the balance between freemen and slaves too greatly.

In A. D. 61, not long before Paul wrote to Philemon, a tragedy was enacted at Rome under the sanction of the law. Possibly it occurred when Paul began his imprisonment there. At any rate, Paul had likely heard about it. As the historian Tacitus relates it (*Annals* XIV:42), Pedanius Secundus, a senator, had been slain by one of his slaves in a fit of anger or jealousy. The law demanded that in such cases all the slaves under the same roof at the time should be put to death. On this occasion 400 persons were thus condemned. However, the populace interposed to rescue them and a tumult ensued. But the law was put to force. To prevent a popular outbreak, the roads were lined by a military guard as the prisoners were led to execution.

This incident illustrates both the extent of slavery and the general wretchedness of their position under the law. The general picture was extremely shocking at the time when Paul wrote to Philemon, and the general picture must be kept in mind if the letter is to be properly understood.

Philemon Reads Paul's Letter

The long journey by land and sea from Rome to Colossae has ended for Tychicus and Onesimus. Tychicus, himself an Asian (Acts 20:4), has carried in his scrip three letters dictated by Paul: the letter to the Laodiceans, which we believe is the letter known as Ephesians (very likely a "circular letter" intended for all the churches in Asia, beginning with the mother church at Ephesus); secondly, the Letter to Colossae; and finally the personal letter to Philemon. One may reasonably conjecture that the travelers who had started out from Laodicea reached Philemon's home at nightfall. The dramatic way in which the runaway slave's name is introduced in the letter (v. 10), after a tactful approach, makes it probable that Tychicus made his entrance into Philemon's home alone, while Onesimus waited outside under cover, nervous and apprehensive. After the formalities of welcome Tychicus took out of his scrip the little missive of Paul that tenderly pleaded the case of the runaway. Subsequently, perhaps after the master's reconciliation with his slave, the larger group addressed in the beginning of the letter was called together to hear Paul's touching letter. Thereupon, one may justly surmise, the letter addressed to the believers in Colossae received its first reading, a letter which John Knox observes is as a whole "more or less overshadowed by Paul's concern about Onesimus." (Knox, 35). (For Scripture background on Tychicus see Acts 20:4; Eph. 6:21-22; Col. 4:7; 2 Tim. 4:12; Titus 3:12.)

OUTLINE

Abbreviations

RSV	Revised Standard Version of the New Testament (1946).
KJV	King James Version (1611).
NEB	The New English Bible: New Testament (1961).
TEV	Good News For Modern Man: The New Testament in Today's English Version. New York: American Bible Society (1966).
LW	*Luther's Works:* American Edition (Published jointly by Fortress Press, Philadelphia, and Concordia Publishing House, St. Louis). The first number after *LW* indicates the volume, the number after the colon (:) indicates the page.
(Name)	Author's name in parentheses refers to the author's work listed in the Bibliography. Number after name indicates the page.
(Par.)	Paraphrased version as given in Appendix.

References to passages from ancient authors are placed in parentheses.

Commentary on Philemon

INTRODUCTION OF THE LETTER   1-7

Salutation   1-3

¹ Paul, a prisoner for Christ Jesus, and Timothy our brother,

To Phile'mon our beloved fellow worker ² and Ap'phia our sister and Archip'pus our fellow soldier, and the church in your house:

³ Grace to you and peace from God our Father and the Lord Jesus Christ.

Paul in his letters adopts the Greek-Roman letter form: (1) *Preface* (or salutation): writer, addressee(s), a word of greeting; (2) *Body* of letter, usually beginning with a declaration of thanksgiving; (3) A brief word of *farewell*. But while Paul adopts the forms, nothing is stereotyped; everything is Paulinized, throbbing with the new life in Christ mediated by His Spirit. This lifts even the short letter to Philemon high above the great mass of letters that have come down to us from the time

245

of Paul. The charm of this letter is matchless. A commentary can only seek to bridge the gap of centuries and try to show what the letter meant to the readers then and there. When the commentary has been read, the reader might well forget the commentary and let the letter itself make its impact, the time gap perhaps having been somewhat bridged.

As in all his letters the introductory preface of Philemon is closely related to the central concern of the letter, and every word bears weight.

1 "Paul." One must sense Philemon's thrill and pride to receive a letter from the foremost Christian leader of the day, his own father in Christ (v. 19b). But this pride at once gives way to pang at the next words: "a prisoner." Usually Paul begins his letters with the claim of authority lying in the title "apostle of Christ Jesus." But in this letter Paul is a suppliant. He writes as a friend to a friend with the object of winning him over to a course of Christian conduct which may come a little hard for him. Paul therefore drops the note of authority and instead lets Philemon hear at the outset the jangling of the chain on his wrist. Five times more Philemon will hear this jangling (vv. 9, 10, 13, 22, 23). The RSV renders: "a prisoner *for* Christ Jesus," while the KJV and NEB have: "a prisoner *of* Christ Jesus." In point of fact, in Paul's Greek there is no preposition but the very versatile Genitive case of the noun which admits of various interpretations. Paul is a prisoner *of* Christ in the sense of belonging to Him, "bought with a price" (1 Cor. 6:20). He is also a prisoner *of* Christ in the sense that Christ has "apprehended" him (Phil. 3:12) and as the conquering Lord leads him as a willing captive in His triumphal procession (2 Cor. 2:14). Paul is that whether he is a free man or, as is the case as he

246

writes the Letter to Philemon, a man with a chain on his wrist and shackled to a Roman soldier. This was the treatment of one under "military custody" as Paul was, even while living under house arrest in his own rented apartment in Rome (Acts 28:16, 20, 30. On the "chains" see Josephus *Ant.* 18:6-7; Seneca *Ep.* 5:7). And further, Paul is a "prisoner *of* Christ," since, in Paul's conviction, suffering is part of the Lord's will for him (Acts 9:16). He feels that his fetters were finally forged by the Supreme Strategist who knows how and where to place his campaigning soldiers. In regard to the RSV rendering: "prisoner *for* Christ," Paul would endorse the thought, for in many ways his imprisonment served to glorify Christ and served to advance the Gospel (see especially Phil. 1:12-14). "Paul, a prisoner of [for] Christ Jesus" involves the paradox of trial and privilege, of indignity and honor. This first note of the letter must go to Philemon's heart and lend all but irresistible force to the request soon to follow. Who could deny a petitioner chained by Christ and for Christ? It is the first of many notes in the letter of which Luther says in regard to Philemon "that even if he were made of stone, he would have to melt." (*LW* 29:93)

The name of Timothy is associated by Paul with his own name. This is not without significance. The article before "Timothy" in the Greek text suggests that he was well known to Philemon. He was associated with Paul in his 3-year ministry at Ephesus (Acts 20:31) and may well have had a hand in the development of the work at Colossae. While his mother was a Jewess, his father was a Greek, perhaps of the same old Phrygian stock as Philemon (Acts 16:1). The mention of his name evokes happy memories and adds strength to Paul's plea. It also hints that Paul has talked over the case of the runaway slave with his young aide-de-camp upon whose shoulders much of Paul's work would soon devolve (see First Timothy), and, happily, Timothy was of one mind with Paul as to the proper procedure in this matter.

Of the three persons addressed (vv. 1b, 2), Philemon, Apphia, and Archippus, we know only what is contained in the letter itself, plus a few inferences that may be drawn from the Letter to the Colossians. Since our letter is occupied with an incident of domestic life, it has been commonly and reasonably held that the trio represents husband, wife, and son. At any rate, if not a son, Archippus stood in an intimate relationship to Philemon and Apphia. The letter shows (v. 19) that Paul was Philemon's father in Christ. Very likely he and perhaps also Apphia and Archippus were converted through contact with Paul in Ephesus, some hundred miles west of Colossae. Colossae almost certainly was the place of Philemon's residence, since in Col. 4:9 his slave Onesimus is identified with the Colossian community.

(In the Introduction we have dealt with John Knox's reconstruction in which Archippus is made out to be the real recipient of this letter and the owner of the runaway slave Onesimus, while Philemon is taken to be the spiritual leader of the churches in the Lycus River Valley. We have presented the arguments that in our estimation make this reconstruction untenable. See pp. 224 – 228.)

Apparently Philemon was a man of some wealth, as is seen from the fact that his house was commodious enough to serve as an assembly place for those who are called in the greeting "the church in your house," and from the fact that his Christian charity extended

to a rather wide circle of fellow Christians (v. 5). We
have no way of determining whether "the church in
your house" was coterminous with the total body of
Christians to whom the Letter to the Colossians was
addressed. Perhaps it is not, since the address in Col. 1:2
is not identical with that in Philemon 2. In Col. 4:15
"Nympha and the church in her house," as a part of
the Laodicean Christian church, are distinguished from
the more general "brethren at Laodicea." The situation in Colossae may well be the same. (On these house
churches, see also 1 Cor. 16:19; Rom. 16:5; cf. Acts 2:46;
5:42; 20:20.)

Colossae, with its neighboring cities of Laodicea
and Hierapolis, lay in the valley of the Lycus River,
a region mountainous and volcanic, with excellent
upland pastures ideal for sheep raising. The chief in-
dustry of these cities was trade in jet-black wool naturally dyed by the minerals in the waters of that region.
It is therefore not farfetched to see in Philemon the
owner of a wool factory or a weaving establishment — an
early Christian industrialist who after his conversion
used his position and fortune in the service of Christ.
Paul calls him our "fellow worker," thus affectionately
linking Philemon's work with his own. The term "fellow
worker" is by no means confined to full-time servants
of the Gospel like the men who in v. 24 join in greeting
Philemon. All who toil for the furtherance of Christ's
work, however glamorous or unglamorous their work,
have a share in one great common work for eternity.
Philemon must thrill with pride to have the Lord's great
servant Paul reach down his hand to him and say: "My
fellow worker."

It is of some importance to note that the RSV adds
to the first addressee's name (Philemon) "our *beloved*

fellow worker." But the literal translation is "our beloved *and* fellow worker," making "beloved" a coordi-
nate epithet and thus assigning to Philemon preemi-
nence among the three addressees. This is contrary to
the view that Archippus is the one primarily addressed
(see above p. 224). In v. 16 the same adjective is applied
to the slave Onesimus. This emphasis on "beloved"
reminds Philemon that he belongs to the fellowship
of mutual love (vv. 5, 7, 9). The love in which he as a
Christian lives and walks and which he shows in action
may therefore not be withheld from his slave whom
Paul calls "beloved brother." (V. 16)

2 The Christian husband has at his side a Christian
wife. As mistress of the home her friendly reception
of the runaway would be quite as important as his own.
Paul gives Apphia the title "sister," assigning to her
a position of equality before God with Timothy, who
bears the corresponding title "brother." As later in
the letter we shall see the Gospel bridging the gulf between master and slave, so we see it here bridging the
gulf of sex, which was still wide and deep both in Jewish
and, still more so, Gentile circles of that day.

As Philemon is honored with the title "fellow
worker," so Archippus (perhaps his son) is similarly
honored with the title "fellow soldier," the veteran
general clasping the hand of the young sergeant and
calling him his comrade. In one of the closing sentences
of the Letter to the Colossians Paul tells the congregation: "And say to Archippus, 'See that you fulfil the
ministry which you have received in the Lord.'" Since
"ministry" here is not the designation of an office but
of function, we cannot tell precisely what his position
in the Colossian church was. Was he perhaps assigned
to take over some of the spiritual work of Epaphras,

who founded the Colossian church (Col. 1:7)? Epaphras had gone to Rome. As Paul wrote the Letter to Philemon, Epaphras was still in Rome with Paul (v. 23; Col. 4:12). He had gone there to consult with Paul about a peculiar hodgepodge of error that was making progress among his people. Young Archippus might have felt a little inadequate to handle the responsibility devolved upon him in Epaphras' absence, and so Paul told the congregation to charge him not to feel discouraged but pursue his task with vigor. That congregational letter was in the hands of Tychicus as he reached Philemon's home.

This, then, is the Christian master and the Christian household from which Onesimus, inwardly alienated at that time from the Christian atmosphere in this little colony of heaven, had fled. And this is the household to which the fugitive slave *voluntarily* returns — an unheard of act! What will be his reception? We, like Paul, have no doubt about the nature of the reception. 3 For here is a house where the Christian greeting: "Grace to you and peace from God our Father and the Lord Jesus Christ" is no mere formula but a fresh bestowal of the blessings invoked by the writer. We confidently look for grace also from the earthly master to his offending slave, and for peace — the peace of reconciliation — that Paul now tactfully asks for.

Thanksgiving   4-7

4 I thank my God always when I remember you in my prayers, 5 because I hear of your love and of the faith which you have toward the Lord Jesus and all the saints, 6 and I pray that the sharing of your faith may promote the knowledge of all the good that

251

is ours in Christ. [7] For I have derived much joy and comfort from your love, my brother, because the hearts of the saints have been refreshed through you.

These verses are the most difficult part of the letter. The words are simple enough, but their order is not at once apparent. In places the language admits of different interpretations, as is reflected too in the numerous current English translations. The thought, simply stated, in our own understanding of the passage, is that Paul thanks God for the genuine Christianity of Philemon *while he prays for its increasing growth.* That lays the foundation for the appeal to follow. There is no greater encouragement to growth than the assurance that one has made a good start.

4 Here we have a picture window admitting a look into the soul of this pastor of pastors. Paul has his definite times of prayer when he intercedes for the churches of Christ which he has founded, as well as for others, and makes specific mention in prayer of a host of individuals, like Philemon. Paul's very first spiritual impulse is deep gratitude for the victories that God Himself has achieved through His Word. Gratitude then leads to confident intercession (v. 6) in the assurance that God will further secure and extend His victories. Take Philemon. Paul remembers well the day — it was some 8 years ago, wasn't it? — when Philemon and Apphia and that splendid young fellow Archippus were baptized into Christ over there in Diana's big city (see Acts 20:23-34). The verb form in v. 5, rendered "because I hear," suggests that report after report from Asia brings word of Philemon's constancy, of the depth of his faith, of the devotedness of his love (v. 5). Especially the tidings of a recent act of loving-kindness on his part

in relieving the anxieties of God's people (v. 7) have brought a waft of coolness and refreshment into the hot prison house of Paul.

May we try to verbalize Paul's prayer as he thinks of Philemon at his prayer hours? "O my God, I thank You for Your gift of faith and love to my friend in Colossae. Grant to him the light of Your Spirit to penetrate ever more deeply into 'the unsearchable riches of Christ,' that he may be shielded against that 'philosophy and vain deceit,' which is currently assaulting the pre-eminence of Christ in Colossae. And by the contemplation of Your loving plan, keep his love strong, strong enough even to take to his heart his slave Onesimus, once a scalawag but now a saint."

5 In this verse some difficulty arises in connection with "all the saints." "Saints," of course, are ordinary Christian believers, not special virtuosos of the good life, not people sinless but people rejoicing in the forgiveness of sins, men and women whom God has called to be His own through faith. The NEB and the TEV commendably render "saints" with "God's people." But how does that connect with the preceding words: "I hear of your love and of the faith which you have toward the Lord Jesus"? Are the Lord Jesus and the saints correlated as objects of faith? So the RSV rendering might seem to imply. Of course, that is impossible. Two possibilities suggest themselves as to the thought in the minds of the translators. One is that faith is understood in the sense of faithfulness or loyalty. Love and loyalty to Christ and to His people surely can be attributed to Philemon. But that is hardly Paul's meaning here. When love is connected with faith in Paul's writings, faith must have the full theological sense of the unreserved Yes to God's promise in the Gospel and of

the saving apprehension of Christ and all His benefits. The second possibility is that the translators had in mind that after the words: "faith which you have toward the Lord Jesus" should come the unexpressed thought: "and [which you manifest towards] all the saints." This would be in the sense of "faith working through love" (Gal. 5:4). That indeed hits the sense of Paul's words.

Another construction, however, seems indicated when we look at the companion letter to the Colossians. In Col. 1:4 (similarly in Eph. 1:15) we read: "because we have heard of your *faith* in the Lord Jesus Christ and of the *love* which you have for all the saints." So very probably we have here in Philemon the chiastic, or crisscross, order (a-b-b-a): *love-faith: faith's object-love's object.* (For the reader of the Greek the change of prepositions before "the Lord Jesus" and before "all saints" facilitates the recognition of this rhetorical order. The RSV obscures this fact, using only one preposition. A few other illustrations of "chiasm" in Paul are 1 Thess. 1:8; Col. 1:16; 1 Tim. 3:16.) The TEV, perhaps wisely for the purpose of this notable version, removes all difficulties by translating v. 5: "For I hear of your love for all God's people and the faith you have in the Lord Jesus." This sense-translation, however, removes the rhetorical emphasis of the chiastic structure, which stresses both the words at the two extremes (the thought of "love") and in the center (the thought of "faith"). Our paraphrase tries to preserve Paul's emphasis: "Your love and your faith, the faith which you have in the Lord Jesus and the love which you demonstrate toward all Christians." This retains the order of thought which puts love first and love last, with faith in the center. This order of thought in Philemon is noteworthy. In the Colossian and Ephesian parallels we have faith

254

first, then love; cause first, then effect; first the root, then the fruit. In Philemon we have the reverse: the effect or fruit first and last, with the cause or root firmly embedded in the center. Since the whole object of the letter is to secure for the fugitive slave the master's love, we can readily understand the order here employed: from manifestation to cause.

Paul's heart has often been gladdened by Philemon's manifested faith in his loving service to "all the saints." Will he shut out one of his own household from the wide reach of his heaven-born love? The question is delicately hinted, though not expressed, in Paul's recognition of Philemon's love. With each word and phrase Paul creeps a little closer in his assault on Philemon's heart.

6 This verse has baffled interpreters more than any other part of this letter. If the reader has access to translations other than the RSV, he can see how they differ from one another. Compare also our paraphrase, which was fashioned after considerable reflection on the problem. A literal translation would run something like this: "praying that the fellowship of the faith of you [singular] may become effective in the knowledge of every good that is in [among] us into [unto] Christ." Our paraphrase reads: "My prayer is that your faith which you share with them [all Christians] may become ever more effective as you come to realize the full range of blessings granted to us [believers] for the promotion of the cause of Christ."

This paraphrase takes the position that Paul is praying for the increasing maturity of Philemon's faith and knowledge. The RSV, however, like the KJV, seems to see here a prayer for others, namely, that the exercise of faith on the part of Philemon, whether in personal, vocal witness to Christ or in active serving love, may open the eyes of men to the divine blessings vouchsafed to the Christian community. The words taken by themselves may bear that meaning. But attention to the context as well as to parallel prayers in Paul's letters seems to tip the scale in favor of the view that *Paul prays for Philemon's spiritual growth.* Verse 6 links up with verse 4: "making mention of *you* in my prayers." That makes the view that Paul in v. 6 is making intercession for Philemon most natural. Furthermore, the design of Paul to elicit a certain conduct from Philemon has shaped all his language thus far, and presumably it is so also here. Finally, in the other Prison Letters written in close succession Paul regularly *prays* for the growth of faith and love and knowledge of the *addressees.* (Phil. 1:9: "It is my prayer that your *love* may abound more and more in *knowledge*"; Eph. 1:16-17: ". . . my prayers that God may give you a spirit of revelation in the *knowledge* of Him"; in Colossians, which is inseparable from Philemon, we read, 1:8-10: "Epaphras . . . has made known to us your love in the Spirit. And so from the day we heard it, we have not ceased to pray for *you*, asking that you may be filled with the *knowledge* of his will . . . increasing in the *knowledge of God.*")

Two words in this verse may call for some remarks: "sharing" and "knowledge." "Sharing" renders the Greek word *koinōnia*, which has become domiciled in our current religious-social vocabulary. Its root meaning is "with-ness," togetherness, hence community, fellowship, sharing; also in a concrete sense: gift, contribution, deeds of charity. Here it is followed by the word "faith" in the versatile Genitive case (see note on "prisoner of Christ Jesus," v. 1). This versatility accounts for many variant translations. However, it must be noted that the thing in which one has or gives a share normally in Greek stands in this Genitive case. (Some examples in the New Testament are: 2 Cor. 8:4; Phil. 3:10; 2 Cor. 1:7; 1 Peter 5:1; 2 Peter 1:4.) It is always wise to follow the normal Greek idioms; hence in this case: "Your sharing in the faith," i. e., "the faith which you share." Paul has just spoken of "all the saints," i. e., believing Christians. Therefore we paraphrase: "the faith which you share with them." So already Martin Luther rendered the text. And he has not stood alone.

The word "knowledge" plays a large role in the Letter to the Colossians, which combats the Gnostic ("knowers") movement. Gnosticism prided itself on its possession of esoteric "truths" and formulas which had no connection with ethics. In the Bible, however, "knowledge" relates to the mighty acts of God in history. An intellectual awareness of these acts does not by itself constitute knowledge. Here knowledge is followed by doing, by obedience. Insight is implemented by action (read Col. 1:9-10; Luke 12:47). Here the word is: "If you know these things, blessed are you if you do them" (John 13:17). Here, too, in the highest sense, the dictum is true: "We learn by doing."

Verses 5 and 6 are applicable to all true believers. Verse 7, however, speaks of a particular act by which Philemon aided and heartened the Christian community, perhaps even beyond Colossae. Was it at the occasion of a disastrous earthquake, an event not uncommon to the cities in the Lycus Valley? Whatever the occasion, the news of Philemon's generous aid brought Paul "much joy and comfort."

Philemon was no laggard in the conflict, contest, and race of true Christianity. But Philemon, like every Christian, must strive still higher. The dynamic for

257

such striving is the unfathomable love of Christ—that inexhaustible "good that is ours *in* Christ" and *for* Christ, and for the promotion of His cause (v. 6). **7** The deeper the insight into that "good," the more sacrificial will be the response. Will this response in Philemon's case bring "joy and comfort" also to his runaway slave? Paul now prepares to request just that of his friend.

PAUL MAKES A REQUEST TO PHILEMON IN BEHALF OF HIS FUGITIVE SLAVE ONESIMUS   8-21

Paul Tactfully Prepares His Request   *8-14*

⁸ Accordingly, though I am bold enough in Christ to command you to do what is required, ⁹ yet for love's sake I prefer to appeal to you — I, Paul, an ambassador *a* **and now a prisoner also for Christ Jesus — ¹⁰ I appeal to you for my child, Ones'imus, whose father I have become in my imprisonment. ¹¹ (Formerly he was useless to you, but now he is indeed useful** *b* **to you and to me.) ¹² I am sending him back to you, sending my very heart. ¹³ I would have been glad to keep him with me, in order that he might serve me on your behalf during my imprisonment for the gospel; ¹⁴ but I preferred to do nothing without your consent in order that your goodness might not be by compulsion but of your own free will.**

a Or *an old man*
b The name Onesimus means *useful* or (compare verse 20) *beneficial*

8-12 The reader is asked to read carefully the text of the RSV for this section, noting in the footnotes the

258

variant rendition of v. 9 and the explanation to v. 10.

Paul here approaches the main purpose of his letter. But even now he does not blurt it out at once. With consummate tact he works up to the mention of the name of him for whom he pleads. He waives his right as an apostle to command, resting his plea on the persuasive principle of love and brotherhood, along with the miracle of grace which has made "a man in Christ" out of a slave who had been more of a nuisance to his master than a benefit.

At this point we should like to use our somewhat paraphrastic translation of this section. A comparison with the RSV text will show a different understanding only of the one verse: v. 9. The rest may give a modest measure of help to the reader.

> Consequently, although I am perfectly free because of my relation to Christ to give you orders in a particular point of duty, I prefer for love's sake to make a personal appeal. And so then I, as Paul grown old and finding myself a prisoner for Christ Jesus, make my appeal to you for my son. Son? Yes, I have become a father—behind prison doors! His name?—It is Onesimus! A fine name it is, Onesimus the Helpful. He once was to you anything but what his name implies, but now he is helpful both to me and to you. I am sending him back to you—in his own person; but no, I should say, I am sending you my very heart. I should have liked to keep him for myself to wait on me in your stead as I am confined here for the sake of the Gospel. But I determined to do nothing without your consent. I should not want any kindness on your part to wear the appearance of constraint exerted upon you; it must come from your own free will.

259

In this paraphrase the attempt is made to bring out Paul's almost playful allusion to the meaning of the slave's name which yet seriously pleads for him. Onesimus was a very common name for slaves (Lightfoot, 308 ff.). That bad specimen of a bad class may yet make a very appropriate name of what was once for the master a misnomer. Paul himself has proved the value of the man.

In introducing this paraphrase we spoke of our dissent from the RSV in v. 9. The dissent touches the words: "I, Paul, an *ambassador* and now a prisoner also for Christ Jesus." The footnote, indeed, does offer the alternative "an old man." The NEB, without a footnote, reads: "Yes, I, Paul, *ambassador* as I am of Christ Jesus." The TEV puts the same word into the text in a concessive clause: "I do this even though I am Paul, the *ambassador* of Christ Jesus." We may grant that the word used (*presbytēs*, the root of the English word "priest" and "Presbyterian") may in a secondary meaning designate the high office of ambassador. In this context, however, "ambassador" is altogether out of place. In the foregoing sentence Paul has hinted at his authority "in Christ" but expressly waives such authority over against his friend in the particular plea that he is about to make. Here there is nothing of the approach "by virtue of my office as an ambassador, an apostle." But here the first meaning of the word that is translated "an old man" (along with the reference to his chains) lends singular power and poignancy to love's request. (In Eph. 6:20 Paul uses a form of the verb "to be an ambassador": "an ambassador in bonds." There in a congregational, not personal, letter the reminder of his office is very much apropos.)

The reader of the KJV may wonder what has become of the words in this old version: "being such a one as Paul," which are connected with the preceding sentence: "I rather beseech thee." Those words in spite of their flatness have become classic, serving as theme of sermons and titles of essays and books. Actually Paul uses these words. However, the Greek student would want a comma after "being such a one," since the Greek word translated by "as" is not the natural correlative to the word translated "such a one." This word in Greek naturally looks backward, in this case to Paul's declaration that he waives all authority and grounds his appeal on love. "Being such a one," namely, one who waives authority and pleads for love's sake, he now, "as Paul grown old" and finding himself a prisoner, makes his appeal. We have translated this "being such a one" with the paraphrase "and so then," which we think reproduces the sense. The RSV and NEB simply bypass this little grammatical problem.

The reader of the two preceding paragraphs may have been bored a bit over the technicalities, but the writer hopes that this section has alerted him to learn again from Paul how love beseeches when it might command. Legal imperatives can at best secure a grudging outward obedience, but the appeal grounded in love has more constraining power than all the trumpets of Sinai. As Luther says here: "A man is more easily drawn than pushed" (*LW*, 29:99). Love's yoke is easy and its burden is light.

Onesimus, for one, found it so. We don't know why he ran away from his master. Was he on business for Philemon, perhaps in Ephesus, and then had taken the chance to get away? There were plenty of opportunities to take passage on a ship bound for Rome where, as Tacitus said (*Annals* XV:44), "all things horrid and

261

shameful collect and find a vogue," and whither, in the words of Sallust (*Cataline* XXXVII:5), "all whom disgrace or crime had forced to leave home had flowed as into a cesspool." How did he come to Paul in prison? Paul, we remember, was under "house arrest"; so the runaway could not have been arrested and accidentally thrown into the same prison. Perhaps one day in the streets of Rome Onesimus had come across Epaphras of Colossae (v. 23 compared with Col. 1:7; 4:12) or some other Asian whom he had met in his master's home. There was a time in his flight when the sight of a familiar face was the last thing he wanted to see. The money that he seems to have stolen from his master (v. 19) has run out. His little fling at precarious freedom has brought him to the dregs of a miserable existence. The slave catchers will get their man sooner or later. Perhaps they already have a "Man Wanted" notice in their hands with a detailed description of Onesimus (for an example see Moule, 34 ff.). And then? . . . Now the sight of a familiar face means at least a straw of hope. He tells his story and is eventually brought to Paul's rented quarters.

More than one soldier assigned to guard Paul became a prisoner of Christ (Phil. 1:12-13). So also the fugitive Onesimus. With Paul in prison he found a freedom of which he had never dreamed, freedom from the slavery of sin, and found a new Master who enchains men with His matchless love and makes service to Him a joyful privilege. At the same time, he found a new friend, found a "brother" in his father-in-Christ.

The implication of our letter (v. 13) is that Onesimus stayed in the same home with Paul and did all in his power to attend to his needs in the bondage of his new love. Paul reciprocated this love. He calls Onesimus "my son," "my very heart," "most definitely to me a brother" (v. 16) — dear to him because of his grateful service, dear to him because of loveable human qualities that required only heavenly love to evoke, dear to him because of God's love to Paul revealed in the gift of a "son begotten in bonds." Prison doors have not barred God's presence, power, and love. Of that Onesimus is a visible token to Paul.

In the Introduction (pp. 228 ff.) we have reminded ourselves that slavery was a legalized institution of that day. No man then questioned more the right of a man to hold a slave than we do today to hire an employee. In those days emancipation was not even an inevitable good for the slave. Out of bondage, he might easily be out of work and, unless he had attained a high level of culture and morals, would become a part of the lazy, dole-fed, sensation-crazy, immoral, wenching, and thieving proletariat, which was eating the heart out of the empire. The philosopher Epictetus, himself a freed slave, voices the nostalgia of an impoverished freedman: "Why, what was wrong with me? Someone else kept me in cloth, and shoes, and supplied me with food, and nursed me when sick; I served him in only a few matters. But now, miserable man that I am, what suffering is mine, who am a slave to several instead of one." (*Diss.* IV. 1:37)

As with the political and economic order then prevalent, Paul and the early church also accepted the prevalent social order, seeking the transformation of individuals within that order. Slaves are not upon conversion asked to demand their freedom, nor are masters upon conversion required to release their slaves. *In Christ* all earthly distinctions of race, sex, and class count for nothing, while *in earthly relations* all should be tied together in the bond of brotherly love amid the established orders of society. While not dynamitic, this

263

teaching was dynamic in relieving the oppressiveness of prevalent social relations among Christians and in sowing the seeds for an eventual better social order. (See Appendix II.)

13-14 After Onesimus was converted, there was no question in Paul's mind that he must return to his master Philemon. Also, the law required that one who held a fugitive must return him to his owner. In recent times an illuminating letter touching on this point was published. An official of a certain town writes to the corresponding official of another town concerning an individual whose arrest was required because he had harbored a slave and then himself had taken flight to avoid the punishment. (*Oxyr. Papyr.* XII:1422)

Paul would have dearly loved to retain the services of a man who had become to him as a loving and loveable son. Although he is sure that Philemon, if he knew the situation, would gladly consent to an arrangement whereby through his slave as a proxy he might repay a part of his own debt of love to Paul, Paul will not presume upon Philemon's love. He will not have any kindness on the owner's part even bear the appearance of being forced from him. No, *Onesimus must return*. That is his master's right. Then, too, Onesimus has an obligation resting on himself. He must right the wrong he has done to Philemon. As appears from the letter, Onesimus had been quite a nuisance in general and, in addition to robbing his master of his services, he had robbed his purse. Paul in no way palliates the wrong he has done. Genuine conversion involves the effort to make full restitution. Onesimus agrees with Paul that he must return and make good, if he is to have a good conscience. It was not an easy decision. Onesimus knows that ordinarily when a fugitive comes back there's no killing of

264

the fattened calf but a killing or a near-killing of the prodigal slave. It still rests with Philemon whether he will punish or forgive. But Onesimus goes — goes because he has become a Christian.

But as he goes, a letter goes along in which Paul, so to say, wraps himself around the man: "I am sending you my very heart." Thus Onesimus comes back to Colossae with a kind of halo around him, now that he is Paul's friend, a part of himself, his very heart. What will Philemon do to a slave with such credentials?

The Request Is Made   15-21

¹⁵ Perhaps this is why he was parted from you for a while, that you might have him back for ever, ¹⁶ no longer as a slave but more than a slave, as a beloved brother, especially to me but how much more to you, both in the flesh and in the Lord. ¹⁷ So if you consider me your partner, receive him as you would receive me. ¹⁸ If he has wronged you at all, or owes you anything, charge that to my account. ¹⁹ I, Paul, write this with my own hand, I will repay it — to say nothing of your owing me even your own self. ²⁰ Yes, brother, I want some benefit from you in the Lord. Refresh my heart in Christ.

²¹ Confident of your obedience, I write to you, knowing that you will do even more than I say.

Carefully Paul has gone forward in his siege. He is ready for the final assault. The letter goes on (vv. 15-17 paraphrased): "Why, it could be that he was separated from you for a short time so that you might have him back forever, no longer as a slave, but something better than that, a beloved brother. Most definitely he is that to me. How much more so must he be that to you, both as a man and as a Christian in the service of the heavenly Master. Do you count me as your partner in Christian blessings? Then welcome him as you would welcome me."

Onesimus' flight was a nasty affair, perhaps more so than we may surmise, and every thought of the rascal may have been a sore irritation to Philemon. In the sacred confidence of confession Onesimus had laid bare the sordid story to Paul. But Paul's love covers all up, and only a word here and there delicately alludes to it. We have noted the psychological skill and evangelical tact with which Paul tried to soften Philemon's heart before he even mentioned Onesimus' name, and then only to take away its odious sound (vv. 10-11). At once, too, he added that he had personally enshrined the bearer of the name in his innermost heart (v. 12). 15 And now that the request is to be made directly, he first suggests that the whole affair should be seen in the light of God's providence. Charitably Paul does not apply the harsh words "ran away" to Onesimus' flight but says he "was parted," an expression that is not only passive in form but also in meaning, as the following purpose clause indicates. Paul thus suggests that behind the slave's flight there was another will at work, a will turning Onesimus' perverse will and act into good for both him and his injured master Philemon. "Perhaps," says Paul, "it could be . . ." Paul does not profess to have the key to God's eternal council chamber, nor does he know what Onesimus and Philemon will do in the future. But in running away from the master the slave was apprehended, not by the slave catchers but by the victorious Christ. Reverently Paul suggests to Philemon that this capture by Christ indicates the divine purpose that the master should have the runaway back as a *brother for ever;* for this brotherhood endures forever. Will Philemon thwart what seems to be God's design in this matter?

16 What precisely is it that Paul asks for here? Not, as so often supposed in 19th and 20th century thinking, that Philemon should release Onesimus from slavery. The words do not bear that out. What Philemon is asked is simply that he love and forgive Onesimus — and that is a much harder thing to do than grant him freedom. One little word is often overlooked — the word "as" (*hōs* in Greek). Paul does not say "no longer a slave" but "no longer *as* a slave," Both the RSV and NEB preserve that "as," which in English, however, is not so strong as the Greek word in indicating the point of view that the reader or hearer should take. The TEV gives the right emphasis: "For now he is not *just a slave*, but much more than a slave." Four times in this little letter this "as" is used in the idiomatic sense just indicated: v. 4: "as [thought of as] Paul the aged"; v. 14: "kindness wearing the appearance of constraint," literally, "lest it be *as* compulsion"; then, besides v. 16, the next verse: "receive him *as* me," i. e., "looked upon as though it were I myself." Luther saw clearly. He remarks on this verse: "Paul does not release him from his servitude or ask Philemon to do so; indeed, he confirms the servitude" (*LW* 29:100). Lightfoot's comment hits the mark: "St. Paul does not say 'slave' but 'as a slave.' It was a matter of indifference whether he were outwardly a 'slave' or outwardly 'free,' since both are one in Christ (Col. 3:11). But though he might still remain a slave, he could no longer be *as* a slave. A change has been wrought in him, independently of his possible manumission: in Christ he has become a brother." (Lightfoot, 340 ff.)

The words at the end of v. 16: "a beloved brother . . . both in the flesh and in the Lord" need a bit of comment since this combination of terms is unique in the New Testament. Both prepositional phrases are very common when taken individually, the context in each case indicating special nuances. Here "in the flesh" designates the sphere of everyday life (see e. g., Phil. 1:22-24), while "in the Lord" designates the new state of existence in which believers have become members of the body of Christ. This is implied in the very frequent formula "in Christ." The same is implied in the formula "in the Lord," the word "Lord," however, reminding us that Christ is and remains our Master and we are His blessed slaves. The Greek word for "Lord" (*kyrios*) is the regular title for the master of a slave. The fivefold use of "Lord" in this letter (v. 3, 5, 16, 20, 25) may be intended to remind Philemon that he, too, has a Master, as Paul makes explicit in the companion letter to all the Colossians: "Masters, treat your slaves justly and fairly, knowing that you also have a Master in heaven" (Col. 4:1). We have paraphrased the words under discussion to read: "both as a man and as a Christian in the service of the heavenly Master." (Compare the NEB.) The TEV, convinced as this version is that Paul is not asking for the freedom of Onesimus, does not hesitate to translate: "How much more he will mean to you, both as a slave and as a brother in the Lord!"

We call attention to the surprising rendition of these words in The Jerusalem Bible which, since its publication in 1966 (Doubleday & Co., Inc., New York), has achieved high acclaim throughout the English-speaking world. There we have this translation: ". . . a dear brother; especially dear to me, how much more to you, as a blood-brother as well as a brother in the Lord."

"Blood-brother" — how do the translators understand that? In the absence of any explanation in the notes we can only surmise. Is it the thought of racial brotherhood, perhaps of fellow Phrygians? Or is it the thought that Paul adopts the Stoic teaching of the equality of all men as sprung from the same seed, breathing the same air? (Of course, that is also the Old Testament teaching. The Stoic view can be seen, for example, in Seneca *Ep.* 47:10.) Or could it be that these translators are following the view presented categorically a half century ago by a German commentator (O. Holtzmann), namely, that Onesimus was the half brother of Philemon, born to his pagan father from one of his female slaves? Such liaisons, indeed, were common enough (see Martial *Epigrams* VI:39; Plutarch *Praec. Coniug.* 16). The child of master and slave would be a slave also (Westermann, 16). We need not expatiate on the chain of improbabilities in this attempted solution of the difficulty felt concerning Paul's words: "a brother beloved . . . both in the flesh and in the Lord." All these words are readily explainable in Paul's use of them in his writings. Note, too, that "brother" is used four times in this letter (vv. 1, 7, 16, 20), the counterpart "sister" once (v. 2), these terms always referring to fellow Christians. It is perverse to superimpose a biological sense in connection with the phrase "in the flesh." The patent meaning is that as Onesimus was both a brother in Christ to Paul and a dear friend in human relations, so Paul hopes it will be the case also with Philemon, to whose household Onesimus belonged, perhaps from childhood on.

17 Here now is the request to which all the preceding has been moving: "So if you consider me your partner, receive him as you would receive me." The word for "partner" in Greek comes from the same root

as the word "sharing" (fellowship) in v. 6. The "partner-ship" of Paul and Philemon is grounded in their having a common Lord, a common goal in faith and life, a common share in all the blessings of the Gospel of Christ. "Philemon," Paul says, "if you count me as a partner in Christian blessings, then welcome Onesimus as you would welcome me." As in v. 12, Paul once again identifies himself with Onesimus. Love to Onesimus is love to Paul, and love to the brother is love to the Lord. (V. 2; Heb. 6:10; 1 John 4:19-20)

The word "receive," or "welcome," in this verse is the same word that Paul uses in Rom. 14:1-3, there addressing the "strong" in faith and telling them to "welcome" also the "weak" into full religious fellow-ship. Again, in Rom. 15:7 Paul says: "Welcome one another, therefore, as Christ has welcomed you, for the glory of God." In these passages the verb means to wel-come into full religious association, into the fellowship of the forgiven and forgiving, into the company of "God's chosen ones, holy and beloved" (Col. 3:12). If Philemon heeds Paul's appeal to "welcome" Onesimus, though the outward form of slavery may remain, the essence of it has been completely transformed. Since the times were such as they were, it may well have been best for Onesi-mus to remain a slave outwardly. But though a slave he is to his master a "beloved brother."

18-20 Before closing, one further thought suggests itself to Paul. Onesimus has caused loss to his master, if by nothing else then through the loss of his services occasioned by his flight. But behind Paul's hypothetical "if" — "if he has wronged you at all, or owes you any-thing" — lies the strong hint that Onesimus has caused his master financial loss. Like a father assuming a son's debt, Paul, with a bit of fine humor, writes a formal "bond," "a certificate of indebtedness" (see Col. 2:14): "If he has wronged you at all, or owes you anything, charge that to my account. *I, Paul, write this with my own hand, I will repay it* — to say nothing of your owing me even your own self." It is hard to prove that Paul wrote the entire letter with his own hand. Perhaps, taking the secretary's pen, he personally wrote only the words that we have just italicized.

Our paraphrase suggests a slightly different understanding of Paul's meaning in one point, presented here as a possible, even probable, alternative to the RSV text. The point at issue lies in the two phrases given now in italics: "If he has caused you any loss or owes you any money, charge it *to me*. (Here is my I O U. I write it in my own hand: 'I, Paul, will repay it.') I could, of course, have said: 'Charge *it to yourself*,' for you owe me your very soul." The difference is one of punctuation: "not *to say to you that etc.*," or alternatively: "not to say: *to yourself*," namely, *charge it* to your own account. This latter would balance the words "charge it *to me*" (v. 19b). This has the support of the word used for "owe," the full force of which is "to owe *besides*." Besides what? Besides Philemon himself taking over Onesimus' debt instead of charging it to Paul; in other words, canceling the debt. For, besides that, he owes to Paul his very self, his soul, his new life in Christ. Thus instead of Philemon's being the apostle's creditor, he was in fact his debtor. Not only was the debt canceled but the balance had turned *against* Philemon. This commercial language means simply: "Forgive Onesimus as you have been forgiven by the Lord." (Col. 4:12-13)

20 Here once again we apparently have a play on Onesimus' name: "useful," "beneficial" (cf. v. 11). "I want some benefit" represents one word in Greek:

onaimēn. Onesimus is a derivative of the same Greek root. Hence our paraphrase: "O dear brother, will you not be an Onesimus to me, helpful in the Lord?" There is here also a second reminiscence of earlier language in the letter (v. 7). To bring this out we have paraphrased the last sentence of v. 20: "As you have cheered hearts of your fellow Christians, cheer my heart because of the Christ to whom we belong."

21 "Confident of your obedience, I write to you." In our paraphrase "compliance" is used instead of "obedience." "Obedience" in English suggests response to authoritative order. In v. 9 Paul has waived all authority and based all of his appeal on love. The Greek word can well be more general than "obedience," namely, "the readiness to hear," or "compliance."

Paul is confident of Philemon's response to love's appeal. What does Paul mean with the phrase "assured that you are going to do even more than I ask"? Some hold that Paul suggests that he send Onesimus back to Paul the prisoner to serve him. But the next words about an anticipated early visit in Colossae after release from prison almost certainly precludes that. Others contend that Paul also here quite strongly hints at his expectation of the manumission of Onesimus, now that he has become a brother in Christ. But while that is possible, it is not certain. Lightfoot makes the cautious comment: "It is a remarkable fact that St. Paul in this epistle stops short of any positive injunction. The word 'emancipation' seems to be trembling on his lips, and yet he does not once utter it" (Lightfoot, 321). We must be careful not to attribute modern sentiments to Paul in this case. It could well be that he is not at all hinting at any definite action, but is only expressing his confidence in his friend that his love and willingness to please Paul will far exceed his expectations, just as the heavenly Father's love goes far beyond what we ask or think. It is best to leave the phrase in its lovely indefiniteness. Paul's great loving heart is confident of a great loving heart in his friend.

CONCLUSION   22-25

Paul Expresses His Hope Soon to Visit Philemon   22

²² At the same time, prepare a guest room for me, for I am hoping through your prayers to be granted to you.

22 Full-scale accounts of Paul's life and career will present and evaluate the data we have for the belief that Paul walked out of his "hired apartment" in Rome (Acts 28:30) a free man, once more able to go about his evangelistic work with no chain hanging on his wrist. The historical data in First Timothy (1:3) make it probable that his hope to visit Philemon was fulfilled. As a prisoner, Paul, confident in the power of prayer, requested the intercessory prayers of his congregations and friends all over the Christian world. It is not so much for his own sake that he longs for his release but for their sake, for their "progress and joy in the faith" (Phil. 1:25). Note that the "your" and "you" is plural as he writes (v. 22): "I hope that in answer to *your* prayers I shall be set free as God's gift to *you*." (Paraphrase)

Greetings   23-24

²³ Ep'aphras, my fellow prisoner in Christ Jesus, sends greetings to you, ²⁴ and so do Mark, Aristar'chus, Demas, and Luke, my fellow workers.

273

23-24 The list of Paul's co-workers who join in greetings to Philemon is the same as the list in the letter to the whole Colossian church (Col. 4:10-14), with one exception: "Jesus who is called Justus," who perhaps was absent from Rome at the time this letter was written. (For data on these men, the interested student may consult a concordance or a Bible dictionary.) By adding these names Paul intimates that other servants of Christ besides Timothy (v. 1) have learned to know the converted slave so devoted to serving Paul the prisoner, and now they share his concern about a happy conclusion to the affair that had such a sorry beginning.

Benediction 25

25 The grace of the Lord Jesus Christ be with your spirit.

25 The final benediction is almost identical with that in Galatians (6:18). In both cases Paul uses the plural "your" in the closing words: "with your spirit." This plural indicates that the entire letter is to be read to the church that meets in Philemon's house (v. 2). And not the least important reason for this is that Paul is lending his aid toward the complete rehabilitation of the fugitive slave who from now on will pray and commune with the whole Colossian brotherhood. Therefore, too, in the letter to Colossae Paul, so to say, takes the repentant slave by the hand, presents him to the whole congregation with the words: "Onesimus, the faithful and beloved brother." (Col. 4:9)

The Sequel

Did Philemon respond favorably to Paul's appeal to "welcome" and forgive the runaway? The very fact of the preservation of this letter by the recipient and its subsequent incorporation in the body of Pauline letters when these were collected by the early church entitles us to give a confident yes to the question.

Did Philemon grant freedom to Onesimus and did this former slave become a full-time servant of the Gospel? Our answer is that we do not know. Later legend that has no historical authority makes Onesimus a bishop in Ephesus or in Berea of Macedonia; an evangelist in Spain; a martyr in Rome, being put to death by the breaking of his legs.

John Knox in the work discussed in the Introduction (pp. 223 ff.) is quite certain about his hypothesis that the bishop Onesimus of Ephesus, whose name is mentioned with great respect by Ignatius in his *Letter to the Ephesians* (about A. D. 110), is Paul's convert Onesimus of Colossae (Knox, 71-108). He bases this view not only on the identity of the name (a very frequent one!) but also on some phrases that appear to be designed reminiscences of language in Paul's letter, particularly the probably intentional pun of Paul on the slave's name which we have noted in our comments on v. 20 *(onaimēn)*. Ignatius uses the same word. But does he, too, intend a pun *(Ig. Eph. 2:2)*? We doubt that, since Ignatius uses the word five more times in his letters where a pun is out of the question. In the entire New Testament this verb occurs only that one time, in Paul's Philemon, although it is exceedingly common in classical and post-classical Greek. In Ignatius it is a mannerism of the writer and thus a weak basis for Knox' argument. Paul's convert may indeed have become the bishop of Ephesus, still active and alive as an old man in Ignatius' time, although our reading of Ignatius' letter suggests that the Onesimus mentioned there was no septuagenarian but a

275

much younger man. Knox further conjectures that this Ephesian bishop had some hand in the collection of Paul's letters and supervised the writing of the so-called Letter to the Ephesians in our New Testament, the latter to serve as a "covering letter" to the collection of Paul's epistles. The discussion and refutation of this theory must be looked for elsewhere — in commentaries on Ephesians and books of New Testament Introduction (e. g., Guthrie, 99-128).

John Knox's teacher, Edgar J. Goodspeed, went a step further than Knox, seeing Onesimus as probably also the writer of Ephesians. "I don't know," he says, "how this mere conjecture may strike the reader, but it fills my eyes with tears. The emancipated slave lives to build his protector a monument more enduring than bronze! Why, whoever he was, he made Paul a lasting power in Christianity, second only to Jesus himself!" *(The Key to Ephesians,* University of Chicago Press, 1956, page XV)

We would suggest that Paul himself, without intending it so, has built for himself that monument, not only in his own authentic Letter to the Ephesians but even in this shortest of all his letters, the Letter to Philemon. And many eyes have grown misty as they closely read this plea of a greathearted prisoner who illustrates for all time the heart and soul of living Christianity: "Faith working through love." (Gal. 5:6)

Appendix

PHILEMON PARAPHRASED

(Words in italics are interpretative and not part of the original text.)

> *Rome, the Capital of the Empire*
> *No. 1 Christ Street*
> *The Xth year of Nero's Reign*

Dear Philemon:

I greet you from the prison to which Christ Jesus has brought me. Timothy, the well-known brother in Christ, is at my side and joins me in greetings to you, our dear fellow worker, and to *your wife*, Apphia, our sister in Christ. We would also greet Archippus, our companion in the good fight, as well as the church which meets in your house. Upon all of you we invoke the grace and peace that comes from God our Father and Jesus Christ our Lord.

I thank my God at all times when I make mention of you at my prayer hours. For again and again word comes to me about your love and your faith, the faith which you have in the Lord Jesus and the love which you demonstrate toward all Christians. My prayer is that your faith, which you share with them, may become ever more effective as you come to realize the full range of blessings granted to us *believers* for the promotion of the cause of Christ. Indeed, a recent report of your active love brought me great joy and cheer, since through you the hearts of your fellow Christians have been cheered, my brother.

Consequently, although I am perfectly free because of my relation to Christ to give you orders in a particular point of duty, I prefer for love's sake to make a personal appeal. And so then I, as Paul grown old and finding myself a prisoner for Christ Jesus, make my appeal to you for my son. Son? Yes, I have become a father — behind prison doors! His name? — It is Onesimus! *A fine name it is, Onesimus the Helpful.* He once was to you anything but what his name implies, but now he is helpful both to me and to you. I am sending him back to you — in his own person; but no, I should say, I am sending you my very heart. I should have liked to keep him for myself to wait on me in your stead as I am confined here for the sake of the Gospel. But I determined to do nothing without your consent. I should not want any kindness on your part to wear the appearance of constraint exerted upon you; it must come of your own free will. Why, it could be that he was separated from you for a short time so that you might have him back forever, no longer as a slave, but something better than that, a beloved brother. Most definitely he is that to me. How much more so must he be that to you, both as a man and as a Christian in the service of the heavenly Master. Do you count me as your partner *in Christian blessings?* Then welcome him as you would welcome me. If he has

278

caused you any loss or owes you any money, charge it to me. (Here is my I O U. I write it in my own hand: "I, Paul, will repay it.") I could, of course, have said: Charge it to yourself, for you owe me your very soul. O dear brother, will you not be an *Onesimus to me*, helpful in the Lord? *As you have cheered the hearts of your fellow Christians*, cheer my heart because of the Christ to whom we belong.

As I write I am confident of your ready compliance, assured that you are going to do even more than I ask. And by the way, make ready to receive me as guest. For I hope that in answer to your prayers I shall be set free as God's gift to you.

Epaphras, who is in prison along with me for the cause of Christ Jesus, sends his good wishes. And so do my fellow workers Mark, Aristarchus, Demas, and Luke.

With my prayers that the grace of the Lord Jesus Christ may be with your spirit, I am

Most cordially yours in Christ,
Paul

A Summary Note on Early Christianity and Slavery

The Letter to Philemon is a classical expression of early Christianity on its position with regard to slavery. Here it is not exhibited in a formal didactic way, but in an actual life situation. Two errors must be avoided in estimating this letter. The one is to contend that Paul defends slavery as an institution. The other is the view represented by a noted French Protestant scholar, F.

279

Godet, who entitled an essay on this letter: "The First Anti-Slavery Petition." It is safe to say that Paul was neither protagonist nor antagonist with respect to this social order of his day. The question of legitimacy or illegitimacy of slavery as an institution was not at all raised by him nor even by Christ and, before Him, by the writers of the Old Testament. In fact, to our best knowledge, no *ancient writer, whether pagan, Jewish, or Christian, expressed, either as a distant hope or as a fleeting desire or as an hypothesis, the thought that some day slavery might be abolished.*

The Bible of the early Christians was the old Testament. From this they knew that slavery was not forbidden by Moses and the prophets, though their injunctions served to ameliorate the institution among Israelites as compared to the situation prevailing in Greek and Roman areas. At the same time their Bible inculcated the dignity of labor. This encouraged the growth of free labor and reduced the number of slaves among the Jews, so that in comparison with the Gentile world the slaves constituted but a small fraction of the total population. (Good Bible dictionaries or the encyclopedias listed under "A Select Bibliography" in the Appendix will help readers who desire further information on this particular area.)

Slavery, indeed, is not an "order of creation" like matrimony, but a social order arising in a sinful race. In the light of Paul's powerful passage on the revelation of God's wrath upon man in revolt from their Sovereign (Rom. 1:18-32), St. Paul would no doubt have agreed with St. Augustine's words: "Sin is the mother of servitude, and first cause of man's subjection to man: which notwithstanding comes not to pass but by the direction of the highest in whom is no injustice, and who alone knows

280

best how to proportionate his punishment unto man's offences." (*The City of God*, XIX: 15, John Healey's translation)

The God of wrath is also the God of mercy. He trains His own people to love their neighbor in imitation of His own redemptive love. He injects into the social orders the salutary leaven that so alters the essence of these orders that their evil is overcome for His children and that through their influence the whole order may be transformed and eventually overthrown. But never are His people exhorted to take violent measures to destroy an existing order.

Suppose that Paul had told converted Onesimus: "Don't return to your master. He is a Christian and has no right to own slaves. You are a Christian and so you are free from all earthly controls since Christ is now your Master. Go out into the slave quarters of Rome and preach social revolt in the name of Christ." What then? It would have been *finis* for Onesimus and Paul and the whole small community of believers, for they would have been charged with constituting an antisocial order. The Rome of Paul's days still had a fearful memory of the furious Servile Wars in the last century of the Republic. In the War of the Gladiators under Spartacus two Roman armies were defeated by 70,000 fighting slaves and all Italy was laid waste. Finally, in 72 B. C., they were utterly defeated. Sixty thousand slaves fell; 60,000 more were captured, and subsequently 60,000 crosses bore carrion for vultures.

Actually, Paul teaches Onesimus that he must return to his legal master and make good his wrongs, while at the same time with delicate Gospel persuasion he teaches the master that, though he may retain his ownership of Onesimus, in his relations to him he must treat him as a brother in Christ. So Paul taught and so the whole church taught. It is as someone has said: "Christians retained slaves and remained slaves."

To use the formulation of Ernst Troeltsch (*The Social Teaching of the Christian Church*, 1936, pp. 82 – 86), there existed side by side in the Christian approach to social orders a *radical* and a *conservative* element. The *conservative* element bids Christians to submit themselves to the political, social, and economic orders in which they find themselves. Here we must not forget that for centuries Christians lived in nondemocratic societies. They had no vote. And it was a long time till Christians occupied positions of political power that might enable them to work towards improved social orders. On the other hand, there was among Christians the *radical* principle: their new life in Christ, which frees them inwardly from all coercive bonds and unites them to their Lord and their brethren in a fellowship of love which transcends all earthly orders and bridges all gulfs of race and class and sex.

We see this radical and this conservative principle in beautiful harmony in the precious letter of Paul to Philemon of Colossae. We see these principles didactically applied in the longer letter to the Colossian congregation. Chapter 3 begins with the *radical* thing:

> If then you have been raised with Christ, seek the things that are above, where Christ is, seated at the right hand of God. Set your minds on things that are above, not on things that are on earth. For you have died, and your life is hid with Christ in God . . . Here there cannot be Greek or Jew, circumcised and uncircumcised, barbarian, Scythian, slave, free man, but Christ is all, and in all. (Col. 3:1-3, 11. Cf. Gal. 3:26-29)

But now Paul goes on (Col. 3:18 ff.) to affirm the mundane orders as the areas in which the new life in Christ is to find expression in the self-surrender of love and service (the *conservative* principle). We look particularly, for our purpose, to the words addressed to Colossian slaves and masters, addressed as members of the body of Christ.

> Slaves, obey in everything those who are your earthly masters, not with eyeservice, as menpleasers, but in singleness of heart, fearing the Lord. Whatever your task, work heartily, as serving the Lord and not men, knowing that from the Lord you will receive the inheritance as your reward; you are serving the Lord Christ. For the wrongdoer will be paid back for the wrong he has done, and there is no partiality. *Masters*, treat your slaves justly and fairly, knowing that you also have a Master in heaven. (3:22 – 4:1. Cf. Eph. 6:5-9; 1 Tim. 6:1-2; 1 Peter 2:18-25)

The link that binds the radical and the conservative principle is love – the love of Christ to his Onesimuses and the love of the Onesimuses, the Pauls, and the Philemons to the Lord and all the redeemed. In the words of Luther:

> A Christian lives not in himself, but in Christ and in his neighbor. Otherwise he is not a Christian. He lives in Christ through faith, in his neighbor through love. By faith he is caught up beyond himself into God. By love he descends beneath himself into his neighbor. Yet he always remains in God and in His love. (*LW* 31:371)

Two significant quotations are added here, one from the theologian Rengstorf and one from the historian

283

Westermann. The works listed in the Appendix bibliography from which the quotations are taken will hardly be readily available to most readers. The theologian says:

> When a slave had the chance of freedom, he was to seize it joyfully, though recognizing that in the last analysis it made no difference whether he was bond or free (1 Cor. 7:21). More important, indeed the only important factor, is the active and passive subordination of slaves also to the rule which fashions the life of the community. This is the rule of love, which is rooted in the fact that all members of the community stand in the same level in Him. It is obvious that this must finally lead to the abolition of slavery amongst Christians. Later developments took this direction, especially when Christian ideas began to acquire normative significance for civilization generally. (Rengstorf, 272. German edition, 274 ff.)

The final quotation is from the great study on slavery in antiquity by the late William L. Westermann, professor of history at Columbia University. We quote the final paragraph of his book:

> It was the convergence of the effects of different ideas — those of Christianity, the humanitarianism of the eighteenth century, and finally the idea of democracy — which eventually brought about the abolishing of human enslavement. It was the necessity of the development of these ideas, and the long wait for their convergence until the time arrived when material conditions were favorable to it, which best explain the failure of the anti-slavery feeling for so many centuries to culminate in abolition. (Westermann, 162)

A Select Bibliography

(Selected especially for readers in college and upper high school classes in religion and ancient history)

A. New Testament Introduction

Guthrie, Donald, *The Pauline Epistles*, Chicago: Intervarsity Press, 1961.

This volume, a part of the author's *Introduction To The New Testament* in three volumes, deals fully and fairly with all questions relating to the usual topics of Introduction. On p. 309 there is a long list of other works of Introduction (mostly in English) as well as of commentaries.

B. Commentaries on Philemon

(Scholars able to handle Greek and German will know how to get at the bibliographical data regarding the commentaries by the following scholars whose names are here alphabetically arranged: Dibelius, M., and M. Greeven, 1953; Ewald, P., 1910; Friedrich, G., 1962; Lohmeyer, E., 1959; Lohse, E., 1968.)

English Commentaries

a) For scholars able to handle Greek (also others):

Lightfoot, J. B. *St. Paul's Epistles to the Colossians and to Philemon,* London: Macmillan and Co., 1875. (References in the commentary are to the reprint of 1904.)

Vincent, M. R. *Epistles to the Philippians and to Philemon.* International Critical Commentary, Edinburgh, 1897. (References are to the reprint of 1955.)

Moule, C. F. D. *The Epistles of Paul the Apostle to the Colossians and to Philemon.* Cambridge Greek Testament Commentary. Cambridge: University Press, 1957.

The general reader will be able to profit from the respective introductions of the above three commentaries, each one having its own points of excellence.

Knox, John. *Philemon Among the Letters of Paul.* Revised Edition. New York and Nashville: Abingdon Press, 1959.

While not a formal commentary, it may be more stimulating than such, even when one is led to reject many of the author's positions.

b) For the general reader:

The Epistle to Philemon. Introduction and exegesis by John Knox; The Interpreter's Bible, Vol. 11. New York and Nashville: Abingdon Press, 1955. pp. 555–573.

Knox here presents more briefly in both the introduction and the commentary the hypotheses in the work referred to immediately above.

Hendriksen, William. *Exposition of Colossians and Philemon.* New Testament Commentary, Grand Rapids: Baker Book House, 1964.

This work is quite satisfactory, fuller than most commentaries designed for the general reader.

Preiss, Théo. "Life in Christ and Social Ethics in the Epistle to Philemon," *Life in Christ.* Studies in Biblical Theology, No. 13. Translated by Harold Knight. Chicago: Alec R. Allenson, Inc., 1954. Pp. 32–42.

Richardson W. J. "Principle and Context of the Epistle to Philemon," *Interpretation*, XXII (3, '68). Pp. 301—316.

These two articles are essays which will be useful for readers interested in the role that Philemon may play in current discussions of Christian ethical principles in relation to our contemporary society.

C. On Ancient Slavery

Encyclopaedia Brittanica (as well as other universal encyclopedias).

The *Encyclopaedia Brittanica* in the post-World War II editions treats also contemporary slavery. If the student desires to read the reports of the Anti-Slavery Society of Britain, he may consult possible references to "slavery" in what may be at the time of his research the current issue of *Reader's Guide to Periodical Literature* (H. W. Wilson Co., N. Y.) and work backward through this Guide, which should be found in all good libraries, until he reaches the date of the article in the latest available edition of the *Encyclopaedia Brittanica*.

Encyclopaedia of Religion and Ethics, 13 volumes, ed. by James Hastings. Edinburgh: T. & T. Clark, 4th edition, 1958.

Vol. XI, pp. 595—631, has six articles on various aspects of the subject of "slavery," each by a different author and each with select bibliographies. Students desiring to pursue the subject in breadth and depth may find this encyclopaedia more readily accessible in libraries than the works listed above.

Harnack, Adolf. *The Mission and Expansion of Christianity in the First Three Centuries*. Trans. and ed.

James Moffatt. London: William & Norgate, 1908. Reproduced in *Harper Torchbooks*. New York: Harper & Brothers, 1962.

Pp. 167–171 present this historian's brief but perceptive and instructive treatment of the "care for slaves" on the part of the early church.

Lea, Henry C. "The Early Church and Slavery," *Studies in Church History*. Philadelphia: Henry C. Lea's Sons & Co., 1883. Pp. 523–576.

The balanced judgment with which this professional American historian treats the subject makes this study worthy of attention even today.

Rengstorf, K. H. *Theological Dictionary of the New Testament*, Vol. II, ed. Gerhard Kittel; trans. Geoffrey W. Bromily. Grand Rapids: Wm. B. Eerdmans Publishing Co., 1964. Pp. 261–280 (pp. 264–283 in the original German edition). Consult *"doulos,"* "slave," and cognate words.

This article of relatively moderate compass is a masterly treatment of the subject of "slave" and "slavery" in both its Old and New Testament aspects. The reader who cannot handle the Hebrew and Greek words and quotations can yet peruse the article with profit.

Westermann, William L. *The Slave Systems of Greek and Roman Antiquity*. Philadelphia: The American Philosophical Society, 1955. Reprinted 1957.

This is the acknowledged masterpiece on the whole subject, with a splendid bibliography. Chap. XXIII "Upon Slavery and Christianity" (along with Chap. XXIV "Conclusion") is especially enlightening.